Conmen, Cheats, & Liars.

by Ron Dawson

To Mary,
Keep smiling like me
when the going gets heavy
Best Wishes Ronnie.

Conmen,
Cheats,
& Liars.

by Ron Dawson

First published by Ron Dawson, May 1998.

Second edition reprinted Sept. 1999.

Published by: Classic Publications © 1999

Apt. 249

Mijas 29650 Málaga

Tel.: 952 486 894

Design & Typesetting by Jon Harper

Set in New Century Schoolbook 10/12pt.

Imprente by: Gráficas San Pancracio, S.L.

29006 Málaga - Tel. 952 34 24 00 / 04.

Depósito Legal: MA-1.013/1999 • ISBN: 84 - 6059457 - 2

*T*his book is dedicated to my Mum, "World Wide Elsie;" a lady who brought three sons into this world when times were not easy. My Mum has never had a bad word to say about anybody. I'm just so proud of her.

I would also like to acknowledge Josephine Quintero for her valuable editorial assistance.

Author's Note to Revised Edition

When I first thought of writing Conmen, Cheats and Liars, I was always intending to write it at a later date, when I was more certain of my financial fate. I have also more evidence now, in my opinion, to show that there was, indeed, a conspiracy against me and my son by the Jockey Club. It therefore seems logical for me to re-write my story.

I have not altered the essential story of Conmen, Cheats and Liars, but a number of significant changes, as well as minor ones have been made. Also, I have added for humour, some of the true stories in racing.

Ronnie Dawson

PREFACE

So, here I am, sitting in the shade by my sun-soaked pool at my luxury villa on the Costa Blanca. I am already halfway through a chilled bottle of Dom Perignon champagne as I reflect on the past few weeks when so much has happened in my life.

I have been warned off for ten years by the Jockey Club for supposedly "bringing racing into disrepute". I have been visited by sleuth reporter, Colin Cooper and exposed in The News of the World. The Sunday People have slammed me in a column written by Brian Radford ...And, for the umpteenth time, The Racing Post has published an article by Graham Green where, once again, he puts the boot in while Andrew Sims of The Sporting Life for the fifty-sixth time in under four years (yes, I counted!), is returning to his pet aversion, namely the Dawsons, my son, Tim, myself and, of course, Classic Bloodstock with his strongest words yet: "It's enriched the Dawsons beyond their wildest dreams ... this family from Hell."

My home town newspaper has accused me in bold headlines of masterminding a multi million pound scam.

I just rang Mr. D.J. Granger of the DTI Investigation Department in Nottingham for a meeting in England. The purpose of this will be to discuss the supposedly missing millions of pounds from Classic Bloodstock plc. I say "supposedly" because it would seem that everyone believes the press reports. I'm amazed at how easily people are conned by what they read in the newspapers.

Right. I will finish the Dom Perignon, have a nap and then get down to telling you the TRUE story.

CHAPTER ONE

Conmen, cheats and liars .... All despised by the estab-lishment, probably quite rightly so. But how about love-able rogues? Those Jack the lad characters that respect-able folk love to hate (but tolerate all the same).

I like to think I fall in this latter category but I'm an optimist, as well as being a great believer in fate. Some-how it was all meant to be.

So, do I look back and wish I had done something different?

I'm beginning to.... The reality is the following: I be-came a millionaire through horse racing although I am no jockey so, for me, it was no easy ride!

I have been accused of many things but, in return, have witnessed the sheer hypocrisy of the so-called racing press and the establishment. That is why I have relished every penny of every tenner I have made in racing. Yes, you may call me 'Jack' today but, tomorrow I may go by a different name; that's just the name of the game. My game.

I want you to read this book and then put me in the frame that fits. Am I that conman, cheat or liar? Or just a guy trying to make money from horse-racing? A tip-ster or bookmaker may tell you: 'A mug is born every minute and thank God most of them live.' But when you read this book I guarantee that you won't be one of those mugs. For me that is a good feeling and the only satis-faction I seek.

This is an autobiography written from the heart and soul. It is a truthful story that I hope will move you from the heights of optimism to the depths of my despair and sorrow. My book is a true roller-coaster ride and, more than that, it is an honest look at the complex underworld of horse racing which is rife with rumours of corruption, criminality, humour, emotion, dreams and (believe it or not!) joy.

So, keep reading ... but hold on tight!

I was born in Barrow-in-Furness, the son of a shipbuilder. I was just a typical eighteen year old, maybe more arrogant than most. A 'teddy boy' with slicked back hair, full draped jacket, velvet collar, half moon pockets, blue suede shoes and string tie. This was the look for the era.

All week I waited for Friday and Saturday night; ten pints of Thompson's Best Bitter (no one drank lager back then). Then it was down to the local 'Palais' with my mates to 'Rock Around The Clock' and, hopefully, pull a girl. Yes, it was all skin deep, but it was living, it was great. I was one of the pack; the rewards of a week of work, sweat and toil. And, if you didn't score, then it was ten pints more. But, God how I suffered for it the rest of the week!

Far too soon, the noise of the alarm pounds into my brain like a jack hammer. It's 6.30 a.m., Monday morning. "Eat your bacon sandwich, Ron," my Mum says, concerned and frowning. There's no time, so I wrap it up in a brown paper bag and put it into the pocket of my overalls, holding my breath, the bile rising bitterly in my mouth. I breath deeply, inwardly cursing for drinking away my pay packet - again. I can't even smoke a fag, my mouth feels dry and bitter like I've had a dose of Redimix concrete for breakfast.

The weather doesn't help. It's pissing down with rain. There's no shelter and the bus is late. Finally, I arrive at the shipyard and at least I have my mates to commiserate with - at least those who turned up. I won't dry out today, inside or outside. But it's not so bad because I'm young and tough; a shipbuilder, an apprentice plater earning top money like the rest of them in the shipyard.

The familiar banter, smells and noise; the hammering, pounding, grinding... the dirt and the grime and dodging danger everywhere I step. 'It's an unlucky ship where someone doesn't get killed in the yard,' is a familiar saying. True enough, plenty got killed on that ship. There were no safety nets in the shipyard in those days.

The day grinds to an end and it's still pouring with rain, the grey clouds are so dense and suffocating that I feel I can just reach up and touch them, typical Barrow weather means rain for days. I'm getting soaked to the skin and need an umbrella. But I'm a shipbuilder, I'm tough, a man of steel, it doesn't matter if I get wet. No shipyard worker has an umbrella, it's an unspoken sign of weakness unless you're on the staff; one of the office's white collar workers.

To hell with it, I think and stop by the small corner shop which sells everything from meat pies to girlie mags. As I walk out with it held up high I can hear the jeers of my work-mates. I don't give a damn. They are the stupid ones, not me because I'm going to be dry as a bone while, as usual, they will be wet through.

It's funny really but I think that incident with the brolly changed my life. I was no longer one of the pack, I had struck out on my own and that was the way it was to stay for the rest of my life. I never worked again as a shipbuilder (or in wet weather!) without a brolly. I was the laughing stock of the yard. But once I set my mind on something, I was like a bulldog and wouldn't let go. You will see what I mean later in the book; a time when, perhaps, I should have let go - but couldn't.

Many years later, I returned to Barrow to see my kinfolk in my Rolls Royce accompanied by my lovely wife, Maureen. Many of the familiar old faces were still there. They all remembered that day so long ago with the brolly. It seemed to have made just as much an impact on them as on me.

Sadly, most of these men are out of work now and Barrow is little more than a ghost town; the ship-building industry has been swept away in the tide of so called progress. Ten thousand men worked in the shipyard at Vickers when I was a lad, with up to six ships on the stocks at any one time. Jeff Davies, my best mate then, became head foreman plater later in life.

But one very good thing happened to me on that last trip to Barrow in July, 1996. Two of the horses that belonged to Classic Bloodstock plc were expected to win that week. Both were trained at my own luxury racing establishment in Newmarket. I told everyone I met that day, all my old good mates from the shipyard, to be sure to bet on those two horses. I told the truth. "Look lads, you've got to have a few quid on those two. Lady Luck smiled on me and both won. *Classic Affair* went in at 25/1, *Classic Beauty* did the business at 11/4. A friend of mine, a fellow horse lover from Barrow called Pauline Corbett, phoned me. I had once given her a horse as a gift called *Dvorak*.

"Ronnie," she said "You are a legend in this town! The bookies couldn't even pay out straight away. They had a pasting!"

Obviously, the name of those two horses got all over the town. 100/1 the double. I still chuckle when I think about it. It was the best feeling in the world for me, giving those two winners to those smashing old pals from the shipyard.

So, if any readers find themselves in Barrow-in-Furness some day, be sure to call in at the Barrow Island Workingman's Club. Say you're a friend of Ronnie Dawson's and you're certain of a free pint or, come to think of it, perhaps just a half (I expect they've drunk away their winnings long ago). Now, where was I? Oh yes, I'd just left Barrow in the early 1960's to earn my fortune.

I was well hooked on betting in those early days. The Sporting Chronicle was my daily paper; a real racing paper, not like the rubbish we have today written by hypocrites who can't tip the winners because they're too busy chasing their tails after stories of sex and scandal.

But then I was a working man and I loved a bet on the horse races. It was part of our life, like a fag or a pint. Although in the future it would usually be big cigars and champagne. The difference for me was that I learned all about the darker, seedier side of gambling early on in life - and it got worse, instead of better.

One of my early girlfriends was called Jean Nightingale, the daughter of a Police Inspector. Her Dad, Jack loved a bet, as have a lot of coppers I've known over the years. But Jack had a bad reputation following a major sting operation with his trail hounds. If you've never been up north to Cumbria for a trail hound race, make a note in your diary, it's a must - ten miles following a scent laid in advance by a man with a rag coated in aniseed. When the lead dog comes over his last sandstone wall to win his race with the baying pack chasing behind him it's a fantastic spectacle - a sight you never forget, especially when it's your dog - or the one you've backed.

Black Diamond was the champion trail dog in my day. Nearly unbeatable. A lion of a dog. Jack also had trail hounds. He was just a street bobby then who wanted to pull off a betting coup. In this particular race, his dog had been a 20/1 outsider in the early betting but he finished up the favourite and, after a huge gamble, was a winner by some distance.

Jack loved to tell me the story. Obviously, the man who had laid the scent was part of the scam. He had laid it into a barn two miles from the finishing line, going in one door and out the other. When the dogs following the scent entered the barn, they were all trapped. Jack's dog was released a full five minutes ahead of the rest of the pack by a couple of guys in on the job, so came in way ahead. 'No danger' as they would say in horse racing.

'Five minutes lead? I had only wanted two minutes!' Jack would exclaim to me, over and over again. But that was what gave him away, of course. If his dog had been released just a minute or so ahead of the rest of the pack, he still would have won - but not so obviously. The bookies never forgot Jack. Some kind of cheating continues to this day, both in dog racing and horse racing - and with serious money involved. However this happens mainly abroad now, racing in this country is pretty straight, although not one hundred percent.

Later, I married Jack's daughter and became a part of his family. He had been promoted to Police Inspector by then and we were good friends. Jack taught me how to catch salmon with wire snares as they lay motionless near the shallow river bed. I remember one memorable day when he caught a twenty pounder in a snare; a huge fish, and walked calmly down the High Street in Cartmel, Lancashire with it stuffed down his trouser leg. He loved his life, his beer, a bet on anything. He was a great character, the type who passes through your life and leaves a mark. A bloody good copper at his job, mind you.

But Jack had not been so amused some months earlier when I was courting his daughter. Stupidly, I had got her pregnant. I was twenty, she was just seventeen. I went to the police station in my lunch-break, wearing overalls and covered in muck, to break the news to him. I was apprehensive but determined to state the truth, clear and simple. He was alone in his office and listened without a word, his face turning gradually paler. Surprisingly quickly, he seemed to be resigned to the situation and shortly after Jean and I got married, and had a baby girl 'Linda', sadly for me, I have not seen her for over thirty years. I treasure the few photographs I have of her. One an action photograph of her and her pony in full flight jumping a high gate, the other in her glider. Linda is a career woman, I am told, she is obviously clever, who I suspect got her brains from her mother Jean, who was also a Grammar School girl, when we fell in love

I don't know what he or his lovely daughter, Jean, saw in me. On the face of it, back then, I had no real prospects, I was an apprentice at Vickers Armstrong with just a few

Linda Dawson, the daughter I never knew and never see, which now I am older causes me much sadness

Linda, my lovely daughter from my first marriage to Jean Nightingale, on her pony in full flight jumping a high gate.

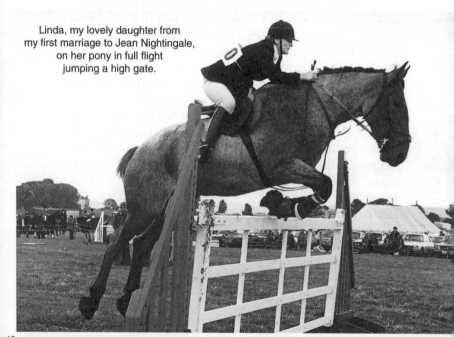

Linda, an qualified
pilot with her glider

My Grandad and Nan
with my Mum, years ago!

quid in my pocket and the gift of the gab when I needed it. But I did have something of value; two Lurcher whippets. One, in particular called Red-Ley became the champion of England. I took him to Stoke-on-Trent once to race against their champion, *Blue Smoke*. Five white fivers, £25 was the side stake. Jack Nightingale put up the money. It was a lot of money then, *Red-Ley* won by half a dog. I was the proudest man in England that day. Jack drove us all the way back from Stoke. *Red-Ley* could have won the Derby the way Jack felt right then.

That dog was marvellous and I loved him to bits. At about the same time, I bought two more racing dogs. Even then, I seemed to have an eye for picking the winners. Jack liked to take on the bookies and sometimes I'd stop my dogs from winning two or three times by feeding them heavily before a race and collect a few quid off a couple of bookmakers who laid them for me. Then I'd have a go with them. We very seldom lost. Jack had got some medicine, a tonic from his chemist friend just to make sure that, when the money was down, my dog had that extra yard or so. But I never gave Red-Ley anything, dogs like him don't need it.

Of course, I'm not proud of all this hanky panky but, if you're going to tell a true story then it's got to be the warts and all. I can't blame anyone else for my decisions. No one led me down the path, I happily ran all the way!

But my life was soon to change. National Service was obligatory and my fate was happily to serve most of my two years serving in Malta. I loved every minute of it and had the best job of all! I was responsible for the company's bar and function hall. I ran the regiment's bingo sessions, played stud poker better than most and could sell anything to anyone. I even bought and sold potatoes in a deal with the officers mess cook sergeant. This was the time of the Malta potato shortage. It only lasted a few weeks but was very lucrative for the crooked Sarge and me. Before long, I was making more than the officers got paid. I knew a few non-commissioned officers didn't like the fact that I had my own car on the base. They couldn't work it out.

I was also courting a Lieutenant, a nurse in the Q.A.R.N.C. called Jenny. My marriage in England was over by this time. It happenned to a lot of lads doing National Service. Jenny's claim to fame was a nude portrait hanging over the bar in the Five Bells on the Kings Road, Chelsea which dated from her student days. When any of the squaddies went back to the UK for leave, it was a virtual pilgramige to see it.

While in the army, I had a car accident, I drove into a bus at a crossroads, broke a few bones and was in hospital for a month. The crash was entirely my fault, but the army got me off the hook. I was discharged from H.M. Service after serving 22 months of my two years in glorious Malta, wiser, smarter, a predator in the making. today, I look back on those days in the National Service as amongst the happiest in my life.

Back in Barrow-in-Furness, I couldn't settle, had seen a bit of the world and had experienced and done things I couldn't tell my mother about. I got a job straight away back at Vickers Shipbuilders as a plater and it was good money too, but I wanted something else out of life. I couldn't be sure what it was, but something was bugging me inside. Unfortunately for me, my education was basic and I left school with no qualifications; age fifteen was the leaving age back then.

I deeply regret not having a good education. I don't think I would be in the position I am today if I had. But more of that later in the book. I'm taking a pull, to stop myself, running away with my story. I'm like a plodder in the Grand National; a long way to go, obstacles in the way, some harder than others, but I will get to the finishing line in the end.

My story has to unfold slowly, from the day I arrived at my town of destiny, Newmarket, after packing in my job as a shipbuilder for ever. Looking back briefly now, I realise I was happy there, but didn't have the sense to realise it. Now it is 1998 and, according to the press, I'm involved in a tangled web of deceit and dishonesty with millions of pounds involved. A supposed scam that was reported in The Sporting Life on February 23rd, 1998, stating: 'Classic Bloodstock plc enriched the Dawsons beyond their wildest dreams.' Oh dear, am I really that conman, cheat or liar? Or could I have a chance to be Jack? You, the reader will have the truth in this book. Judge me not ... at least not yet.

Aside from a restlessness, there was all the personal tragedy I had to deal with back in the ship yard; like work mates who died on the ships. Just a few weeks after my return, a young boilerman like me had fallen to his death and, shortly before that, two other shipbuilders had met their fate equally horrifically, burnt to death in a confined space. I was getting the message loud and clear - it was time to get out.

"Your family have a long tradition in the shipbuilding business," my boss reminded me sternly when I went to get my cards. "I think you're making the wrong decision here. You are a tradesman now, the best paid job in the shipyard."

The former was certainly true, it was the best paid job, and my father and two uncles worked as platers, but it killed my father in the end; he contracted asbestosis via his work which is a very nasty type of lung cancer. He died early in his retirement after giving 45 years of his life to Vickers Armstrong. His reward? A handshake and a gold-plated watch.

I missed my father a lot. He was a good man; hardworking, solid and dependable and we always had an honest relationship. Sometimes I wish that I could have

My Dad (centre) on his retirement, receiving his certificate and watch after 45 years service in shipbuilding.

My Dad and Mum celebrate their Golden Wedding with our family at Newmarket.

A law abiding, tax paying family who, according to Mirror Group Newspapers PLC's main racing paper, Sporting Life, are the "Family from Hell" it's little wonder my poor mum was so upset

inherited that same conscientious hard working reliability he had. I just wasn't cut out to be a shipbuilder, although I was good at my job. A good tradesman after six years apprenticeship. I wasn't going to wait for 45 years for my gold plated watch.

They say that all roads finish at Newmarket in racing, but it certainly took me a while to get there! A few months in different towns, living on my wits, sometimes sleeping rough. Like all gamblers, I had my ups and downs, especially when I was betting solely on the strength of the form book. I shudder when I think of all the non- triers that I must have backed around that time. The "man in the street" has very little chance of beating the bookie. I think betting shops are money factories where many a man's wages are lost.

There was one bet which has always stayed in my mind. It was a particular tip I was given and really got me thinking. It had no chance at all on the form book. A chauffeur who, by chance, I helped to change a tyre on a nice car. (I wasn't much help really, but I did my best). After thanking me for my assistance, he suddenly asked, 'Do you bet on horses, son?'

'Yes,' I replied. 'But my luck's out at present.'

'Listen lad, Frankie Durr will ride a winner this afternoon. Keep it to yourself. It's called *Blazon D'Or* runs in the 2.30 race. Back it each way to be on the safe side, son?' (How could I imagine then that in the not too distant future, Frankie Durr would be riding my own racehorses).

Now I knew my racing form inside out and this horse could not be remotely expected to win. That's it, I reasoned. It just has to be genuine information.

That was the very first time that anyone had given me a tip, other than other punters which went in one ear and out the other. But this was different. I just had a gut feeling. The problem was money; as usual, I had none. I did have a decent watch though; a 21st birthday present from my Mum and Dad and I went round 'to uncle's' (which is what a pawn shop was known as in those days). A fiver was his top wack offer. I wasn't too happy about it, but went ahead. I knew I just had the one chance and I wasn't going to let it slip by.

I was advised to back each way and reasoned that if this animal was there to do the business, it would win or finish nowhere. *Blazon D'Or* was never headed. Price 33/1. £170 returned, counting my stake. Up until then, this was the biggest win in my life.

My first call was back to the pawn shop to recover my watch. Then I headed for Newmarket, the capital of horse racing. I never made it there. The Lincoln race-track was in my way. I backed three of Doug Smith's rides, all favourites, all lost and I felt as sick as a parrot. Half my money gone. That day I learned the hard way again - the key is information. You can't back winners and win consistently without it.

Betting on the form book alone will never be good enough. I never repeated that mistake since leaving the old Lincoln racecourse that day. Nowadays, it's no longer in use. The old grandstands are still there with all the memories though. What tales they could tell! A few years ago I went past it. It seemed an eyrie place to me. Lonely and unhappy in its decay.

After more escapades and reflections, like Dick Whittington, I continued on to Newmarket where I was sure my destiny lay and where I was going to make my fortune. Back in those days, Newmarket was a sleepy, small town, except on Saturday night that is, when it was more like the Wild West. Stable lads are a strange breed; horse lovers built like pocket battleships, drunk on three pints and ready to punch anyone on the nose who they don't like the look of. A rough and ready lot. Lads from all corners of the country - Irish, Scottish, Welsh, English. One obvious thing in common (aside from jodhpurs and riding boots!) they stick together, bonded via their passion for horses, betting and drinking. All hoping to be a top jockey some day, only one percent achieving that objective.

The first real work I did in Newmarket, before I started tipping, was for a trainer called Percy Alden who lived in a great big house on the Bury Road. I had heard on the grapevine, via Percy's gardener, that Percy wanted some concrete steps built leading down to his tennis courts. I was hungry and skint so that afternoon I knocked on his door and offered my service to do the job for £20, cash in hand. Percy was delighted. He had all the stuff: tools, sand and cement. Well, I had never mixed cement in my life, but couldn't imagine there could be much to it. I did a nice job. Percy was over the moon and gave me £20. Two days later in the pub, Percy's gardener came up to me. "Hey son, Percy's looking for you." I rubbed my hands together enthusiastically. Must be another job, I thought optimistically. "Okay," I replied. "What's up?"

"Well son, Percy stood on his new tennis steps for the first time this morning and went straight through them!" I never did see old Percy again. I had some laughs in those days!

Nothing's changed today. Newmarket is still a great town, albeit a little larger with some London overspill living there now. A boiling pot of boisterous high spirits and night life, pubs and clubs. Come Sunday morning though, and the scene is more sobering; broken windows, blood on the pavement, broken glass everywhere.... But Newmarket life goes on as normal. Six days a week, horses are out from 5 a.m.. Sundays are a bit easier but they still have to be fed and watered, hangovers or not. There may be a few headaches, black eyes, even a limp or two but the racing boots are shined and the hair slicked back and combed. In my opinion, these lads earn a pittance for the job they do, but they never short-change when it comes to hard work. Why?. Because they love their horses. That simple.

Today conditions are a little better and perhaps they earn a little more. but the majority of lads still go around on foot or pedal bike. (You're still called a lad if working in racing, and youcould be fifty years old!). After all, think about it. If a stable lad can't do better for himself at backing winners instead of losers when he's right there on the spot working in racing, then maybe you should look elsewhere for your tips. A lot of lads are poor judges. they do their best but can't get it quite right. Always beware a stable lad tipping a horse to win that he looks after personally. The lads are very biased towards the abilities of these horses.

Now lets get this straight. I do personally know a few lads who do very well out of racing; nice car, nice house, plenty of punters. But the bottom line is that they are in the minority. My advice is, get a real good lad under your wing, from a good yard who rides a bit of work on the gallops. His judgement is respected and he is on good terms with the trainers, that's my advice. Many owners listen to a knowledgeable lad and slip him their phone number with a few quid, telling him to be sure, "to keep in touch..." It's a bit like an insurance policy. Some trainers will lie to the owners about how well the horse is going, forgetting to mention, for example, that its been sick, off its food, lame, got a virus, won't try its best to run, bone lazy, needs more time.... In other words, its bloody useless. But if the naive owner is shelling out two hundred quid a week, best to keep him guessing.

And I know about this first-hand. I had a trainer called Jeff Pierce who strung me along with a horse called *King Menelaos* for over two years and nearly £20,000 in training fees. It never did anything, a waste of training fees. It's common practice but more about Jeff later in the book. I am galloping away with my story here, it's time to tighten the reins and take a pull.

Many punters try and chat up the stable lads trying to get information for that day, sometimes those who are leading up their horse at the racecourse,. My advice is that you would probably do as well by asking the horse. Read your racing form then, with a little good information from a proven good judge working in a stables, you can possibly make it pay. I get both the Time Form prospectus and Super Form to keep me on my toes. I also study the entries very carefully. Certain trainers like to win on certain courses. Also, if a horse carried big race entries for the future, you have to be sure to keep that horse in mind if its going to, say, Pontefract for a small race before its main objective. This type of research is one of the finest ways I know of building up a picture of how much potential a trainer may consider the horse in his care has.

Peter Gordon's, Future Form, an excellent publication, was based on this formula and, in my view, is an important aid in racing for the punter. Mind you, it had the trainers spitting blood when it became popular with serious punters. Their secrets of the best horse in the yard were for all to see, except perhaps in the case of the mega rich Arab Sheikh entering two hundred horses in the Derby. For the Arabs it is run of the mill stuff, paying fees for big race entries. The few trainers who train for these rich Arabs are on a gravy train, while a great many trainers struggle to make ends meet.

CHAPTER TWO

Back to the story. Things started slowly for me at Newmarket. In effect, you were either a stable lad sort or a townie; the two didn't mix. For me that was difficult because I wanted to drink in the stable lads' pubs and was only interested in racing gossip. Slowly I started to make friends, although I still had my head in the form books. I liked 'the crack' as you say in racing for chat and, more importantly, I was starting to get some inside information, particularly from two excellent work jockeys who were employed in Harvey Leader's and Bruce Hobb's yards. Of course, I was seeing the work jockeys all right with a tenner here and there. And nothing's changed today, except if you want to know the secrets of a racing yard, the fifty pound note does the business instead of the tenner

I remember once that I had seven bets from Harvey Leader's stables in a space of a few months; six were winners. Naturally, my main man in the yard gave me more than seven horses to bet on during that time, but I had the knack of sorting the wheat from the chaff. The Bruce Hobb's information was also top notch.

It was around this time that I started slipping away to Cambridge or Bury St. Edmunds to place my bets. In a small town like Newmarket with the betting shops full of racing folk, it was best you kept your bets quiet. Lads in racing don't take kindly to townie's knowing more about the game than themselves. Now if I backed a winner in the bookies, I could give it the full vocals during the exciting commentary of the race without looking over my shoulder.

This is a funny little story. It still makes me laugh when I think of it! Sean Rogan, the jockey, was a friend of mine. He was a real hard case and, I believe, had done a stretch or two for grievous bodily harm..

At the time, Sean was courting a girl called Irene who worked as a secretary for the trainer, Robert Armstrong, Lester Piggott's brother-in-law. Irene used to finish work at about 1 p.m. and we would wait for her. She would tell us what bets she had phoned up to McClaghlan's bookmakers in Scotland. I know Lester Piggott always rode the horse she gave us. They were never big prices, but would invariably win. And, in turn, we would have a few quid on them. I was tipping from Towerflat Stable's at the time which was a run down derelict joint that had seen better days, but was now Sean's home.

Anyway, Sean was going to ride a possible winner at Newbury in a condition's hurdle event. We couldn't punt it because the trainer wouldn't tell Sean if it's off or not (trying or not trying to win) until he was in the saddling enclosure.

So I decided to go down to Newbury Races to back the horse and put Rogan's money on as well. If it was there to win, Sean wouldn't find out until the trainer told him. But I couldn't seem to get any nods or winks from Rogan while he mounted up. So, on his way out from the parade ring, I found a strategic spot where he had to walk past me on his horse in order to reach the race track from the saddling enclosure.

"Is it off?" I hissed to Sean through gritted teeth.

"No," he replied. "But I'm off at the first." I was puzzled by this remark until the race began and then up the runners came to the first hurdle and the horse went over it very nicely indeed, but without the jockey! As Sean had said, "off at first." This still makes me laugh out loud to this day.

Even now, although racing is straighter and horses aren't stopped as blatantly as they were then, trainers still do stop them. I can't think of many trainers who have never stopped a horse winning by, say, running it over a mile when it really is a five furlong horse. It's all so easily done.

Within two years of first arriving in Newmarket, I bought a new M.G. sport car and proudly drove home to my town of birth, Barrow. I knew it to be true that, if I had stayed in shipbuilding, I would probably never have earned the money to run a car, never mind own one. The long three hundred mile journey back to Barrow in that car was very enjoyable. My old Mum and Dad were impressed. A couple of years later when I went home again, my Dad had had a garage built. My parents had never owned a car, never would, couldn't afford to, but they were so pleased and happy to put my car in that garage. I loved my Mum and Dad so very much. I wish I had told them that more in my life.

All my ex-work mates were still in the shipyard, working the same daily grind. A few days home with my folks and I was itching to get back to the action in Newmarket. I knew I could do even better, much better in fact and, upon my return to the town, I set up in business.

I started to advertise my information for sale in the Racing Handicap book and The Sporting Life. I also formed a business called Infoform Race Ratings which was based on my own formula, information and forms. Over the next few years, I built it up to several hundred clients. For only a pound a week, you got my racing assessments of each race and for as little as 50 pence my Saturday only clients got the Saturday form cards. I used to sell my form cards at the race meetings. I even had my Mum once sat outside Ascot Racecourse selling my form cards. I was pretty proud of the publication and was negotiating to buy the 'Gold Form' from Lord Avonbury who marketed his own guide. His publication was not as successful as mine at finding the winners, but I reasoned that, once I got his business, I would have his client list and could scrap his book - which I did once the deal was completed.

My far superior guide was based on my winning formula and gave my clients information like "Harry Wragg

Me and my Mum, when I drove back to Barrow in my first M.G. sports car.

My mum
'World Wide Elsie'
with my Jack Russell
bitch Meg who later died
of poisoning

On old Barrow Island
with my Mum and
my Rolls Royce,
outside the house
I was born in 1938,
at Abercorn Street

RHD 1

has two runners in the 2 pm race at York on Tuesday. One will be favourite and ridden by the stable's retained jockey. The other will be an outsider in the betting and will be ridden by the stable's apprentice, Graham Sexton who rode this one in a bit of work in a Newmarket gallop last week. I can tell you that the outsider is the better of the two horses by a long way. Take my advice and back this one."

The result was as I promised and the horse won at 20/1. Graham rode the horse. Around that time I had come to know Graham and later when I worked for The Sunday Mirror I wrote an article on the lad to help his career.

I will quickly explain how I got a job on The Sunday Mirror. During my early days in Newmarket, I was stony broke, so I called in at the local fish and chip shop and cheekily asked if they would feed me until I found a job or got some money. The owner, Bert and his wife, Doll, for reasons best-known to themselves, did just that. In other words they took a chance with this scruffy, cheeky kid, Ronnie Dawson and fed me like a long lost son.

A few weeks later I repaid Bert in full. I knew no other way, but I realised later why that must have made an impression on that wonderful couple because very, very few people paid their debts in Newmarket. I suspect it's not changed much today.

Anyway, Bert's brother, George was the Mirror's Sport's Editor. Bert put in a word about the race-horse fanatic, Ronnie Dawson and before I knew it, I'm working for The Sunday Mirror. Well, there you go. So if you ever want to get a step up in life, always pay for your fish and chips!

Later, as I got to know Bert and Doll and his two daughters as a family, they unknowingly moulded my life for the better. I had great respect and love for them. Wonderful people that leave their mark on one. I owe them so much for their guidance. But, of course, back then, as is usual with all young lads, I didn't listen as much as I should have.

Do trainers bet? Is a question I have often been asked. Of course, the answer is "yes". But I know one trainer who lost everything and not solely by betting - but betting to get out of financial trouble. And he was so unlucky, it's almost unbelievable.

Old Arthur Freeman lived and trained on the Bury Road where a lot of major Newmarket trainers have their training yards. Arthur was only a small job trainer (laid horses out for a certain race for betting purposes); a blunt man and not given to fools. I got the feeling from the stable lads that not many people liked old grumpy Arthur. He was tetchy to say the least. Anyway, for reasons best known to Arthur, he liked me, possibly because I stood up to him.

I first met Arthur when I was working for The Sunday Mirror and called at his house to ask if I could interview his apprentice jockey, Tommy Reidy, take a photograph and do an article as part of a series I was doing at the time on young up-and-coming jockeys; trainers ruled the roost in those days. They ran their yards like Sergeant Majors.

Arthur stood at his door with a bleak face and gruffly said, "Piss of, son!" I recoiled at his remark and tone, but gave him as good as I got,

"You may be king of your manor, but you ain't nowt to me! I was doing the kid a favour. I don't even want to do an article, I'd rather be in the betting shop!"

Old Arthur was stunned and speechless. "Come in son and have a drink. I need one!" So I got to know old Arthur and, of course, his good apprentice jockey, Tommy Reidy; a real nice lad. Anyway, Arthur needed a touch (to back a winner) around that time to keep the wolves from the door. Over a short period, he laid out three horses to win. Arthur was a very shrewd trainer and didn't mess about when he had got his horses ready for a tilt at the bookies and put his betting boots on.

So, there were three big bets on three horses. Any one wins and old Arthur is back in front in the financial stakes. I was also on them at the time. Do you know that every one of those three horses was beaten in a photograph? Right on the line, 'on the nod', so to speak.

Poor old Arthur never recovered from such misfortunes. Any one winner from the three would have done the trick for him. Tommy Reidy rode all three horses and they were all very big prices. Arthur packed up training and some time later my good friend and wonderful rider, Tommy Reidy, was killed in a tragic car accident with a trainer's young son. I was greatly saddened by this cruel blow to people I knew so well.

Yes, I was doing okay, but there were still better days to come and fate dealt me a winning hand. Up until that time, I was getting some good information, but I needed more. I needed to cover more racing stables for my business, Infoform. But the majority of lads still kept me at arms' length. But that was something that was to change virtually overnight.

Black Malcolm was the hard case in town and feared by everyone, racing lads and townies alike. He hung about in the snooker room at the Carlton Hotel with all the local villains, like Kinlan, Bloater, Irish Collins and one-eyed Jack - a stable lad who had lost an eye years previously in a street brawl, plus a few unsavoury characters besides.

One night I had teamed up with one of my few friends in racing, a work jockey. I had always been pretty sharp with a snooker cue; they say it's a sign of my misspent youth. I would play for money. On this occasion, there was a good crowd of stable lads and townies watching the drama. It was the blue to win my go and it was right over the pocket. I couldn't miss. Black Malcolm started loudly abusing my partner in our doubles game, calling him a stable lad wanker, then he grabbed him very forcefully around the throat. It was typical. He was a malicious nasty bully who ruled the roost at the Carlton Hotel and many of the young stable lads were in fear of him. But trouble was brewing all right. Black Malcolm was just about to lose the game and his money with it. Probably all he had. His beer money for the rest of the week, I would say. Everything happened in a flash. I reversed my cue, grabbed it firmly halfway down the stock and brought it down hard as I could on the bastard's head. I knew if I didn't down him in one, I wouldn't live to get a second blow in.

What a crack! It echoed throughout the room. Luckily (or unluckily) he had a very thick skull but still crumpled to the floor. My blood was up.

"You're next if you want the same," I told his main side kick, one eyed Jack. He backed off. His playing partner, Kinlan, another villain, legged it. Like most thugs, he had no bottle once the pack leader was down. Black Malcolm was dragged to his feet and helped out into the street. He was finished. From that day on, he was never ever seen in town again and The Carlton Hotel became a better place; the lads could play snooker on the only table without asking his permission. But don't get me wrong. I don't believe in violence and can honestly say that it was the only time in my life that I willingly hurt somebody and, in this case, I certainly have no regrets.

The news of the demise of Black Malcolm soon got round the town. Lads in racing, especially after this incident, would seek out my friendship. I'd stood up for one of their own. I was well-respected now. The knowledgeable lads would regularly stop me in town for a chat and tell me just what I wanted to know. Many of them are around today and still good friends. Believe me when

I say that it's a dog eat dog situation in the racing business and you have to always keep one stroke ahead of your competitors and watch your back. I certainly became street-wise over the years, but had to stay always alert in order to stay on top. But any of the lads in trouble or needed money to help them out of a fix could rely on me. I was a soft touch. Some of those lads are jockeys or trainers today. They are still my friends.

One of my good friends at that time was Tony Orange. Tony was a local villain with a bit of known form, but knew his horses all right. He started out as a stable lad at Major Holliday's and then moved on to Jack Watt's stable. He was a fearless punter and an up-and-coming tipster who had put together a large mailing list. Tony over-stepped the mark with me just one time on a personal matter. A bit of business. I was fuming! However, a few months later I evened the score. I got the message on the grapevine that Tony was planning a big mailing shot to pull in some punters. The day he posted his mail shot out he confided the whole plan to me. (But I already had all the details from a so-called friend of Tony's). Tony was trying to make me envious, showing to me that he could beat me at my own game. Two weeks later in the pub I asked Tony how his mail shot had gone.

"Not one bloody reply!" he moaned. "I just can't understand it. It was a brilliant circular, offering real good information, mainly from Jack Watt's yard. Not one reply!"

The fact was that to even the score with Tony, I had filled in a re-direction form at the post office, signing his alias name, Tommy Jones, and arranging to have all the mail re-directed from his safe house to a particular address; a partly demolished terrace row of houses, all the fronts still standing, but the demolishers were working from the back knocking them to bits. But there was a front door still, with a letter box. That's all I needed.

A few months later I told Tony what I had done. His face was a picture, he couldn't believe it at first but, knowing me, he soon did. After he had recovered from shock, we had a good laugh and a couple of drinks. We were all square now. Still today, we are friends. Tony had a lovely girlfriend at the time called Jenny, who later became his wife. What a winning combination! Their son, Jason grew up to be the millionaire pop star, Jason Orange of the famous 'Take That' pop group. Jason is the splitting image of his father. God Bless Tony and all his family. We had some laughs in those days. Tony now lives near Manchester in relative luxury, thanks to Jason's generosity. I know Tony is dead proud of his son and rightly so. He wasn't born with a silver spoon in his mouth.

Back in the early days there was one particular scam that I pulled off which needed quite a bit of courage, I can tell you. It concerned a particular stable lad called Ally Shaw who worked for the trainer, Humphrey Cottrill. Humphrey was a true gentleman from the old school, upright and solid. As far as I know, all his horses were triers. Ally had only ridden one winner in his life as a jockey. It had landed a gamble for trainer Arthur Goodwill.

One day I persuaded Ally to let me write a letter in his name to a list of punters, glossing over his career and elaborating on his jockey skills. But no lies, just about truthful. I asked for the odds to £10 with a £10 deposit in the mail shot. Ally could keep the deposits for his co-operation. I just wanted their names and addresses to punt horses to. The bait was the address I was to use.

This was Ally Shaw jockey, c/o Trainer, Humphrey Cotterill at his stables in Newmarket. I then re-directed the mail to a different address and just waited for the replies. Ally was Humphrey's top work jockey and had told me the stable would shortly be having a lot of winners. I thought we should cash in on them.

For the first three days, it worked like a dream - then disaster struck; in all its so-called efficiency, the post office missed the re-direction instructions and delivered the mail straight to old Humphrey! Well, they said you could hear his voice all the way from his stable to the Newmarket clocktower. Ally was in deep water and, later, the Jockey Club's investigator was hot on my trail. As it happened, I had committed no crime and they backed off. But it was a close thing and certainly shook me.

The best thing that came out of the whole botch-up was that I gave those people who had replied three winning bets out of three. Ally's info was spot on so at least the punters were happy. Ally made a few quid and I did very well too, thank you. I don't think Humphrey ever quite got over the sheer audacity of this particular scam. But it harmed no one. I did a similar one the following year, but reminded the post office daily of the re-direction forms. I wasn't taking any chances!

Shortly after this, I moved into a particularly smart flat on the High Street but, at the same time, the realisation dawned on me that I really was a very small fish in the large pond of the tipping game. It was a few months after I moved in that I was exploring in the attic and discovered several large tea chests which were crammed full with registered envelopes. These were empty, of course, but I had a feeling that the respective names and addresses printed on each one would come in useful some day. The only major drawback was that they were so outdated; some postmarked back to 1949. Still, I was intrigued and made several enquiries, eventually discovering that a great tipster had lived in this same flat and that such was his coups, that the post-office delivered his mail in a hand cart! Furthermore, apparently this particular gentleman was a right toff (as they say!) and when he pulled off a particularly good coup, it was drinks all round, all night at the Carlton Hotel.

Some things never change! except the hotel's gone, of course, but the tipsters are still in town and the big boys are around as well, although may not be in the physical sense. John Blake is a good example. He lives on the South Coast in real luxury; one of the biggest tipsters in the racing game. Although he is not ethical in his dealings, I never advertised winners I didn't give, John Blake did and the racing public believed him

He also advertises in Newmarket as 'Martin Wells of Newmarket', M. L. Harrington and under many other aliases. Again, it's the re-direction game. All his mail was sent back to his bunker in Hampshire. John Blake uses many aliases and unethical ways of claiming winners; something I have never been guilty of. The Sporting Life and John Blake constitute the truly despicable side of racing to the man in the street while maintaining the face of respectability on the surface.

I tried to expose Blake as a conman but didn't get any where. I suppose because that particular paper, The Sporting Life, needed his advertising revenue; he was a big spender with them so they conveniently turned a blind eye to his unsavoury malpractice habits. Their reporter and chief bottle washer, Andrew Sims fondly referred to Blake as the Chicken Strangler. In my view, both Sims and the editor, Tom Clark are hypocrites of the first order. But more of that particular team later in the book. The latest I hear is that The Sporting Life is in trouble. I certainly won't be shedding any tears. I have a probable court action in the pipeline against this paper and its lies concerning my family and myself.

CHAPTER THREE

Believe it or not, I was becoming a semi-respectable sort of person in Newmarket. Well-liked and an easy touch for a few quid, if I say it myself. That's just the way I was, easy come, easy go. More important to me was the fact that I loved the life. The intrigue, the bet, that glowing feeling that washes over you when you stick up a good priced winner. And the glowing letters from your clients. But then there was the other side of the game - when your bet got beat. What a sickening feeling that was. It wasn't so bad when you backed a loser with your own money, but for my information to cause someone else to lose their money, that was bad news indeed. I genuinely cared about others having a losing bet because of me and it made me even more selective. I've seen the hard case tipsters laugh these losing bets off. I could never do that. I did have principles.

As aforementioned, I was doing just fine and was well-familiar with all the sharks in town. Some I backed away from, some I tolerated. For example, one particular Saturday, I had won more than £500 at the Newmarket races; a fair whack of money in those days. That night I went out to celebrate and, luckily, took the wad of notes with me. Good thing! I eventually returned home in a suitably festive mood, but not for long. When I pushed open the front door, hanging off its hinges, I was greeted with devastation. Everything had been pulled out of drawers and the floor was ankle deep in papers, etc. There wasn't much I could do that night though so I jammed the door closed with a heavy table and returned to my former state of drunken stupor, trying to blearily fathom out who had done such a thing. Instead of counting sheep, I was counting villains and quickly got up to more than twenty and was soon asleep. That was the trouble with Newmarket, it abounded with petty thieves and the local coppers were run off their feet. To the best of my knowledge, it's exactly the same today.

By this time, I was driving a second-hand Jensen Interceptor; a really flash car which topped 142 miles an hour with ease. How do I know? Because one early Sunday morning, I put it to the test, opened up the throttle and went flat out on a good stretch of road. I realised I was toying with early death and slowed down and never did that kind of speed again. But I had proved a point to a mate of mine with me. His knuckles were as white as his face as he clung on for dear life.

I had a girlfriend at the time. Her name was Jane and she was the daughter of a Newmarket vicar, a ballet dancer, a beauty, well-educated and well-spoken - nothing like me at all! I was a rough diamond - still am, I suppose. But, back then, I had a flash car, a good-looking girl and plenty of money in my pocket. What more could a young man want? My luxurious flat was the icing on the cake. It hadn't been so long ago when working in the shipyard that I had done my courting by bus and if I found a nice hay barn I was lucky. Today, it seems almost unreal. My life and different lifestyles. Today, I'm a bit of a wreck compared to my old self. But, believe me, I've had my moments.

Soon after Jane who went off to university, I moved on to another girlfriend, Carol, a lovely local girl who I married when she became pregnant with our first son, Tim. My job was to make the money and I did, more and more of it. I hadn't realised how well off I really was when single, now my earnings were cut smartly in half. It's not that I minded, but I still wanted my freedom to wheel and deal. Keep tipping and sniffing out those winning horses. Nothing changed in that respect. But my business 'Infoform' went to the wall, the reason? Well, when you have a good idea, everyone jumps on the band wagon and copies you. Very soon the market for form ratings was over-exposed.

By this time, I would go around to the stable yard with those lads who trusted me, usually during the evening or perhaps on a Sunday when the Guvnor (as the trainer liked to be called) was absent. I was gradually gleaning a lot of useful knowledge about bloodstock, including the pedigree and the horse's conformation. I was acquiring a good eye for picking out a decent racehorse. Of course, you need a lot of luck also. The best looking racehorse in the world with the best possible pedigree could turn out a right dud.

It was at John Winter's yard that, for the first and last time, I actually sat on a racehorse, following an all night party at the stable lads' accommodation; many lived on the premises in those days. Bravely (and foolishly) I volunteered to mount one of those graceful, glorious thoroughbreds that morning. The trainer was overseas at a racecourse with one of his horses and I was full of false and boozy bravado. After all, I had worked 200 feet up on a ship before. But once in the saddle, I had misgivings. I may have been only five foot from the ground but my undercarriage was distinctly unstable. I dug my heels in to make him move forward. He spun round, gave a snort and a jiggle and I went sky high landing squarely in the muck heap. How I stunk! Naturally, it was a cause of great mirth among the lads and they never succeeded to persuade me to mount a horse again, no matter how many pints I downed! Although I may have owned up to drinking twenty at one time, the closest bodily contact I had from that day forward was a pat on the neck.

On a more serious note, I have witnessed first-hand how a highly strung thoroughbred can do some real damage. I sometimes think that stable lads deserve danger pay.

In 1997, during my last year as a racehorse owner, there was a lovely young stable lass, just nineteen years old, who lost her life following a nasty fall from a racehorse I owned called *General Shabba* during a training gallop. This horse had been trained in my own racing stables. Unfortunately, it's easy for a horse to stumble, catch his hoof in a hole and lose balance, especially at a high gallop. I think of just one of my friends in racing, the jockey, Brian Taylor who was killed on a race-course, while others like Kipper Lynch had a promising career snatched from him when left with serious head injuries. Several jockeys I once knew have died in racing accidents, but it's a lot safer game now with strong head gear and plastic running rails at the racecourses. At the same time, I realise that jockeys are paid to take the risk, and that they are paid plenty for the privilege..

Just recently my next door neighbour, Declan Murphy, a great jockey over fences had to call it a day after a serious head injury. He does TV work nowadays. But not everyone is so lucky afterwards. I will say this, you are more likely to get seriously hurt or killed in a flat race than riding over fences. The Grand National course may be fearsome, with some mighty obstacles to negotiate, but you are going much slower than 40 m.p.h. which is the average racing speed of a horse running on the flat. I've lost friends, both national hunt jockeys and in flat racing. Broken bones are a very common occurrence indeed. Riding racehorses is a dangerous game, also always remember if ever going round racing stables, horses can bite. You can lose your fingers in a flash. Of course, most horses are gentle, but like in life, you get a few bad apples in the barrel.

Talking of bad apples, Lester Piggott who was sent to prison over tax evasion to the sum of several million pounds, most certainly was not a bad apple in my view. I would suspect over the years, many jockeys made plenty of money in back-handers. All in cash. Racing has always been awash with a cash flow to those highest in the game. Horse racing generates that sort of money. To the one extreme you have Lester Piggott, to the other the much more lowly stable lads who serve an apprenticeship like any other tradesmen and get peanuts in return for their labour. They deserve to get a few extra quid, or as much as they can get out of a horse they look after.

Nothing has ever given me greater pleasure than slipping a stable lad a few pounds for a little inside information. Not necessarily directly for the name of a winner, it's often more subtle than that, like telling me that a particular horse was still short of a gallop or two to be fully fit. That was the kind of information I appreciated, because it meant I could narrow down the field and would often end up with four or five horses in a race that were definitely not expected to win. You can make a few pounds on that information; there's lots of ins and outs to backing winners (or avoiding backing losers). As far as I am concerned, stable staff are the dog bodies of racing. They swear like troopers, they drink like fish, but I personally found them honest and trustworthy. The Jockey Clubs official line is against tipping horses if you work in racing. To my mind, that just encourages the villains and sharks to get in on the action. Let the lads have their punters officially. The Jockey Club knows all about insider tipping, and so do the trainers. It goes on in racing. It will always be the only way a racing lad can make a few extra pounds.

Later in my story, I will tell you my way in full detail; the secrets of betting that made me the owner of one of the finest stables in England with my own string of racehorses. And for any lads who worked in my stables and made a few pounds out of my winners, good luck to them, I say. They deserve it.

As time went by, I was gradually becoming more involved in the racing scene, the social side, the betting, the personalities and also in the horses themselves. Clearly, it was time to buy one. But where on earth would

I start? I was a little unsure of myself and eventually resorted to the impersonality of the sales catalogues. I spent hours studying these in great detail, finding out who had bought which horse, how he had raced, etc. etc One thing was evident; people seemed to invest more often in poor performers than good ones. I was going to make it as safe as possible and buy a winner. Losers are what you can expect to buy. Winners were harder to find. I was sure that I was going to be in the latter category; I couldn't afford it any other way. I also decided that the chances of a bloodstock agent or trainer buying a decent animal were not much greater than my own.

For instance, if Sheikh Mohammed - with all his expert advice, can buy a lot of junk, then buying junk is easy for anyone to do. Sheikh Mohammed paid over ten million dollars for one particular horse which he named *Snaffi Dancer* in Keeneland and it was useless. Along with his brothers, Sheikh Hamdan and Sheikh Maktoum, Sheikh Mohammed spent over $43 million at that one sale in the U.S.A. when they bought that yearling which was later to prove such a waste of money. But more about this later in the book.

There again, all the other country's leading owners have bought plenty of pigs in a poke. Despite all the top expert advice, many millions of pounds end up down the drain. At the same time, I realise that it's not easy to buy a winner, although I would have thought it would be easier if you have a few millions at your disposal. I was in charge of spending the moderate sum of over one million once on behalf of Classic Bloodstock shareholders. Like the Sheikhs with their top advisors, we could get a good one, if lucky, but it wasn't easy. With the Sheikhs, the more mud you throw at the wall, the more will stick so obviously keep throwing big money at it and, as sure as night follows day, you will get lucky someday. Bloodstock agents have it made, buying with other people's money, whether winners or losers, they get their percentage of the price paid for the animal, good or bad.

Personally, I find it amazing really, those bloodstock agents that have, by luck or judgement, managed to secure a decent horse now and again and like the world to know how clever they are. But the one fact that is generally swept under the carpet is that there are numerous moderate or useless animals bought on their advice - 'more bad 'uns than good 'uns'.

Anyway, the time had come for me to buy my very own first racehorse, but I didn't have millions to spend. In fact, I ended up spending just £180 for that first horse, *La Dolca Vita*. Money well spent for that filly, in turn, brought me my first ever success as a racehorse owner. I just bought her because I liked the way she looked in the sales ring. Her mother (*Dam*) had foaled winners previously, though a moderate pedigree, it was full of moderate winning horses.

I wasn't alone in seeing the potential there; that great trainer, Henry Cecil bought *La Dolca Vita*'s mother's next yearling the following year and that filly went on to be a winner as well. Why did I name her *La Dolca Vita* (sweet life) you may ask? Simple, my life was becoming pretty sweet by then. It seemed like nothing could go wrong.

First things first, there I was with a racehorse and I obviously needed to find a trainer. That wasn't difficult. Barry Hills had just set up in training at Lambourn. He had made his money working first for trainer, John Oxley and then being involved in training the Lincoln Handicap winner, *Frankencense* which landed a huge gamble backed from early 66/1 anti-post down to favourite. That filly was a dream machine for a gambler who did the business good and proper for those in the know, when the heavies (money) was down.

I did all right with that one also, punting it at all prices. I knew all about it from one of my inside contacts. But for the first bet of the flat season, I always asked for lower odds and I had lots of new punters on the horse as a free trial bet to sample my goods. So, while I did okay, it was not a killing in any shape or form - but it was for Barrington Hills and his cronies. They got themselves a sackful. If Barry Hills could mastermind a job like that Lincoln winner, he was my man. My judgement was spot on. Barry agreed to train *La Dolca Vita* for me. After all, now he had set up as a trainer himself, with his money won from the Lincoln handicap, he needed horses to train to get him started.

Sunday morning was the time when trainers, jockeys and owners get the ball rolling for business for the ensuing week. It was also the beginning of another new flat racing season and hope springs eternal in the tipster's heart. I was no different. For me, it was like being re-born. Newmarket comes out of its long winter slumber. "Chit, chat, don't back this, chit, chat have a bet on that." The telephone lines are red hot out of Newmarket, you can't find an empty telephone box for miles. In every one, the same scenario is taking place; stable lads giving their last years battered punters the old revival tonic. A typical conversation goes something like this.

"Forget last year, sir, horses were all wrong, they are all back in top form now. The 'Guvnor' thinks we had a virus last year or those that got beat did. Oh, all those other winners from our yard, the ones you didn't back, sir? Well, the 'Guvnor' thought they had no chance, he couldn't believe it himself when they won.

"Yes, I know some were well-backed, it must have been the bloody jockeys, having one or two for themselves. Look sir, it's all different in the yard now. That crook, the head lad's gone and good riddance. Never did like him and two work jockeys have gone away too. Got two new work jocks in the yard. We're best mates. Look sir, as I say, have a good bet on this one for yourself. Put a few quid on for me, if it wins sir, send it cash by registered post c/o the Post

*Office. Yes it's safe, the manager's my uncle. If it gets beat
...? This won't get beat sir, it's a certainty, catching pigeons
on the gallops. Trust me."*

*"Okay son, I'll give it a go, but last year's eleven bets
with only one winner and that was 4/7, a useless price.
The missus missed her usual week's holiday in Benidorm
because of your information. But I promise I will cover
you on this one, odds to a tenner okay?"*

"Better make it twenty, sir."

*"The wife wants to have an operation on her nose. God
knows how I'm going to get the money. I've been promising her since we got spliced. I tried to get the money last
year for the op. Bloody horses, f....ing virus. Okay son, I
will see what I can do."*

"Thanks sir, you're okay. I'll look after you. "

And so it goes on. Every punter gets a similar story
from his stable lad contact. It's all part of the game - the
racing game. And within a few weeks of the flat season
starting, it's a whole lot easier to find an empty coin box.
Many of those punters have been blown to bits. But it's
not from lack of trying; those same lads are genuinely
hoping their horse will win for you. That's what they have
gone through the hard, cold, wet damp long winter for - a
dream. A world apart from the typical spiv in his London
office with an accommodation address in Newmarket or
Lambourn and a thousand punters on his book. He will
give out five horses in a five horse race, two hundred punters on each, with odds to £20. The terms of business? The
spiv tipster can't lose. Any one of the five runners winning will do for him. What an easy way to make money! If
the favourite goes in at, say, 6/4 that means £6,000 to the
spiv. If the outsider wins instead at, say, 20/1 that's £80,000
for that same tipster. Does it really happen? You can bet
your life it does. I know some who do it, albeit on a smaller
scale but, believe you me, these big boys are out there
waiting to get you on their books.

Of course, not all tipsters are con men, but the honest ones are in the minority. I know a few decent tipsters trying to make a living and its frustrating for them to get business when battling against the sharks who make it sound all too easy.

I was never that kind of tipster. I like to think I gave out genuine racing information at a fair price. One thing for sure, I never got any complaints and, to me, that was all important.

After I had bought *La Dolca Vita*, it was always at the back of my mind if she could win a race, I'd stick her up to my punters. (That's racing slang for spilling the beans on her chances in a race - i.e.: that she is expected to win). Barry had only had the filly in training for a few months when he rang me up one Sunday morning.

"I've entered her in a poor maiden race at Wolverhampton, she can go a bit. I think there's a small race to be won." My heart missed a beat.

"At Wolverhampton?" I replied.

"No, not this time. We'll give her a run down the field. She will need the race, then we'll look at a race for her."

"Okay Barry, you're the trainer, but I want my pal, Taffy Thomas to ride her. Is that all right?"

"Yes, that's fine. I'll book him to ride her for you at Wolverhampton," he replied.

Could this be true, here I was, a shipbuilding lad with a race horse. Can't be bad!

The big day arrived and there I was, standing in the owner's ring for the first time in my life. Trainers everywhere, jockeys in colourful racing silks, small men - but in physique only. I felt like a fish out of water, as if I didn't really belong there - at least not yet. Taffy Thomas, my jockey, came out, touched his cap in a note of respect. "Afternoon, sir, " I spun round and looked behind me. No, he was talking to me, the owner. I still couldn't get used to this new sense of upmanship.

"Hi Taff," was all I could think to say. Normally in a pub with the jocks it's so different. "Those blue and white colours you're wearing, they're Barrow rugby colours?" I couldn't think of anything else to say.

"Yes, I know," Taff replied. "You told me the other night when we were on the piss in the White Lion. We listened to you for over an hour going on about Barrow Rugby Club. You bored our heads off." He grinned. I felt more relaxed, one of the boys again. I had always had a soft spot for Barrow Rugby. I went to Wembley once when they won the cup; a fantastic day out. Today they are a shadow of their former glory. They went downhill with the shipyard running down.

We all played rugby as kids. My youngest brother, Dave played for England under 21's in France, scored as well. I was so proud of him. We all were, but an ankle injury jeopardised his career as a professional player. Pity really, he was good. My other brother, Rick, played for the R.A.F. Sorry ... I'm drifting off the track.

Now came the orders. Trainer, Barry Hill's to jockey, Taffy Thomas. Me, straining to catch every word.

"Now then Taff, this filly goes a bit, so be careful. You should have no problem covering her up. Don't be hard on her, but then if you finish out the back, try and beat one or two."

"Jockeys mount!" was the loud cry from the ring steward. Barry gave Taffy a leg up. All the other trainers were dashing about getting their jocks on their intended mounts, then we were off to watch the race from the grandstand. I stood in the stand with my trainer, Barry Hill. "They're off!" was the message over the loudspeaker. My heart was thumping. I was very tense but don't know why. After all, I had not one penny piece riding on the filly. She got one mention on the racecourse commentary, about sixth place, then she went backwards fast, that was it. The race was over in a flash. She was a blur when she went past me. I wasn't crying with emotion, but my eyes were all misty and I was a little disappointed. After all, my trainer Barry Hills had said she could run a bit. Well, she didn't run very well that day. I had imagined that she would run a little better - even if she wasn't going to win outright.

Taffy came in and dismounted in the unsaddling enclosure for the 'also rans'. I couldn't believe the conversation that followed between the jockey and trainer. Taffy made an expression, eyes down to the ground and in a low whisper I heard him say, "I'm sure to get pulled in by the stewards." (He didn't and there was no enquiry). "Look that filly will win next time, but I won't ride her for you," he continued. "The stewards would crucify me." Then, with a nod of the head, he was gone.

Well for the life of me, I couldn't understand it. Back then, I was as green as grass. Win, win next time? I thought. He's having me on and the trainer is too. But I'd heard about jockeys stringing owners along before. No owner wants to hear his pride and joy is useless. And trainers? Well they can all tell a good story if they have to. I was not impressed one bit. Still, I had had a good day out. A runner in my own colours, rubbed shoulders with some of my idols; trainers and jockeys.

That night back in Newmarket, I had a quiet word with Taffy, my jockey in the Bushell Inn, my late Newmarket watering hole. You could always get a drink after time. Official closing in those days was 10.30 p.m.

"So, no good is she, Taff? Shall I flog her to somebody?"

"Don't be a fool, she'll win for you," he answered. "She just wasn't there to win today."

"Okay, Taff, I nearly believe you. I will keep her for another month and see."

The following Sunday morning, Barry Hills rang me.

"Ron, that filly of yours. There's a race up north at Thirsk. She should go there, it's an auction plate. She will only carry 7 stone 7 lbs. Ernie Johnson will ride.

"Right Barry," I replied. "How will she go?"

"She's an absolute stonewall certainty," he said.

I went goose pimply all over.

"She will what, Barry?"

"She will win," he replied. "Have what you like on her, but keep it quiet."

"Bloody hell, Barry, I won't even tell my mother." Then came the bombshell.

"Look Ron, you're the owner, if you don't go, everyone will think she's out for a run or no good. I'll make sure you're on at the best price available on the course."

"Yeah, okay Barry, you have my word. If you think that's best." I put the phone down. So I was going to have my own racehorse winning and I wouldn't even be at the race to lead her in? The thought of it was just unbearable. But I had given my word and I had work to do; my punter's list of letters to write, get that done first. Punters who could only take a bet by post. Then there were the punters I could contact directly via phone. I decided that I would do that the night before the race.

Finally, the big day arrived and I was well set up to make a nice few pounds. But I also sent a friend to the racecourse to back her for me. "If she wins I've pulled quite a coup!" I thought.

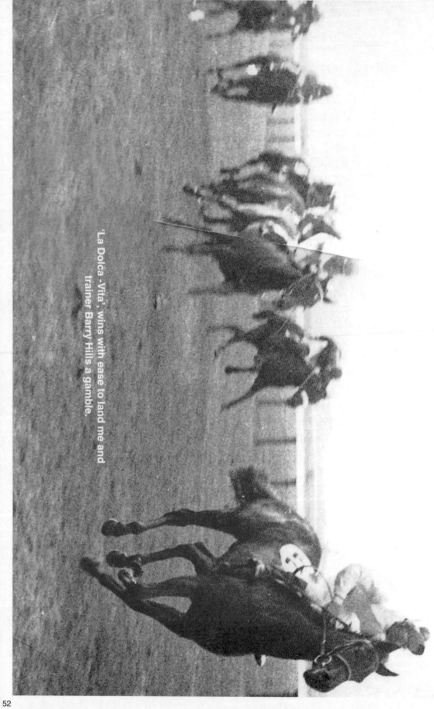

'La Dolca-Vita', wins with ease to land me and trainer Barry Hills a gamble.

CHAPTER FOUR

So there I am, in a seedy Newmarket betting shop owned by the local businessman, Terry Forman. (I was eventually banned from his shop all together for winning too often!). But Terry was okay, I liked him and used to even help him out, doing some nifty book-keeping for his wholesale newspaper business. Terry owned a few horses himself which were trained by Neville Callagan. He always told me when I could have a bet and when not. In the race for *La Dolca Vita* at Thirsk, there were a lot of runners, she was number 42; there were no starting stalls in those days. You just lined up the horses the best you could in front of the tape. Up goes the tape and you're running, easy as pie back then. If you're not there to win, hang back a bit, get caught flat-footed and you have no chance in a sprint race.

In Terry's betting shop, I was disappointed when my horse opened in the betting at only 7/4. I had expected at least 20/1. At least I got those odds myself with some of my betting money sent to the racecourse. My man gradually took all the best odds available down to 3/1 with the money I had entrusted to him. Anyway, there was no TV in the betting shops back then. Instead, the commentary came over the loudspeaker, directly from the racecourse.

"The distance is only five furlongs less than a minute for the whole race!" I listened to the commentator announce. "They're off! *La Dolca Vita* is in the lead. It's still *La Dolca Vita* going easily now, drawing well ahead. It's a one horse race, the further she goes, the further she is drawing away!" Then finally, those magic words ... "It's number 42, *La Dolca Vita*, the winner!"

The other 41 entries never got a mention! I was on cloud nine. So this was what racing was all about. Lay them out to win a race and get the money on. It was also a first for Barry Hills; his first ever winner and marked the beginning of his highly successful career as a trainer.

My next job was easy. I just had to hang in there until Monday morning and wait for the postman to knock. But he didn't just knock once, he knocked for days on end and, pretty soon, my sitting-room floor was littered with money and postal orders. There were very few cheques in those day, it was mainly cash or postal orders which were usually not crossed so just as good because they could be cashed at the post office counter.

I took those winnings and invested in my very first house, detached with three bedrooms. I was the new kid on the block and popular with everyone, from the bank manager to the neighbours. But life has a way of kicking you in the teeth now and again, and the first knuckleduster was to come sooner than I could have imagined. Until that time, however, I was cruising along very nicely, thank you.

It was just a week later when the phone rang. It was Barry.

"Ron, I've entered *La Dolca Vita* in the Selling race at Wolverhampton," he announced. "There should be no bid for her and she'll win again. This time she'll start the favourite though. You can have a big bet on her. The prize money is about £800."

"Okay Barry, but I want Taffy to ride," I replied. "I owe him a winner."

"No problem. See you at Wolverhampton!" He hung up.

A few days later, I presented myself at the Wolverhampton racecourse, dressed to kill in my new patent leather shoes, slick suit and Crombie overcoat. A suede trilby completed the look. My mother wouldn't have recognised me, I chortled to myself. For that matter, I hardly recognised myself.

At Wolverhampton, I quickly found the saddling enclosure which was exclusive, for owners, trainers and jockey. I looked disdainfully around at the other horses. As a typical owner, I only had eyes for my horse. As usual, there were some last minute instructions from the trainers to the jockeys.

"Okay Taff, she will win okay, but the ground's very heavy, so keep her up to her work."

I hadn't punted her this time. I never did like punting short priced horses. Anyway, you're not telling anyone anything they don't know already. Most people can guess those sort correctly. But I had told any punters who rang me to back her, but not to put anything on for me.

I sent a £1,000 with my main man to the London betting shops, reasoning that she could be a slightly better price off course. For me, it was a big cash bet. I also had two £500 pounds bets at evens at the track. I had guessed right, she went to 5/4 off course which was okay for the thousand I had sent down to London but, after I paid my man's expenses, there wouldn't be much in it at 5/4. There again, she could have been 7/4, in which case a journey to London would have been well worthwhile. I had £2,000 on the filly in total, a nice easy way of doubling my money if she won.

I watched the race through my brand new top-of-the-range Zeizz binoculars. I always bought the best of anything when I had the money. No danger! She won on a tightish rein easily by twelve lengths. Not Taffy's fault for winning by so far! If you slow down on a heavy going surface, you can get stuck in the mud. Anyway, the problem was that another trainer, Pat Rohan, started to bid for her in the winning enclosure which is the well-known practice in selling races. I had to go to £1,000 to retain her. At the end of the day, with prize money and winnings, I still had only cleared about £2,000. If there had been no bid for her, it would have been nearer £3,000, still I was happy, arms swinging, a spring in the step, I must get a money belt, I thought!

She never won again.

A third and then fourth place in a good quality race showed her true colours and I sold *La Dolca Vita* at the end of the season.

This is another little story which is completely true. A good few years ago, I was at the races when a guy approached me about a horse a friend of mine was riding at Yarmouth that day.

"Will it win, son?" he asked.

"Well, it will be a very short priced favourite, but I think it's a good thing, so does the jockey," I replied, thinking that there was no harm in his question.

"Yes, it's a good thing by all accounts," he replied. "There's £500 in cash in it for your jockey friend if he gets beat." Now, that was a good back-hander in those days. I couldn't place this guy, although I thought I'd seen his face somewhere before. "Okay," I said. "I'll ask my mate, the jockey. I should think that £500 in cash would be fine."

But the more I thought about it, the more I didn't like it. In the end, I didn't say anything. I had a feeling that my friend was likely to have said no, and the very question to him could damage a good friendship between us.

It was only about an hour before the race. I made myself scarce until the start. I didn't have a bet. The favourite was odds on "under starter's orders." The stalls open, the horse rears up and the jockey is unseated. I couldn't believe it. Obviously, in my mind this was a pure fluke, an accident and coincidence. I thought no more about it that day. Only that I could have taken a chance and told the guy a lie, saying the horse had been stopped.

I was driving jockeys and the object was to get away fast after the last race. While rushing on my way out to the car park someone pushed a package right at me. I honestly thought someone had given me a sandwich by mistake. I automatically grabbed it, got in the car and opened it and there was a wad of notes. I thought there had been some mistake of identity!

I put the package in the glove compartment, spun the car around, got the jocks in and set off like the clappers back to Newmarket and the White Lion which was the main watering hole for jockeys after a race meeting.

Much later, I slunk back to the car and counted the money, £500 exactly. I didn't know who that guy was or why he had given me the money, for certain. I most certainly had not confirmed any deal. I obviously kept it, reasoning that, if it was a mistake, they would ask for it back.

A week or so later, I was at Windsor Races when I spotted that same guy who had first approached me on the racecourse at Yarmouth talking to a well-known bookmaker. He spotted me at the same time, winked and just looked away.

I kept the money.

I was now in the market for buying another horse. I put my ear to the ground and, sure enough, soon heard about a horse called *Hickleton* which was due to run in a 'seller' at Newmarket that coming Saturday. He was owned by Lady Halifax, trained by John Oxley and ridden by Grenville Starkey; the jockey who had landed the Lincoln Handicap two years earlier aboard Barry Hills' famous coup on Frankincense.

My informant proved spot on. There was a job on and, furthermore, an owner who was friendly with the jockey, Grenville Starkey would be there to bid for the horse (after he had won!). I punted *Hickleton* well up and, as I had the information to hand early on, I did the letters three days before and the phone-calls the evening before the race.

Basically, if I knew about a horse and gave it to my punters, I always backed it myself with my own money. That's just the way it was and I reasoned it like this: if it's good enough to give to someone else, it should be good enough for your own money. (Remember, at the beginning of the book when I asked you which frame would fit me best? I hope you continue to bear this point in mind ...).

I have felt the pain first-hand of losing money betting; it's a pain that settles deep in the pit of the stomach. And this principle of also backing any horse I punted has helped me keep my feet on the ground. Please accept this as the truth. It is important to me. I can't stand tipsters who tip horses to others, yet won't risk a penny of their own. In fact, I can tell you now that that is exactly how 99% of them operate, By the time I've finished this book, my credibility may be zero, so allow me that one indulgence. Actually, I feel pretty good that I am not a shallow, uncaring tipster....

Back to the *Hickleton* horse. Needless to say, he won with ease. The horse had a bit of class. He was miles better than a selling plater

Now, when a horse has just run a race, he is very sweaty and not looking his best. *Hickleton* looked a sorry sight indeed. He was a very small horse with a light frame but I knew that he was well-thought of in his stables and that his owner, Lady Halifax had paid about thirty-three thousand guineas for him as a yearling which was mega money in those days.

I had had a nice winning touch. Now it was time to play up my winnings. I decided to bid up to £2,000 for him in the ensuing auction which took place fifteen minutes after the race. This was my limit and, in my opinion, what he was worth. The auctioneer was asking for bids starting at five hundred guineas. I thought I would start the ball rolling and got his attention with a nod. Okay, we're off. I've a bid for five hundred guineas. He repeated it once, and then again and rattled on trying to get a better bid. I could hardly believe my ears! There was a silence which seemed like an hour, but was actu-

My lovely ex wife Carol
with me at Churchills Caberet Club,
New Bond Street, London, celebrating Hickleton's
win at Ascot.

ally just a few minutes. The hammer crashed down. Sold! He was mine. I later found out that the other interested prospective bidder arrived just twenty minutes too late, apparently held up in a traffic jam, the only traffic jam I have ever blessed.

This horse turned out to be a real bargain. That night the trainer, Gerry Blum called round to my house and offered me a £1,000 for the horse and a chance to double my money. There is a golden rule in racing which is to take advantage of a profit whenever you can, but I had a gut feeling about this horse, so refused. The next day he was on his way to Barry Hill's at Lambourn and, later that same year, he won his first race for me at Warwick. His new trainer Barry rang and said, "You've got a bargain with this one, Ron. I've been giving him a good bit of work over a longer distance. It's just what the horse wants, a trip. He will win at Warwick for you. He is a good thing," (racing slang for a sure winner). It was the same routine. All the punters on and a good bet from myself resulted in a boost to my bank balance because, as expected, *Hickleton* won very easily indeed.

The jockeys were all getting ready for their winter contracts abroad - Hong Kong, Barbados, India, Ceylon (now called Sri Lanka) - while I settled down to a few months of homely comforts, financially well fixed, playing cards or snooker with the lads and anticipating a successful season to come. But, somehow it seemed a longer winter than most. I was itching to have a few more tilts at the bookies with Hickleton. Another bonus was that, upon his return to England after riding the winter season in India, jockey Taffy Thomas was coming to live with my family as a lodger which I thought was great. But I vowed I wouldn't trouble him by asking him too much about racing information. I thought it would be wiser, and more personally advantageous, if we just drifted into an easy confidentiality.

CHAPTER FIVE

The flat season started off in Newmarket (as it always does); the same old routine, full of hopes and dreams. Like the previous year, I struck early. Barry gave *Hickleton* a pipe opener in a minor race at Warwick. We didn't back him to win, he needed the run. If he had won then he would have received a 5 lbs penalty for the Great Metropolitan Handicap at Epsom and that was the race we were laying him out for. Our plan worked perfectly, he won the latter easily and I profited once again.

The only niggling factor that day was that Barry Hills very nearly took him out of the race! It had poured with rain the previous night and that same morning and the going was heavy. Barry had his doubts and didn't really want him to run.

"Look Barry," I told him. "His sire is Exbury and he gets plenty of winners in France under similar ground conditions. I think this horse is made for heavy ground. He has the light physique. I am pretty sure he's a horse who will act on heavy going." Barry wasn't convinced. We had just ten minutes to make a decision.

"Let's toss a coin!" I ventured. "Heads, he runs; tails, he doesn't. That way, fate will decide for us." Barry agreed and we flipped a coin. It came up heads.

I shot round to the row of bookmakers and sought out my partner, Bunny Warren. I had recently acquired a half share in his bookie business. I told him. "Don't back him, just lay the field and keep him on the right side of our book." Of course, I had to back him. I had stuck him up to my punters. That old principle of mine again. I had punted him, so was obliged to lose cash, along with my clients.

To tell the truth, I didn't have all the confidence in the world that day because of the above-mentioned ground conditions. But the Gods smiled on me and the rest is history. One thing I nearly forgot to mention was exactly how I was spending my winnings. By this time, I was blowing the large majority of it on 'wine, women and song' - as the saying goes.

Just two years previously, The Sunday Mirror had approached me to write a few articles and tip a few horses in my column. I agreed. Although it was an easy job, I couldn't handle it. I just couldn't come to terms with giving away all that inside information to the general public. I struggled with my conscious. (Yes, I do have one!) and did the only thing I could. I resigned. Sometimes I wonder where I would be today if I had stuck that job out.

Monty Court (who later became the Editor of The Sporting Life) was second in command on The Sunday Mirror sports desk at the time. Monty didn't like me, perhaps he thought I was too clever for him. Maybe he thought I was after his job. Although, most people in racing regarded him highly, I wasn't impressed with Monty, nothing personal, just not my cup of tea, that's all..

The main man, the Sports' Editor, George Casey, had me under his wing though and there were plenty of perks back then if you were associated with the newspaper, including tickets to major boxing matches, cricket, football, etc. I took advantage of everything going, particularly boxing and cricket which, after racing, are my favourite sports. In return for those favours, I gave George and some of the lads at The Sunday Mirror a number of good tips which definitely were not for publication.

George used to come and see me at Newmarket and we would typically spend a couple of hours at the pub. I thought he was a terrific guy. Although I only spent a few hours a month at the newspaper offices, I was invited to his home once for Sunday lunch.

I enjoyed it immensely. George treated me like a son. He had a very nice daughter who was about my age and very classy. I would have loved to have asked her out for a date. But it could have been suicidal in front of George, so I played it steady. On the way home from London to Newmarket, I regretted the fact that I hadn't tried to chat her up. Even if she had given me the cold shoulder, at least I would have tried. Instead, I acted like a wimp which was definitely not my style, which was more like 'In Like Flynn'. If knocked back, it didn't matter because, like buses, another would soon be along, and there might be room for you.

It was time for the Chester Cup, a race Barry was desperate to win. We went there with all the confidence in the world. However, *Hickleton* was beaten by just a head. We both knew that he should have won and was just an unlucky loser that day. When you get beat in racing, all the old excuses come out - "he lost a shoe, swallowed his tongue, the saddle slipped, the jockey gave him a bad ride, he wasn't trying, he had a virus...". In fact, anything but the brutal truth - the horse just wasn't up to scratch. "He wasn't good enough and that's that" has always been my saying if beaten when the money was down.

But on that day in the Chester Cup, I have to say that *Hickleton* was just downright unlucky, beaten by only inches after getting boxed in. My jockey, Ernie Johnson couldn't look me in the eye when he came in. Timeform, the Bible in racing, also stated that the horse was unlucky. More to the point, however, was the fact that I had lost big money on that race. It was a very serious setback for me. I had gone in 'with my head down' (put too much money on him). To balance my bank account after that loss, I sold a half share in my horse to Bill Ward.

At the same time, I did have some very big hitters indeed around then who were also putting good money on for me; Irish lads living in and around Dublin. They had been very generous to me over the Great Met. winner and I was on to heavy money if my horse had won the Chester Cup. I was going to the horse sales in Dublin shortly thereafter and would have liked to have a nice winner for the Irish boys under my belt.

It was a long journey by car back for me from Chester to Newmarket, made worse by my switching on the radio for the Sports Report and hearing the race commentator, Peter Bromley saying, "There's been a drama in the Chester Cup! The winner should have been *Hickleton* but the jockey, Ernie Johnson was not at his best." Johnson had rode a Derby winner the year before on Blakney but was apparently having a bad day at the office at Chester. That radio report made me feel worse. If *Hickleton* had done the business as expected, I would have cleared £100,000 from my own bets and my punters, the prize money was just incidental.

Royal Ascot follows the Chester Cup meeting and that was the venue for Hickleton's next objective. The Queen Alexandra stakes at Royal Ascot with all its pomp and ceremony with everyone dressed in all their finery. It was not for me in those days, I felt I would be so out of place in topper and tails. So I stayed home and watched the race on TV. The horse finished second. I have always regretted missing out on that Royal Ascot experience, more for personal feelings. I thought that, for some reason I didn't fit (it was a working-class attitude, it's hard for me to explain). *Hickleton* returned to Royal Ascot the following year and this time won the Queen Alexandra stakes but, like the fool I was then, I had sold the horse. Later I bounced back from those alcoholic hazy years. And, indeed, I went to Royal Ascot in topper and tails as an owner of another horse.

Hickleton made up my losses for me at the next Ascot meeting later that season when he won the Brown Jack Stakes. Lester Piggott rode him that day. The Irish boys were well suited. A week later, they flew over and settled their dues, paying me off with brown envelopes, sealed with wax by the Irish Bank, each containing £500. I tossed them carelessly on top of the wardrobe, unopened. Things were going great. The plan was that Taffy Thomas and myself would fly to Dublin at the end of the season for an Irish shindig at their expense; the full works with all the comforts laid on. And I mean all the comforts, if you get my drift.

But I already had an Irish girlfriend who I had been introduced to the previous year by her father, a punter of mine and keen golfer. On his invitation, I had flown to Dublin for the Irish Golf Open for a few days and met his daughter, an Irish beauty called Breeda Caitlin O'Prey (Caitlin is Irish Gaelic for Katherine). We hit if off right away - sweetly so. She came to London a few times for the weekend and I would shoot down to stay at her hotel. At other times, we would meet in Douglas on the Isle of Man.

I was, of course, married at the time but she was very special to me all the same. Still today, years later, she is often on my mind. I can close my eyes and picture her laughing with those beautiful twinkling Irish eyes. But I knew that we had no future together. My prospects for making money lay in Newmarket while Breeda loved her home in Killarney, County Kerry too much to ever contemplate leaving.

I truly hope that some lucky guy has made her very happy. Girls like Breeda Caitlin don't pass through your life often yet, when they do, the memories last forever.

The Irish boys put us up at the Druries Hotel, the best one in town. Three years ago I returned when in Dublin to buy horses at the Bloodstock sales. I was sad to see that it is a mere shadow of its former self.

Back then, though, we had a great time, witnessing true Irish hospitality first-hand and at its best. Taffy Thomas was treated like some sort of God by the Irish boys. Although he wasn't the jockey of my greatest coups, he was the 'Jock on the Block' - part of the team. One little story here: When Lester Piggott came into the saddling ring at Ascot, he doffed his cap to me and said, "I don't known how this horse got beat at Chester. He won't get beat today." That was enough for me. The king has spoken. I hurriedly said goodbye and rushed round to the betting ring, emptying my pockets, completely on Lester's confidence. *Hickleton* only won by a neck. When Lester came into the winning enclosure, I told him. "You just made it Lester!" He replied with that grin of his,

"No, he won easy. Always had a bit in hand. Nice horse this." Then he was gone. So was I, round to the bookmakers to collect my money. That night Carol and I threw a party for our friends at Churchill's Cabaret Club in Bond Street, London.

I never asked Taffy at any time for a bit of inside information. Perhaps he would say something one day, perhaps not. It was up to him. I was happy just with our friendship.

However, out of the blue, one morning at breakfast, he suddenly said, "I'll ride a winner today!" It was the way he said it, the tone of his voice. I quickly looked through The Sporting Life, 20/1 was the price, not one expert tipped him. I ran through the form. No wonder, he was 20/1! On paper, it looked like it would be a struggle to win any kind of race. I looked up at Taffy. He said nothing, just looked piercingly back at me. I decided that I wasn't going to question him further and knew straight away that it was a job, the job I was waiting for. 'Help yourself boyo,' went through my mind.

Breakfast was at 10 a.m. in my house in those days, after the early morning first lots in the stables. Jockeys didn't go back for second lot. Anyway, down to the business in hand. Obviously, my letter men had no chance. The information to hand was far too late. I also couldn't back Taffy's horse in town with heavy money at the bookies in that area as it could get back to the wrong people and I could lose Taffy's confidence. Quick planning was called for. I had about four hours before the race.

I had built up a decent number of punters in Trinidad over the years, those lads love a bet; the same in Barbados. If my memory serves me right, there was five hours time difference and I had one very big hitter in Ceylon (now Sri Lanka) who was a tea baron. That was the only way to operate; the coup for my business, all the bets out of the country. It worked like clockwork, of course. I had a few grumbles from the Caribbean, though. Those lads don't like to be disturbed from their business without prior arrangement. But my big hitter in Ceylon was a real gentleman and always ready for a big bet. All I had to do was leave a message with his house boy and tell him that this was a bit special and I would be well taken care of financially. And special it turned out to be.

The horse won by ten lengths that day. As usual, I stuck to my principles about backing these horses myself. I just had a fiver each way, a fun bet as it drew no attention to me. A couple of days passed and I received a call from Ceylon. No problem. A very good bet indeed had been struck on my behalf and a substantial cheque was in the post. That was excellent news indeed! The main punter had done the business. Anything coming from the Caribbean team was a bonus.

I had another good betting tip from Taffy later that season and it won at 100/7, but, again, I was informed very late and my Ceylon punter was in Africa, while the Trinidad team were in business in South America at the time. So I couldn't take maximum advantage of the job.

After *Hickleton* won the Brown Jack stakes at Ascot, I sold all my share in the horse. What a mug I was! He finished up winning close to £28,000 in prize money all told and was sold to stand at stud in South America as a

Hinckleton spreadeagle his field to win the Great Metropolitan Handicap at Ascot

Beaten by a head in the Chester Cup, and it cost me £100,000.
about £10,000 per inch on the line!

Me with my wife Carol, and our four lovely children. My eldest son Tim stands behind me.

Building sandcastles with my boys at Blackpool, on a rare day off from racing

sire for £60,000. Remember, he only cost five hundred guineas when I bought him. I did well out of the old boy but if I had hung on and kept him I would have done a lot better. In those days, you could buy a very nice house for £5,000.

From that day on, it was a downward spiral and I seemed powerless to stop it. I was very much into partying then and there was a group of jockeys who were my drinking buddies. The private parties were pretty wild at my house and other 'safe' houses, but clean (to a point, anyway...). For instance, Willie Carson and a few other racing people would swap their outfits with the girls and vice versa. I vividly remember how I was wearing a very flattering gold lamÈ dress one time while Willie Carson was in a nice white dress. From then on, we always referred to Willie as Kitty Carson.

Peter, another friend from those days, was tragically gunned down some years later in Newmarket High Street over an affair with a woman by her ex-boyfriend. Peter was a nice guy. The only illegal vice in the town back then was cannabis and Newmarket was close to the American Airforce Base where it was readily available. Although I never saw any of the jockeys using it, they certainly knew how to drink! And I was no different. My personal champagne bill at the White Lion was always in the high figures. I threw a lot of parties in those days. We called ourselves the 'inner circle'.

For me, the money was easy come, easy go. However, in my case, it started going faster than it was coming in. Drink was slowly destroying me, especially my sense of judgement. I was also losing heavily at cards schools in Newmarket and the Playboy Club in London. I even had girls from the then infamous Stork Club sent up to Newmarket's White Lion pub by taxi for the 'inner circle' boys. I paid the bills. I'd started getting a taste for the high life the previous year when I drove several jockeys to the

Top left. Peter, who was murdered in Newmarket High Street. Jockey Willie Carson (front) in a dress, me (far right) in a dress. One of our 'Inner Circle' parties at a safe house in Newmarket.

Trainer Barry Hills with my horse Hickleton in the winning enclosure after winning the Great Metropolitan Handicap at Epsom

Hilton Hotel for the stable lad boxing finals. Afterwards I would typically go clubbing with a crowd of about eight jockeys. We usually went to the Playboy Club and The Stork Club. There was no stopping me. I was having a ball (or being a wally!), spending my money like a fool.

To my mind, jockeys are randy little sods and it wasn't unusual for some to have two different girls during one evening, straight after another. That wasn't my weakness. By this time in life I loved only one thing, and that was the bottle; champagne and brandy then Bacardi and coke when I was cutting down.

The jockeys were (and still are) a close-knit set. Sunday lunch-time was the day to meet at our local watering hole, The White Lion. I remember once how I followed three smart suited Indian blokes into the toilet because they, in turn, had followed in a jockey friend of mine and I thought there might be some trouble. As it turned out, they were just paying him the money due for racing information. I duly apologised, turned around and walked straight out. It was none of my business. Many jockeys had private punters; it was all part of the racing game.

You'll like this story.... Bill Ward who had bought *Hickleton* off me wanted to call at Lester's home in Newmarket following a race Lester had won for him. He had an envelope with £500 in it for a present for Lester. Bill said to me as I waited in the car. "He is sure to give me a bit of info. He will probably invite me in. See you in a while!"

Within two minutes, Bill was back in the car. "Not in, Bill?" I asked.

"He was in all right," Bill said. "I gave him the money. He thanked me, then shut the door in my face and left me standing there. Typical Lester, I thought and Bill was a typical mug. That was £500 of his money down the drain.

The following two years I had bad seasons I bust up with Taffy Thomas and he moved out of my house. A few of the other jockeys cold-shouldered me and my information was fast becoming inaccurate rubbish. The drink was seriously starting to affect my once reliable judgement.

The previous Autumn I had bought a two year filly in Ireland at the Dublin horse sales. As usual, the Irish boys laid on all my comforts, but I had Breeda to meet me as usual. I was drinking far too much though. Breeda Caitlin was a real head turner, a top notch Irish Colleen and I was trying hard not to blow myself to bits with booze; a difficult task in those dark days.

One night during the Dublin horse sales, we had dinner in our posh hotel and stayed at our table having yet another bottle of champagne. At the next table was Henry Cecil, he was also drinking a lot in those day and smoking big cigars. I invited him to join us and told him that I had just bought a horse at the sales. We chatted easily. Henry didn't even seem to notice me. His gaze was fixed on my beautiful Irish girlfriend and they seemed to get along really well - although Henry did most of the talking as I recall. When she went off to the powder room, he laid his cards straight on the table.

"I'll train that new filly for you," he told me. "Come and have dinner with Julie and me at Warren Place when you return home to Newmarket."

Back then, Henry wasn't the high flyer that he is today, but he had class and style and my lady companion was clearly impressed. "Any 'chance' with the girl?" he added in a hushed whisper, "... and I will do you a cheap deal on training the filly."

I turned him down flat. I like to think that I couldn't be bought on some things, but the truth was that I was jealous of his obvious charm. Deep down, I was still just a working class lad. Looking back, I guess that Henry was pretty inebriated at the time so perhaps it was nothing more than a bit of a joke. One fact was sure, he liked the ladies! But I always liked and respected the man, and there aren't too many of that breed in the racing world.

I never did go to dinner with him and Julie but that was my fault, not his. I spoke to him many years later when he signed a copy of his latest racing book for me. I happened to lightly mention the incident but immediately wish I'd kept my mouth shut! He just smiled that supercilious smile and said that he couldn't remember the occasion. Game, set and match to Henry. May he remain a top trainer for many years to come.

CHAPTER SIX

The new filly of mine was my final throw. I just couldn't seem to back or punt a winner. My judgement had gone haywire. The bottle called the tune. Arthur 'Fidler' Goodwill was my new trainer in whom I placed all my faith. Barry Hills and I no longer saw eye to eye. Barry was training for the big boys now and certainly didn't need the likes of me by then. Fidler did, however. He was perfect for me, desperate for horses with little money to his name, but a more decent chap you couldn't meet. We struck a deal straight away. The problem was the horse, not Fidler. She was named *Highly Perfumed* and Fidler trained her the best he could and eventually found a couple of races to run her in to increase her level of fitness. Then he ran her a few more times out of her distance in order to get her handicap down.

All this was taking time, however, and I was getting nervous and running out of money fast - very fast. My luck was at rock bottom; my golden touch succumbed to the devil drink. Finally, my last reserve of those famous brown envelopes with the Irish money was gone and the debts started mounting up at a steady pace. I was still living it up, but on credit now. I was in serious trouble with no one to blame but myself.

According to Fidler, I had one big chance. He was confident that the filly would win the seller at Newmarket. The South African jockey, John Gorton was to ride her. I knew that he was good enough, it was the horse that was the problem. Was she good enough? My punters had lost enough for this season and the Irish boys were out of the game altogether. They were skint too. Not one winner. My confidence was zero. But it wasn't just me who had failed the Irish boys. I never gave out many bets. Another tipster had got them in his clutches.

My Ceylon man had also disappeared underground and wouldn't surface from his bunker to take my phone calls. The only chance I had was with a couple of big hitters in Trinidad; unsavoury characters but with plenty of money. I had received a visit from this particular team two years previously; a couple of them were built like gorillas and dripping in gold jewellery. They were a flash lot, that's for sure, and I knew I could easily place myself on a knife's edge. Anyway, the horse would win, I tried to convince myself continually. It had to, there was no other choice.

I spent a lot of time on the phone to the boys in Trinidad. "Look," I pleaded. "I need this one badly and so do you. Please, put me £4,000 on and if it loses I will pay you back." I was so bloody desperate. "And you lads have £1,000 on for yourself. If it gets beat, I will pay you that money back, as well - £5,000 in total." Little did they know that I didn't even have this amount available. I always suspected that they were involved in drug smuggling or distribution. They had lots of readies (cash). But that was their business, I just wanted that £4,000 on my horse desperately, so that I would be out of debt and back in front. "Please God," I prayed." Let my horse win this time. I really need this one to do the business for me."

I stayed awake the whole night before the race, despite being spaced out with booze. At the race track in *Highly Perfumed's* race, in the betting she opened up 5/1 then to 4/1 to 7/2. Who the hell is backing her? I thought. Must be Fidler's punters. I knew I could only be on at starting price in Trinidad. The market move had already cost me £6,000 if she won at 7/2, I reasoned. 7/2 would do me fine. Don't be greedy, son, I thought. Keep your composure. Get them off starter, I prayed silently, ... before she shortens again.

I looked down at the bookies boards from the grandstand, 3/1. Hell! Anyway, as long as she wins, I thought, that is all that matters. £12,000 will do. It would have been £20,000 if she had stayed at 5/1 in the betting. The market moves had nicked £8,000 off me, I reasoned.

They were off! She was soon going nicely and hit the front with a hundred yards to go. I lost my cool completely, shouting my head off. "Go on, girl. Go on, you beauty!" A multitude of thoughts flashed through my mind. Fifty yards to go and she was still in front. She must win!

Next, there was a scene that has stuck in my mind like a Technicolor nightmare. Gorton cracked her with the whip and she swerved abruptly sideways across the course. She was beat right on the line! I was rigid with shock, still standing there, half an hour later in the same spot in the stands, my jaw set solid. My God! This time I am really done for, good and proper, I thought.

The Monday following the race at Newmarket was the worst day in my life. I went to the estate agents to sell my lovely house, having to first explain the situation to my wife. It was her palace, her security and, while she had enjoyed the fruits of my early success, she was in no way to blame for the downfall. Just the previous winter, we had spent three weeks holidaying in the Canary Islands, all first class. I had honestly believed that I had the world at my fingertips. I had bought a new sport's car every year and drank champagne continually. The money had been so easy to get, so why not? Now I regretted not having saved for 'a rainy day', let alone a downpour. I had no choice. It was too late. I had to pay.

I was grimly aware that the Trinidad lads would have to be paid their money fast. They were not the kind of people you mess with. At least my house was worth a lot more now. I had spent some of my winnings building two extensions and paid for the same in cash.

At least I was in luck there. Someone who lived close to us had apparently had his eye on the house for some time. There was no quibbling over the price and we shook hands on the deal in my lounge. He was delighted.

Then something very strange happened. Now this is most bizarre. Later that night, just after midnight, I was awoken from my sleep by a very loud urgent banging on the door. I went downstairs and opened the door. Standing there was my brother, Rick and his wife, Helen. They said that they were very worried about me. Apparently, they had heard my voice in their garden moaning and calling out. "Help me! Help me!" They decided that I was definitely in trouble but searched the garden and I was nowhere to be found. Hence their arrival on my doorstep from their home which was right next door to the man who was buying my house. I was still standing there by the open door listening to this strange story when I felt something touch me as it glided past and went upstairs. I felt the coldness and the hair on the back of my neck stand up. It was a very odd experience. I immediately followed this thing - whatever it was, upstairs and sensed that it was in my son's bedroom.

I was right, I was convinced it was somewhere in the room. My small son was there in bed, apparently sound asleep but with his eyes wide open. I had a strong sense that whatever this strange force was, it meant no harm. I picked my son up, still apparently asleep and carried him to my bedroom. When I returned back to Timmy's room, I felt the icy cold again. I slowly opened the bedroom window and said. "Please go, please go. You don't belong here." And the spirit was gone.

I was very shook up, I can tell you, but the shock was greater the following morning when I discovered that the gentleman set on buying my house had been killed instantly at midnight in a car crash a few minutes before my brother and his wife had called round. I know he loved the house and he had a young son about the same age as Tim. A priest told me later that this man's spirit had gone to my house as he considered it his. And it would have been. I shook hands on the sale. Although this story has nothing to do with racing, it is one of several strange experiences I have had which I feel are worth recounting.

Another incident took place when I was in Malta with some army lads. We were trying to conjure up spirits on a ouiji board and a message was spelt out for me - with the upturned tumbler - Uncle Gilbert dead. I took it with a pinch of salt, although I was puzzled as I couldn't imagine how any of these army mates could possibly know the name of my uncle. Imagine my surprise later the next day when I was called to the commanding officer's office and handed a telegram which read that my Uncle Gilbert had, indeed, died that same night. Needless to say, I never messed with a ouiji board again! But I will say here that I do believe that I have someone up above that looks after me. Seven times I have been close to death and seven times saved; all in different circumstances. My present wife, Maureen and I go to church now and again, but I have no strong convictions, expect that I don't fear death in the least.

My house was sold shortly thereafter and the Trinidad crew came and collected their money and did some business of sorts in London. I only had a few thousand pounds over from my house sale and no doubt enough for another house, albeit with a mortgage round my neck for twenty-five years. But with no steady job and my only real talent before my drink problem being backing winners and tipping. I felt I was careering more rapidly on that downward spiral and had to get off. It was time to try my hand at something else. Returning to shipbuilding was out of the question. My hands had gone soft and I knew that I wouldn't last half a day in that industry. In any case, I hadn't worked properly for a few years and lacked the motivation to start all over again.

Then I did something that I have never regretted since. With the balance of the house sale, I bought a huge gypsy caravan to live in and a large brand-new Landrover

From my 'gypsy' days with our caravan parked in a farmers field,
to the Jockey Club rooms, Newmarket,
where I conceived the idea for Classic Bloodstock PLC,
which led to my eventual ruination in horse racing,
and my son and I being banned by the
Jockey Club for 10 years.

to pull it with. I gave away or sold my furniture. Carol, my wife and our three children packed up our personal belongings and set off on a brand new adventure! "Good-bye Newmarket and your streets paved with gold. You beat me fair and square, but I will return someday," I thought out loud. I didn't know then that, when that time came, I would become a millionaire.

The next two years we were on the road, travelling all over England and sometimes staying on a gypsy site, sometimes on the side of the road or in a field. One gorgeous summer I do remember well. We parked ourselves in a secluded field on the banks of a river in Oxfordshire. There were no neighbours, just the countryside and wild life for company. We ate well, I was pretty handy at snaring a rabbit or two or using my two ferrets, with nets, both of which I had got from a gypsy, in trade for the Landrover spare tyre (thankfully, we never had a puncture!).

I was not so bad at poaching; a few pheasants at night with the help of a torch or hooking a few trout in forbidden trout runs. For the other necessities of life, I used to go round houses with my camera taking photographs of children and babies. These mothers always seemed to be good for a few pounds for a nice photograph of their little treasures.

It was a wonderful, carefree life but did have its negative points. For example, we were living in a caravan with no electricity or running water which is no fun in the winter. Our only luxury was a small portable black and white TV which ran off a small generator to keep the kids happy.

Life is funny. Only a few years ago, I was having dinner with a real Lord, negotiating to buy his horse racing form guide business off him in order to upgrade my own form guide mailing list, Infoform Race Ratings. Now I was negotiating with gypsies to buy a better generator to run my electrics. (It was actually a lot easier dealing with His Lordship!) The gypsies are tough and bargain long and hard. One thing for sure, life is never dull!

Of course, I had changed. The best thing of all was that I had dried out and the bottle was no longer my best friend. It took a long time to dry out completely, and the damage to my health had already been done (as I was to discover in due course). I was never an alcoholic of the common type, starting with a drink early in the morning and having a few all day. No, my problem was not that sort of alcoholism. My type was that I could never stop at one drink, only when I had had a skinful. Hangovers for days on end. Alcoholics usually don't suffer from hangovers. Once alcohol passed my lips, I craved drink - a fix until I was spaced out.

Throughout this period in the caravan I still kept my hand in with the racing form. I would pick up a racing paper if I saw one when I was in a town or village and I always purchased the Timeform year book. (Today, I have the full set). I purchased all the early publications over the years, from bookshops, racecourse stalls, etc. I have publications from 1945 including a rare one for which I paid £2000 pounds. I love my collection and the tenacity I showed in building it up to completion.

I knew I would return to Newmarket. I wasn't finished with that town by a long shot. But wasn't ready to go back yet. I needed Newmarket like a drug, but I still had to stay in the wilderness, leaving it to fate as to when I would return, still reasonably happy, but life was too quiet. I was missing 'the action', the excitement - the bet. I knew that, sooner or later, I had to get back in the game.

Fate set the wheels in motion. My wife, Carol became pregnant and we had already run out of space in our caravan. Five was maximum and it was obviously not suitable for our new baby. I decided to sell up and invested our money in a house in Newark-on-Trent which was the cheapest place to buy a house in the country back then. Still is, I believe. Of course, selling a gypsy caravan is not easy. So I took a big loss on it. But it had served me well. The Landrover was easy to sell on; a twelve-seater and very much in demand. I secured nearly as much as I had originally paid for it.

The house we purchased in Newark was big and old, it was great living with a proper roof over our head again. I don't regret my gypsy life. I reckon I was lucky to have had the experience. You could advertise racing information from Newark-on-Trent, as you would from Lambourn or Newmarket, but you couldn't rope in as many customers. At least you can make a living and I had learned a lot from my earlier mistakes, such as don't throw your money around and stay sober.

For instance, I knew all too well that you can't tip winners all the time. So when you did you should put some of your returns away for a rainy day. I also did what I thought was a cracking idea, I got the Horses In Training book and wrote to all my best contacts care of their last trainer employer. Racing lads are always moving digs or from one trainer to another, so their mail was forwarded on. I got about a dozen good replies and, in return for inside racing information, would see them okay for a bit of money, deals were struck and arrangements made. I was back in business. And, even though it wasn't in Newmarket yet, it was a start. I ran my business with the old proven routine. And I knew if I stayed sober I would get on top of the game again.

I rented an office in Newark, called it 'Limerick House' and started advertising in the sporting papers. True, I was only making a fraction of what I had made previously, but I wasn't spending the same as I had, at least it was a living. I now had four children to feed and they never went short. But it wasn't Newmarket and, frankly, I was bored, even though I made some good friends. Essentially I just missed the buzz of racing and all the lads who worked in racing.

After a particular good summer of punting, during which I had a golden run of winners, I decided to take my children to the Costa Blanca in Spain for a month's holiday. My wife, Carol stayed behind at her mother's house in Newmarket with our new baby boy who we named David . As I sat in sunny Spain, I was busy making plans for the future and how I could return to my beloved Newmarket. I phoned Carol and told her to look for the smallest, furnished accommodation she could find to rent in Newmarket with a maximum of two bedrooms. She was puzzled by this but did as instructed and found a small flat in Derby Way. The way was open now for my return. I couldn't afford to buy a house in Newmarket. It was too expensive.

So I returned from my long winter holiday, picked up a few of our family personal things from our home in Newark-on-Trent, hired a van and, within twenty-four hours of my return, we were installed in our rented flat; Carol, the new baby and myself were crammed into one small bedroom, while the other three children were in a box room. Tim, the eldest, was in a tiny bed with the girls sleeping on the floor.

The first thing I did was to ring the Newmarket Council and arrange for them to visit. It worked! Within a month we had been moved into a spacious council house on Manderston Road, Mayfair it was not, but to me it was the start of my second chance. I then quickly sold my house in Newark-on-Trent for a profit, having spent a lot of my racing money earned on building an extension and general refurbishment.

So, at last I had a home again in Newmarket, some money in the bank and a wedge (money) in my pocket for smoothing my path and more importantly, my drinking was under control. I had severe health problems, but more of that later....

CHAPTER SEVEN

The important thing was that Ronnie Dawson was back in town. It was time to make plans which was all going to take time. The main thing was to keep my feet on the ground.

I was continuing to build up my racing contacts, slowly and surely through trial and error, putting a good team together. I got a few top class work jockeys in tow. I was the 'guvnor' again. At last I could afford to be, but not stupidly so. If you did business with me, you got paid, plus a bonus. I had Newmarket information nicely sewn up, although I still needed a couple of very good contacts in the southern stables to complete my team.

At that time, I was racing pigeons which the council wasn't too happy about. The rule was that, if you lived in a council house, you couldn't keep pigeons. Back then, several racing people had racing pigeon lofts in their stables, including the trainers Jeremy Hindley and Robert Armstrong. Needless to say, I had an ulterior motive in the beginning as the Pigeon Club was a good source of information. Other regulars there included Michael Stouts, head lad; Andy Andrews; Robert Armstrong's head lad for Alister Veitch; and several ex-professional jockeys who were now top work riders. It was a mixed bunch of mostly racing people in the club but I kept my ears open and got some useful information for my little black book on club nights, Fridays and Saturday. Of course, the pigeon racing bug got me and my birds became an important part of my life. It's a truly wonderful hobby which requires great skill from you, the trainer and dedication to your racing team of birds.

However, the council was cracking down on me with my pigeon loft which was not allowed for council tenants. I had two warnings by letter and it looked as if I was to lose my pigeons pretty soon. But I was too smart for the council's petty rules. I went up to Norfolk and spent a few hours with Len Rush, the loft manager of Her Majesty's racing pigeons. I knew the racing birds like I did my race-horses. I had read everything I could get my hands on about racing pigeons for the previous couple of years.

As I said farewell to the loft manager of the Queen's birds, I had six of the young beauties, all cooing away in my pigeon basket which I had taken with me. Good job I did. I looked upon the six young birds as a gift of sorts from Her Majesty, Queen Elizabeth, albeit by her loft manager but, the fact remained, that she owned the birds and they were all rung on their leg with that special prefix, E.R.

I was now ready to do battle with Newmarket District Council.

"Okay, I will get rid of my racing pigeons," I told them on the phone. "I will have to kill them, they're no good to anybody else to race because they will always come back to my loft. It's a pity really especially the lovely six from Her Majesty, the Queen; all ringed with her personal prefix, E.R. I will phone The Sun newspaper to witness the dastardly deed I have to perform and, of course, I will have to write to the Queen to say how sorry I am."

That same afternoon, two council officials were at my front door. "Don't be hasty Mr. Dawson," they told me. "Let's talk about this. We can't have all this trouble." With difficulty, I managed to keep a straight face.

"It's funny you getting here right now," I replied. "This very afternoon I was going to neck them and bury them in the front garden with a plaque that read: 'Here rests six of the Queen's racing pigeons. Born to fly, not to die.'

"Don't do it," they begged.

"I have no choice," I replied. The rule is you can't keep pigeons if you live in a council house.

"We will change the rules at the next council meeting," they replied. "We'll call for an extraordinary meeting to be held right away." Just don't kill the birds.

My house in 1989 at
Manderston Road.

My pigeon loft and some
trophy's won.
Home also to some of her Majesty's
Queen Elizabeth's birds which were
given to me as a gift.

"Okay," I replied. "I will give you a week."

Only a few days later, I received a letter from the Newmarket Council stating that tenants were allowed to keep pigeons. Victory!

A few days after this, I rang the telephone company to complain about telephone wires that were running across my garden and which I wanted re-routed. They were not interested. However, they soon were when I said that the birds from Her Majesty's loft which had been given to me as a gift could decapitate themselves if they flew into the wires. A week later they had been duly re-routed. A little name dropping can do wonders at times!

Later, when I was the Chairman of the Newmarket Pigeon Racing Club and also winning a lot of cups and trophies with a good team of birds, I had built up, I supplied top trainer, Dick Hern's wife with some of my best racing bloodlines, as well as Dick Hern's main work jockey, Brian Proctor with a few good ones. In return, Brian gave me some good racing info and a few useful winners from the yard. One, in particular, he rode himself and won at 33/1, a very nice tip indeed.

During that period of my life when I was Chairman of the Pigeon Club, I received trophies for every race and competition we had in the club for members to win, thanks to the generosity of Newmarket racehorse trainers and jockeys.

In my business, I was still struggling a bit to attract customers, mainly due to the fact that the big boys in the tipping game had it well sewn up. The Sporting Life and Racing Post were well aware of this. For instance, John Blake was using seven different aliases over the year which may not be illegal, but is certainly unethical. There were full page advertisements in these papers which showed that he had proven winners. Typically, they would be under the name of an alias, say Martin

Wells or Harrington or R. J. Francis (or any alias he chose), and would give the names of several horses to the sporting press on the pretence that he was giving those same horses to clients. Then, under his proofing to the racing rags, he was sure to hit lucky under the name of, say, Harrington with two nice winners. The following week, his ads would include the blazoned headline that Harrington tips had resulted in winners for all clients, eg: 'Last week, all my clients were sent the names of two horses only and these two horses. Both won 10/1 and 10/1: a 100/1 double, etc etc. Send your money now for next week's coup and why not take ten weeks or even twenty weeks for 'x' amount of money!' Now in his report on tipsters in The Sporting Life on the 4th August, 1997, Sims sees nothing wrong in his paper being used by this advertiser to con the public.

Naturally, once you had sent your money, the information you got was absolute rubbish but Johnny Boy didn't care a monkey. He had your cash. A few weeks later another one of his bogus tipster names would scream out a couple of winners in this name or that and the same old routine would carry on. The News of the World exposed John Blake, but he carried on regardless, roping in the mugs. I complained to The Sporting Life about his unethical practices, but they didn't care twopence.

John Blake used to phone me from his bunker to see if I could give him some racing information for his personal use, but I was wise to him and his scams and he got nothing from me. But in his advertisements he wrote glowing stuff, full of untrue drivel and the punters fell for it every time thinking that, if it was in The Sporting Life or Racing Post it must be true. I nailed Blake eventually but it made The Sporting Life my enemy for life. The message was out. 'Get Ron Dawson.' And they did, good and proper. But my day will come in the High Court soon in a serious libel action against The Sporting Life, (incidentally, this paper is fondly referred to in the racing set as The Sporting Lie) - and we shall cross swords then.

My son, Tim was now in the tipping business under his name and from Lambourn. He had been doing well, using his father's principle. In other words, the form book and burning the midnight oil until your eyes won't focus. Remember all you read and keep it at your fingertips, that's the key. But, most important of all, is to look after your punters and get some top inside information.

Some of the best national hunt racing information we ever got out of Lambourn came from Nick Deacon. I sent him a monthly cheque for years. Later he was given a job by The Sporting Life. He deserved it, but I still kept him on my payroll for a few more years. He was good. He went on to win the Naps Table for The Sporting Life which was no mean feat, but I have a better Lambourn informant now. I can tell you why Nick doesn't do so well these days, it's due to success. It's okay if a few trainers confide in you with their bets, but after a while if you're tipping them in the paper, they wise up because too many punters are backing horses which they shouldn't. So the trainers keep the best info back. My new Lambourn mole is happy. He doesn't need to show himself on the surface. I pay him well. Tim is also very well-connected. In fact, he went to school with several top jockeys.

Tim landed some memorable bets in those golden days with information from Nick Deacon. Nick still gets to know a bit and if you follow him and keep records, you will soon learn which stables still give him good information and those that don't....

As mentioned earlier in my story, I have had health problems over the years and by this time in my life, they were starting to catch up with me. I had spent a few weeks in Newmarket Hospital on several occasions with

Systemic Lupus, a nasty insidious disease. My next attack damaged my heart and kidneys and put me in hospital for six months and two weeks. More to the point, this coincided exactly with the flat racing season! I couldn't get out of bed at all for four months of that time, although I was not in much pain so couldn't really complain. But it was a long time for me. I ran my tipping service from the Newmarket hospital ward and the nurses were my runners with any bets I would want to put on. I was lucky really because the staff nurse on my ward was the mother of a jockey so was sympathetic! Tim called at the hospital every morning to collect my mail for posting and delivering my tipping mail.

During my hospital stay, I had several visits from racing friends, including one jockey called Alan Mackay. He always bucked me up with his wisecracks about horse racing folk and also asked me if I could be his manager when I was discharged. This meant that I would book his rides and liaise with the trainers.

To me, this sounded like a heaven sent opportunity. I would be responsible for phoning various trainers every morning and would surely be able to glean a little inside information at the same time.

Upon my discharge from the hospital, I set the wheels in motion to becoming a jockey's agent. This was a part of the racing scene which was just becoming established back then. Nowadays, all jockeys have agents or managers to book their rides for them. It can be a hectic business though, especially when the jockeys are riding at two different meetings on the same day.

There may be one race meeting during the day and another one elsewhere in the evening. You have to get the timing exactly right in order to allow your jock the time to get from riding his last booked ride at one race meeting to his first booked ride at another race meeting.. Then a quick dash by car to the next meeting which

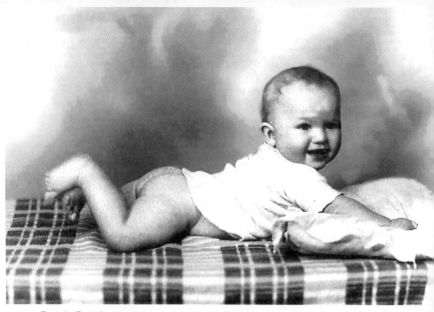

Bonnie Ronnie, aged one year in 1939. Do I look like a 'Conman, cheat and liar'? or could I just grow up to be 'Jack the Lad'?

Dawson's Fish & Oysters:
My great, great uncle Jack, Gold prospector and shopkeeper.
Resident of Dawson City, U.S.A - circa 1800

could be a hundred miles away. Very often you had to use helicopters or light aircraft to make life easier, "to do the two" as the saying in racing goes when you are booked to ride horses at two different meetings on the same day. I have booked the same jockey to ride, say in Edinburgh in the afternoon and then again in Windsor that evening. You can do this if the timing's right and you use the schedule aircraft on that Scotland to Heathrow route with a car and driver waiting at the airport to whisk you away.

As I was to manage rides, I decided that more jockeys I looked after and managed, the more viable it would be as a business and I soon had a few jockeys on my books. Certain trainers liked to use certain jockeys or a good apprentice who could claim up to 7 lbs off the horse's weight it had to carry in a race. I had up to six jockeys on my agency books, taking 10% from each one's prize money. For example, if a jockey won a race of say £10,000 pounds, that meant a jockey earned 10% of that amount which was £1,000 so you got paid £100 as his agent. Of course, you also got 10% of his basic riding fee of £60 which meant an additional £6. So, if you had one of your jockeys riding six mounts that day, you had made £36 for yourself from just one jockey - and I had six. And then there is the 10% cut on prize-money won by the jockey whether it comes 2nd, 3rd or in 4th place.

In short, it doesn't take much working out to realise that, with up to six jockeys being booked for rides by you each day, it is a very lucrative business indeed. Of course, the flat season was only from about March 27th to the 10th November so, even though it was hectic, you had a long rest to look forward to.

It is not quite like that these days as there are races all year round now, thanks to the special all weather surfaces installed at the race tracks of Wolverhampton, Southwell and Lingfield. And, with floodlights nowadays, many of the racetracks also provide night racing which adds a bit of glamour to tracks like Wolverhampton where I have spent many an enjoyable evening.

But racing is all about backing a winner or two and being a jockey's agent provided me with a few good sources of information, although it took a while to get it sussed. Many trainers talked a load of drivel. They would tell you that they thought the horse in their charge would win, in order to get you to book a certain jockey on your books to take the ride, probably because the racehorse owner liked that particular jockey.

I was wise to all this jiggery pokery and knew the form and abilities of many horses. In fact, nearly as much as the trainer himself. But, yes, of course other trainers who I respected a great deal would book a jockey on your books for a certain race and tell you it would win and you knew that it probably would. Sunday morning was full steam ahead, booking your jockeys all that week for rides from Monday to Saturday. You also had horse race meetings in the summer evenings and now on Sundays, so that means you are working seven days a week. In my view, this is far too much racing. The jockeys are getting burnt out and the public is witnessing over-kill at race meetings. If I was on the planning committee of the Jockey Club, I would sort it out for them because, in my view, they certainly can't!

CHAPTER EIGHT

Obviously, it took me some time to know which trainers you took notice of when booking a ride. For instance, if Clive Britain was booking one of your jockeys, for a horse, he would generally never say any more than ... "it should run well."

In fact, if Clive had said to me: "I think this horse will definitely win!" I doubt whether I would have taken much notice. Clive's strike rate (percentage of winners to runners) had never particularly impressed me.

On the other hand, if the trainer John Sutcliffe had said the same thing, then I would sit up and take notice because, chances were, that he was probably spot on or, at least, the horse would come very close to winning. Sutcliffe sometimes told me outright: "I think this one will win." It usually did. He liked to use Taffy Thomas as his lightweight jockey, especially when he had a horse in a handicap that he thought had a very good chance of winning. This was a good sign for a bet in my book, especially if I knew that some of the other runners in the race were not fancied by connections. Incidentally, by this time, Taffy and I were friends again.

Bill Whitman was of a similar vein and also booked Taffy Thomas for around a weight of 7.12 particularly when he booked Taffy weeks in advance for a big handicap. On these occasions, you could normally anticipate a good bet was on the cards. However, most weeks, your jockeys were just doing bread and butter riding; small races with horses which have a small chance of winning and no betting opportunity. But if one did win a race, you had your 10% and a week would hardly go by without your jockeys winning a few races between them.

Alan Mackay was always in demand as a good strong lightweight jockey. That's why later, when that mega punter, Hugh "Shuggie" McDonnell was having very big money on his horse, Alan was the main man for the job.

Ensuring the jockeys are on the best mounts available is the responsibility of the agent, as not many trainers ring you directly. It is up to you to chase them up. I made it a policy always to be first on the blower to pester trainers for rides for my jockeys and not one other agent was better at the job than me. I was right on the ball. I practically knew the very minute a trainer would be in his house for breakfast after seeing to his first lot. (The horses trained before breakfast; second lot after breakfast).

After a while, it's all first names, "John this," "Bill that," etc., except in Mark Prescott's case, that is. I used to ring him up for rides and got a few for Alan Mackay. I was always very polite and referred to him as 'Sir Mark'. However, it's a small world at times and, as always, there is a story to tell.

I had a good friend from Barrow-in-Furness. We were good mates and went back many years working together in the shipyard. He bred the finest fighting cocks in the country, bar none; they were legendary. In the old days, if he put down ten birds in a ten match set of battles (ten consecutive fights) and lost just one bird from the ten battles that would be par for the course for this lad. They were that good. I went to a match just one time. There were about a hundred people there betting big money on every match, mostly gypsy types. We didn't get to know the exact venue until one hour before the start, only the area where we would be going.

Cock fighting wasn't for me after that day. I just didn't have the stomach for it. It still goes on today in close secrecy, I am sure, but the police are very quick to act if they get wind of it.

Anyway, my friend had arranged a visit to Sir Mark and told him that he was bringing a friend along - me. I explained that I had spoken to Prescott many times on the phone and it would probably do my jockey business no harm to actually meet the man in person. My friend brought Prescott a couple of hen birds as a gift. They were of a certain pedigree strain to assist Mark in his breeding programme and ideal for out-crossing his bloodlines.

So, there I was, round at Sir Mark's one Sunday with my long time mate from Barrow. We were sitting there in Prescott's racing office drinking his best Scotch while he was ringing his owners with news of how their horses were getting on. Naturally, I was all ears. Afterwards, we went outside to look at his team of fighting cocks. I'm sure that Sir Mark didn't use them for fighting. They were more show bird types and didn't look as though they would have the tenacity to battle until death. They were nice to look at though, all tethered up in their individual tepees with just enough space to strut about in style, but not enough to enable them to get at an adjacent bird. Anyway "they were a grand lot of chickens," as they are fondly called in the fighting cock world.

Afterwards, we all went back to the house where Mark gave us a guided tour. There were pictures of fight cocks and sporting country events of all kinds hung in every room. The huge master bedroom was adorned with exquisite rare prints and paintings. Greyhound champion coursers were also displayed all over the house. Sir Mark was a Waterloo Cup enthusiast, as was my friend.

In my earlier days, I also liked to go to this sporting spectacle (greyhounds chasing hares). There are two dogs in every heat, then one hare is released with a start and the dog who turns the hare the most is the winner of that heat and goes through to the next round. Over the 1,000 yards course, the hare is usually too smart and fast for the dogs, although obviously there are times when the hare is caught and killed. Of course, the dog who kills the hare is not automatically the winner of that heat. It's the dog who works the hardest and turns the hare; a dog could turn a hare a dozen times, only the last time into the jaws of the other dog. The winner of each heat goes through to the next round. Finally, two dogs chase the last hare for the overall champion and the glory of winning the Waterloo Cup. Of course, bookmaking betting, as well as illegal betting accompanies every event.

I think the animal rights people are trying to stop this event. In fact, they may well have done so by now. Anyway, we said goodbye to Mark and thanked him for his hospitality.

"Give me a ring in the morning, Ron," he told me on leaving. "I may have a ride for your jockey, Alan Mackay during the week. Of course, I wasted no time and telephoned him as instructed, cocky as anything.

"Good morning Mark," I said as he answered the phone.

"Sir Mark to you," he replied. In other words, he put me in my place, but he gave me a ride for my jockey, Alan Mackay, all the same.

Despite him getting on his 'high horse', I have great respect for the man as a trainer although I have to say that, as far as I know, he never really earned that title he was so proud of. It was passed down from his father. Anyway, good luck to him. If he suffers from delusions of grandeur, that's his problem. In later years, I occasionally mixed with titled folk, but they never imposed their titles to my face like Sir Mark did!

The only thing Sir Mark and I had in common was our penchant for the exclusive Reeds Hotel on the island of Madeira. "Nice place to take a bird wasn't it Mark" No I don't mean a chicken.

Working as a jockey's agent was a good life and I had a few perks, like free trips to Cyprus to meet owners who, in turn, usually became my punters. On one particular occasion it was the winter season; one of my jockeys working there on a retainer rode two well-expected winners (they were 'jobs'), so I returned to England a bit richer than when I had left!

People in racing have always asked me why I am so loyal to jockey, Alan Mackay. Well, the main reason is that he is honest with me. If, say one of my own horses runs disappointingly, he will say to me: "It's no good - useless," or something like that. He most certainly wouldn't try and pull the wool over my eyes.

That's what I want to hear - the truth, not a load of bullshit which is the norm when a jockey rides for an owner. Bruce Raymond rode a horse once for me at Windsor. It beat one in a twenty runner race. His comment on dismounting afterwards was, "Nice horse this Sir, another 1/4 mile further and it can win for you." That sort of remark to me meant one thing - the jockey would never ride for me again. But many owners are fool enough to take it in but then, of course, many owners wanting to impress their cronies want to hear a load of bullshit. They don't want to hear the hard truth about their pride and joy, especially in front of others they want to impress.

The Gullible Owner

This story starts like most good tales
In a dark hotel saloon
Where an innocent fool
With hard earned cash
Is persuaded to spend it soon.

He's taken to the Newmarket sales
They go there in a cab
But at the end of the day
There's one man who'll pay
The new owner picks up the tab.

The bidding is fast, they urge him on,
He begins to stall and stammer,
But they nudge his arm,

99

Just one more bid
Will catch the falling hammer.

He's escorted over across the yard,
The trainer shakes his hand
He looks in dismay
At the flashy bay
That has cost him fifty grand.

They smile and wink
New owner buys the drink
They pat him on the back
And he takes them out to dinner
This horse they say, will be a winner.

"I'll be in touch" the trainer says
"We'll enter him in September,
But all his family needed time,
He's a big horse please remember."

The owner smiles, he understands
Though he doesn't quite get the jargon
Of course, he'll pay the hotel bill
After all, he's got a bargain.

A month goes by and not a word
The owner lives in hope
But the first account arrives on time
In a plain brown envelope.

The months roll on, the bills roll in
He gradually comes to his senses
They never said at Newmarket sales
There'd be additional expenses.

"Convital plus - plus vital con.

Authority to act
The farrier, the tack man
They all must think I'm stacked.
"He's coming on," the trainer says
"He's schooled and jumping well
But whether we will win a hurdle
Only time will tell."

In February he gets the virus
In March his shins are sore
In May he's off his food
New owner's in a depressed mood.

In July the trainer has a plan
We'll give him a quiet run
There is a race for him at Southwell
"You'll enjoy it, it's a bit of fun".

The big day dawns, the owner's there
In his very best bib and tucker
But no-one's told him
It's on the sand
The stupid looking f***er!

The wiry jockey taps his whip
As the trainer gives instructions
"I like this horse Don't knock him about
If you do there'll be holy ructions."

The race is run, they cheer them on
The horses gallop past
The owner puts his glasses down
He's finished a long way last.

"He didn't stay," the jockey says
"They went a fair old clip

He hated the ground
He's finished unsound
And he wants a longer trip."
"Come on old chap" the trainer says
I'll let you buy me a stiff drink
I think it's time we face the facts
We'd better sit down and think".

"I hate to admit
He's not worth a spit
There's no point messing about.
All of us know
The horse is slow
Let's cut your losses and get out."

There's a decent trade
In a horse that's made
I'm sure he'd make a hunter
There must be some fool
With a riding school
I'm certain we'll find a punter."

The owner sighs, he shakes his head
It's hard for him not to cry
But the trainer winks
Orders two more drinks
And says with a glint in his eye.

"Don't worry old boy, the thing to do
Is to try to find another
As a matter of fact I've one in the yard
He's this one's three parts brother.

R.I.P.

The Gullible Owner. 1998

CHAPTER NINE

It was my health problems that finally put paid to my jockey agency business. Two years later, during the summer, I was back in hospital. Obviously, while I could just about run my tipping business from Ward C5, I most certainly couldn't book my jockeys for rides. There is a limit to how much business you can do from your hospital bed, especially when you are having continuous transfusions. To this day, I have fond memories from my days in the jockey business. It was a hectic life, but an enjoyable and challenging one.

I emerged from hospital six months later after another Lupus attack. It was a long time out of circulation in racing but, as long as I kept taking the many drugs prescribed, I was told I could stay reasonably well until succumbing to the next attack of Systemic Lupus. I was also informed by my doctors that there was no cure and that I would have flare ups of this disease throughout my life. This has proven to be a true statement. Systemic Lupus is a malfunction of the immune system. The disease has been working round my body for years now, sometimes attacking my kidneys, sometimes my heart. It just goes on attacking the vital organs. Indeed, it can do this to the brain also. Then it's goodnight

Meanwhile, I was still comfortably off and, having made a bob or two from the horses over the years, I decided to spend four months during the winter in the Canary Islands. My wife, Carol wasn't so keen on the idea as she wasn't too fond of hot weather. Instead, I took my four children with me, the two eldest, Tim and Jane and the two youngest, Sarah and David who, of course, had to miss school which was naturally wonderful for them. I rented a luxury villa and had the most fabulous eighteen weeks although, during that time, I realised how demanding looking after children can be.

I went back to England a far fitter man and ready to continue my tipping business at the start of the new flat season, which was just two weeks later.

I started off with a nice winner at Doncaster and settled into a familiar, comfortable routine. I was doing okay, still living in my council house and with no financial problems looming on the horizon. 'Everything looked rosy,' as they say.

I also had my drinking under control. I still loved a few belts, but I knew when to stop.

It's a fact of life that not many people know how to make money at horse racing and, yet, if you have followed my story so far, you will have noticed that I was an exception. Granted, I had a bad run at one time but that can safely be attributed to my over fondness for the bottle. Once that phase was over, I was doing comfortably again with a good run of winners which, whilst not reaching the big time, was making me plenty of money.

My punters were run of the mill chaps who liked a bet but didn't really understand the game as I did. Then I met someone who was to change my life dramatically and a filly called On the House who was, likewise, a winner for my punters and instrumental in shaping my destiny.

At the time, I was advertising my information in the racing press on a regular basis. Odds to £25 winners, deduct any losing bets. I always operated this way; to my mind it was the fairest as far as the punter was concerned.

Years earlier, I had tried to do a deal with Mick Ryan to add him to my team of informants. Mick is now a trainer but, back then, he was the head lad for Bernard (Fingers) Van Cutsmen. Mick was happy to play ball. I would pay him odds to £50 for information from the yard on any horse he gave me to punt, but no deductions for losers.

But it didn't work like this - and it still doesn't. You have to be fair, I let my punters deduct losers and Mick should have done likewise, otherwise you're giving losers and too many bets and not being slammed with a penalty. Mick wouldn't agree to this so I refused to do business with him.

I pulled in a few punters from my regular advertisements. One of these was called Kevin Moorcroft. Kevin liked a bet and I gave him a nice 8/1 winner from Geoff Wragg's stable; the first time out on a racecourse. A few weeks later, I had a good one from Armstrongs that went in at 6/1. It had no previous form, Kevin was no fool, he could see I wasn't guessing. Soon after that, I had my killer bet of the season, the best bet of the year. *On The House* to win the Sussex stakes at Goodwood. I had got the full report of the amazing secret gallop of this filly on the trial ground. My man, an ex-jockey who rode in the workout was on the blower to me within half-an-hour. "This filly worked with two stone in hand," he said. Now, I always half what jockey's tell me, but this was an amazing bit of work considering the other horse in the gallop was a useful four-year old.

At Goodwood in the Sussex stakes, the filly won at 12/1, as I said she would, she had been 14/1 at one time in the betting. Now, this was all very interesting to Kevin. He knew he had at last found a top notch tipster and a few days later he was outside my house at Newmarket to pay his dues. I invited him in for a chat and, within five minutes, I knew I was listening to someone very special in horse racing knowledge. He reminded me of that great professional backer, Phil Bull.

If I was ever at a racecourse and saw Phil I always asked him if he had a bang for the day. Bang was the word Phil used for bet. And, if he was going to bang a particular horse, I would steam in there also. Timeform was at its peak in those days and Phil Bull, a master at backing horses professionally. Although Jack Ramsden, whose wife Linda is a trainer is not bad either. According to him, he won £100,000 one year alone. Me? Well, I won't tell you the most I have won ....

So there I sat with Kevin in my lounge. I knew all too well that he probably wouldn't have bothered coming to see me if *On The House* hadn't won. He obviously respected the fact that I was good at what I could come up with. And, likewise, I respected him because he really knew his racing. In fact, I was impressed to such a degree that I said: "Kevin, you should be living in Newmarket. You would do well here." At the time, he was working as a surveyor in the North of England.

I'm pleased to say that Kevin took my advice and twelve months later he sold his house up north and moved to Newmarket, together with his wife, Maureen and Jack Russell, Nell. Thus was sown the seed of a brilliant financial period of my life. I had decided that I wanted Kevin to be my partner in a plan I was going to proceed with when the time was right. Of course, I was loathe to just go and give Kevin half my current business and make him a partner, (although as it turned out, I was forced to do just that).

Kevin is a very likeable lad and will go out of his way to help anyone. He also has a generous streak (too generous in my opinion) and so tended to be taken advantage of by some of the people in Newmarket.

Notwithstanding, within a year he had started the Newmarket Weekly Newsletter which was sold for only £3 a copy while it was worth closer to £100. He advertised in the sporting press and even on TV.

To say it was good is an understatement. It was too bloody good. The winners Kevin gave in those publications were damaging my tipping business and Kevin was selling top grade betting opportunities for peanuts. It had to stop!

So I roped Kevin into my master plan and a full part-nership which I had had on the drawing board for a cou-ple of years and was now ready to launch. I had been saving all my betting cash up for a major assault on buy-ing up all the names and addresses I could possibly buy from all the racing tipsters in the country who had been advertising in the sporting papers, of which there were dozens.

I did business with the lot of them. Big guys and small guys alike; the only tipster I couldn't get to do business was the biggest of them all - John Blake; the main rea-son was that he was too successful. I would have paid him fifty grand in cash for his addresses, no problem. But John Blake had more sense. Over the years, he had probably spent hundreds of thousands of pounds in ad-vertising and he knew the golden rule, i.e. that you never sell your names and addresses. Blake was no fool. He knew if someone else got them, his own business would suffer greatly. However, he was the exception and I man-aged to acquire plenty of good names and addresses. My son, Tim and I even went into the 'Lion's Den', Hammond (or Ramsden as he is better known - no relation to Jack Ramsden whose wife, Linda is a trainer) couldn't resist the cash on offer. And there is a small story to recount here:

Ramsden operated a devious scam. He advertised as Hammond of Newmarket. From, believe it or not, 'Hammond's Close'. I used to see his flashy advertise-ments in the sporting press costing thousands of pounds and his elaborate mailing circulars to draw in the mug punters. I decided to investigate further.

His Newmarket tipping address turned out to be a lock-up garage with a post box outside, attached to a wire fence. A phone line was set up inside with an an-swering machine which said something like: "Hammond of Newmarket speaking. Hang on a few seconds, please...

and the machine would divert the call to Hammond's lair in Yorkshire. This is the man who later also got his marching orders from the Jockey Club over the Palacegate Corporation fiasco; a big sting by the Yorkshire swindler and his accomplices.

Still, I wanted his addresses and he was equally keen to do business. We arranged to meet at a motel carpark up north. I packed my briefcase with cash and my son Tim who was to accompany me in a minder role packed a baseball bat (just in case!) for what looked like a possibly dangerous mission.

We arrived at the rendezvous point just as darkness fell and waited in our parked car, as arranged, having told him that we would be in a white Mercedes with dark windows and a 'Ron' registration plate. After a few moments, a big, dark Mercedes loomed up and flashed its lights, indicating that we should follow. This we did for about five miles, around small country roads, twisting and turning until we finally turned off down a narrow dirt track and stopped outside a large manor house; the only sound being the eyrie hoot of an owl.

I had a firm grip on the briefcase with the money, while Tim held the insurance (the baseball bat). "Look Tim, we could be in the lion's den here and no one has a clue where we are, but leave the insurance behind, at least for now," I pleaded. He did and the baseball bat was left on the back seat with the door unlocked.

Next, we were ushered into the house which was stuffed full of expensive looking antiques. Then it was straight down to business. I looked through the two sacks full of addresses, briefly picking one at random, like you would in a raffle. The letters showed how much cash had been paid. There were also coupons cut out from newspapers showing the same details

In total, there were around 20,000 names and addresses which seemed about right at the time. I opened the money case and Tim counted out the bills. Finally, we shook hands on the deal. I was pretty happy with the outcome. Tim picked up the dustbin liner sacks, the deal finalised. In fact, I was quite surprised because I found I actually liked the guy, although he didn't say too much. As I left, I mentioned something like, "I hope I don't drive into the river!" It was lit up by the moonlight around thirty yards away and I noticed that it was wide and flowing fast and making that rushing noise water does over rocks, as it obviously cascaded down from higher up on the moors.

"That's my private trout stream," he replied. "I will let you fish it some day."

However, the only time I ever saw Hammond after that was at a race meeting where he had one of his own horses running which did very well for him that day. In fact, his Palacegate Corporation horses were mostly quite good and two in particular very good. But I never had the chance to speak to him after that visit to his 'bunker'!

Gradually, I bought up all the names and addresses that were for sale on the market. They were all original letters or coupons representing a great deal of money spent by various punters over the years. I paid John Jenks of Spyform about £13,000 for his at £1 each. Some addresses I would pay up to £3 each for. Any lists that were typed with punters' names and addresses. I wouldn't pay a penny a million for; a total waste of time. No, they had to be actual letters or coupons with a name and address taken from a sporting paper..

While I was going through Ramsden's list later at my leisure, I noticed one punter who also happened to be one of my clients. His letter read: "Please find enclosed a cheque for £1,500. But the most I had ever got out of the guy was £100! Obviously Ramsden was a real pro in the game. I was impressed. But he was also very hard on his clients. I wasn't, it just wasn't my style.

When I had completed my buying up of all the addresses I possibly could find for sale, the next step was sorting them out. We had about twenty black dustbin sacksfull, all told. Kevin and I rented a spacious office in town and brought in thirty large tables. We employed four young girls up to seven days a week for nearly a year sorting the addresses out. As you can imagine, there were thousands of duplications as the punters tried different tipsters in their elusive search for those few good ones. The sorting and eventual files were all kept on cards, we didn't use a computer. It's too difficult to do the job properly. When you look at a name and address in front of you, all nearly the same, you can have up to a dozen variations of the same address, but different. i.e. D. Jones, no 14a, D.C. Jones, no 14a, Mr Jones 14a, Mr C. Jones 14 and so on. It's a nightmare to do it by computer. It has to be done by hand.

When the job was finished, we found that, from approximately 700,000 names and addresses, we had a final list of about 127,000 names and addresses and those then were put on a computer. This was probably the biggest and best mailing list of racing addresses ever assembled. It took a lot of money and a long time to perfect it. But it was soon to prove its worth.

In my opinion, advertising is a total waste of time, unless you are getting a cheap deal with a newspaper. It's just too expensive. Far better is if you can do a deal with a paper like The Sporting Life whereby they sometimes give you free advertising for a share of your profits like they did with racing commentator and tipster, Derek Thompson. Of course, the beauty of these deals is that you can be as economical with the truth as you want. To the man on the street, any advertising in The Sporting Life must be the gospel truth; they are automatically granted credibility. What these editors don't understand is that the average punter is sick to death of being ripped off which I had no intention of being guilty of.

According to my calculations, the 700,000 names and addresses that I bought represented over £2 million pounds spent in advertising by these tipsters. The reason I needed such an extensive mailing list was because, until then, those punters who were interested in racing were getting a raw deal. They wanted to have a bet, but couldn't trust the information being supplied to them. Now I'm not trying to put myself forward as some sheriff of the people but being an ex-working class lad, I have an axe to grind over rip-off tipsters.

Now I had my mailing list, my master plan was so simple. I would buy around twelve racehorses, say for £60,000 averaging £5,000 each. Then there was the further £125,000 annually to find for their keep and training fees which totalled £185,000. I would send a circular to around 120,000 racing people which would work out to a further cost of around £75,000. The total lay out would be in the region of quarter of a million pounds for everything to be in place. The problem was, would my idea work? If not, I was in a bit of financial trouble. But, as the saying goes, a faint heart never won a fair lady. So, I went in like Flynn. I was confident the punters out there were just screaming out for a bit of genuine inside information and it doesn't come any better when the horses are run for your benefit to bet on. The idea was a winner. And a big one!

Ron and Maureen off to Royal Ascot to support their horse,
Castell Rossello in the "Royal Hunt Cup".

CHAPTER TEN

Going back a little, before Kevin moved to Newmarket in the late 1980's, my marriage to Carol had been going through a very difficult period. No one else was involved but I knew that I was difficult to live with. My illness, S.L.E. was the cause of many bad days when I suffered severe joint pains. We were still living in the council house, it was our little palace by then with a lovely garden and a top of the range racing loft which cost me £4,000. My two Jack Russells, Jack and Meg completed the family.

I had bought the house from the council at a very good reduced price as a long-standing tenant for only £8,000 (due to the Margaret Thatcher 'sell council houses' policy). It had a big garden so I had no difficulty in securing planning permission for building on two spacious extra rooms and a large kitchen. It may not have been Park Lane, but visitors were always pleasantly surprised when they stepped inside. I actually sold it a few years later for £58,000; a fantastic profit of £50,000.

Much of my tipping money earnings was spent on my house and family and, overall, I was content with my life. The only drawback had been the lack of communication between my wife, Carol and myself. It was more my fault than Carol's. Our marriage had run its course. The problems just couldn't be solved

So, ultimately, Carol returned to her mother with the two girls, Jane and Sarah and little David and soon had her own home, while the eldest son, Tim, stayed with me and my two dogs, Jack and Meg.

It seems unnecessary to go into any more details here, except to say that we eventually got divorced but are still close and I gave Carol as much financial security as I could, plus a valuable piece of property I had acquired. In fact, last year I flew Carol and the girls, plus four of my five grandchildren to Spain to join me for two weeks.

It was a wonderful time for me and proved that, essentially, we are still one big happy family - at times, anyway. My role in life is still to take care of my family. I spoilt my children when they were little and still spoil them to this day, especially my two boys, Tim aged 31 and David now 24. Both are now into body-building and fitness and have fine physiques. Unlike his father, Tim is practically a teetotaller. I suppose the reason for that is that he can remember me as a Dad who drunk too much when he was little.

Why have I always spoilt my children? The only way I can justify it is by saying that it must have something to do with the fact that, as a child, I had nothing - although, there again, that's not true, because we had lots of love. But from a materialistic standpoint, I had very little. Although I could drive from an early age, I never owned a car until I was 26 and lived in Newmarket. I drove a hired car all the time when in Malta.

My boys had it easier. When David was just 17, I bought him his first car; a red Mercedes. Tim was driving a Cosworth at the time. He has always loved fast cars. I know I was re-living my life through my children and wanted them to have what I never did. I didn't want them to be tied down and restricted as I was as a young man when I worked at Vickers Armstrong. My motto was: 'Have a good time when you're young and have your health. It's no good later dwelling on the things you wished you had done.'

My girls are no different. If they want something, they know that all they have to do is pick up the phone and I help in any way I can but I have never spoilt them quite like my boys.

I was born on Friday 13th, at the thirteenth hour in May, 1938. So, in May this year I will be 61. I most certainly don't need money for myself, only to give away; you can't take it with you. I only need to ensure that my dear wife and my stepdaughter are comfortably off and my ex-wife, Carol is okay. To my mind, a home is where your heart is and my heart was once in my council house whereas, today, it is in my villa in Spain. And, between those two homes is my racing complex with four houses and sixty horse boxes with barns, horse walker, lunging ring and all the extras required in a top racing yard which has been valued at 3/4 million. But my heart has never been truly there. To my mind it is no more than a soulless monument.

During my school days. I was a poor pupil. The only thing I could do well was play chess. I won the school championship and was far too good for my teacher who ran the school chess club. To this day, I still play a game when I can; at least once a week. I taught all my children this wonderfully pure game when they were very young. Tim is a fine player while David was good enough to play for Newmarket town's team at the tender age of only 11 years, despite his poor education at school. Here in Spain, I play a few games with him every week. He gives me odds of 5/1 and the bet is £50 pounds to £10. I just about win one game in six. However Tim probably could have been the better player. As I say, he is a fine player, an attacking player of great inventiveness, but his defence can have a weakness. He also had a poor education, but at 15 he still managed to win two good chess competitions.

I gave my children all I could in years gone past except perhaps the most important gift of all - education. No wonder my lads are 'Jack the lads'. "Dad didn't do so bad," they probably think. And they're right. My boys try and be 'Jacks' and there is nothing wrong in that. I just want them to be honest, which they are. They have never got into any trouble, like drugs or crime.

Now I send my much loved step-daughter, Kate aged 10 to private school. And it shows. I wish I could have done the same for all my children and, of course, I deeply regret that I never had a proper education. I am known throughout my large family and my close circle of friends as the 'godfather'; a mellowed, rough diamond who listens to your problems and finds the money if needed and, these days, am content with my life.

Here in Spain, I spend hours in my garden, surrounded by colourful flowers and an abundance of fragrant fruit trees, including orange, lemon, fig, apricot and grapefruit. My three little terriers are at my feet and the sun basks me in light and warmth from dawn to dusk. I'm in love; in love with nature and all its beauty, the sunrises and sunsets.....and the blue Mediterranean sea dotted with yachts which I can see from my balconies with the Sierra Bernia mountains looking down on me from behind. As I write these pages, I'm in love with God and all the blessings he has bestowed on me through this journey of sorrow and sweetness that we call life.

And today, what do I have? My beautiful racing stables and rose gardens in Newmarket which I never visit, my town flat which I never use, my Rolls Royce which I never drive.... I could travel anywhere in the world, but this means nothing to me. I realise now that all I wanted was to prove to myself that I could achieve something in my life and that is why I acquired all these possessions. Now I am ready to let go of all these unwanted trappings because, far more important, are my family and memories. As long as I have these, I have enough.

As I write, my dogs are still at my feet waiting for me to move and take them round the garden. My wife, Maureen, went to the beach about an hour ago for her usual jog. She is just 39 years old and still very lovely. Why do women worry so much about their looks, while we men take the lines on our face in our stride? I wear mine with pride - and there are plenty these days. Maureen worries far more about her faintest imaginary wrinkles which I can't see and even talks of plastic surgery - women can be so vain!

Lucky for me, however, that now I am later in life, I prefer the company of women to that of my fellow man. So often, men turn into boring old farts, whilst a woman is far more interesting, (especially when she is suffering from a crisis about her supposedly fading beauty!).

Aside from all that, I believe that women are a lot smarter. The penny never seems to drop with men that we can't do without them, whereas they can get along very nicely without us. Unbearable though the thought may be, it's true!

Now where was I? Ah, yes ... deceit! But first let's hear about P.P.S.

During March 1990, a publication was released on the market called Punters Protection Services (P.P.S.) which changed the racing scene for many people. Using top security and an accommodation address, it allowed its writers to wage a war against various tipsters of ill-repute or, to put it another way, the con-men in racing. Within a few months, crooked tipping services were exposed and dropped like flies. Punters who had been receiving junk mail for years from various tipsters were pleasantly surprised at the falling off of these deliveries. It was only the big boys, like Blake who could survive and, even then, they were also harmed by the exposure of the various scams in the industry.

I know how successful P.P.S. was. I also know that when the P.P.S. team went to pick up the P.P.S. mail from the accommodation address, they wore crash helmets and carried baseball bats following various threats they had received. On one occasion, before the mail was collected, the office girls there narrowly escaped being attacked by a half-crazed man who was brandishing a hammer looking for the P.P.S. lads.

I understand that The Sporting Life was greatly concerned. After all, they had a lot of advertising revenue coming in from some of these tipping rogues and so it was bad for their business. P.P.S. only charged £1 for three months of exposures and to be a member of P.P.S., but with a 35,0000 plus membership, P.P.S. was having an enormous impact on the tipping industry and the word was out about the devious bunch of tipsters operating under several bogus names. After much detective work by Blake and his agents, they finally laid the blame at the feet of my son, Tim. Why? Blake won't or can't give me an explanation.

For the first ever strike with my new massive mailing list, I had all the labels run off the computer, of which the full list was now on discs for the P.P.S. team. My reward was nothing, except that I knew a lot of tipsters were robbing racing punters blind and I had the pledge of the P.P.S. team that they would carry their name on the back of the mail shots they sent to the 127,000 people on my list. All those goneaways were returned and they passed on to me those useful 'return to sender' envelopes. Thus, I was able to clean my master list down by 14,000 to 113,000 names and addresses.

So, at no cost to myself whatever, I had my mailing list cleaned and, at the same time, saw the bogus opposition slaughtered. P.P.S. is to start up again very soon and, once again, I have offered my mailing list to them free of charge. It's around 118,000 nowadays. I have only added approximately 5000 names and addresses to it in eight years. People don't reply to addresses now like they used to. They prefer premium tipping phone lines.

During the P.P.S. exposures, things got pretty uncomfortable for a while. I received nasty threatening phone calls at all hours of the day and night. Then started the poison-pen letters sent to Tim, but usually addressed to the Newmarket Tennis Club or other such venues which he was known to frequent. At the same time, Tim and I were dragged into an income tax enquiry following a tip-off which we were cleared of completely. I am pretty sure that those letters came from somebody with the initial 'B', although I can't prove it.

At any rate, The Sporting Life's reporter called Sims made it his crusade to make the P.P.S. boys suffer, accusing me of being the instigator and telling me: "Don't worry, we'll get you and Tim...". I'm not surprised that The Sporting Life circulation has dropped. Punters are sick of reading about the continuous, never-ending story of Ron Dawson, Tim Dawson and Classic Bloodstock plc. It must bore the pants off the man in the street by now.

For many years, Sims has thrown every supposed ounce of dirt he could get hold of at me and Tim and turned it into tons of victimisation journalism at its best through his paper, along with the apparent blessing of his side-kick and bottle washer, editor Tom Clark. Even considering this, I don't regret giving my mailing list to P.P.S. one bit. I considered it to be a noble cause which received my full backing. As it will again shortly.

In late 1990, I was ready for the list to be used for the benefit of Kevin and myself in our new business, 'Newmarket Racing Club'. It was to prove a big winner with the punters. At last, the man in the street knew that he would be getting a fair deal.

When Kevin and I did our first big circular using our mailing list for Newmarket Racing Club, our turnover was fairly good, just under £300,000. As the word got around, the following year it was generally appreciated that Kevin and myself (the Likely Lads!) were consistently producing winning information for racing punters. Our turnover was a few pounds short of a million pounds. Out of this, we also had a huge training and operating expenses which equalled around a half million pounds.

Apart from the information on our own horses, Kevin Moorcroft was giving consistently winning bets to our clients from various inside connections we had built up; trainers, jockeys ... anyone who could be relied upon. Obviously, they were treated confidentially. In fact, even today, though I am warned off by the Jockey Club, those same inside connections are more than pleased to tell me all I want to know and well-known trainers still take me out to dinner. I spend hours every day on the phone ringing my racing connections. They give the information, how could they do otherwise? I am a good person. If somebody needs something and he is a friend, in my book, that's it. Two years ago, a good jockey came and asked me to lend him £10,000 to buy a new car as he had cash flow problems. I gave him the money, no problem. Three months later, he paid me back in full. I knew he would. He didn't need to, he could have done a runner. He put up no security but with friends you don't need to but I am sure that to be a successful tipster you need jockeys and training as confidants.

We called our business the Newmarket Racing Club during its early days, Jeff Pierce was our number one trainer and he did well enough for Kevin and me. He landed us some good betting opportunities which, of course, benefited our clients. As long as we could control the running of the horses solely for gambling purposes, we knew the club would thrive.

The reader shouldn't imagine here that the trainer is stopping horses for you to win with later. It's not quite like that any more. What a trainer does do, however, is run your horse not fully fit over the wrong distance to get his handicap weight down. Next, when he considers that the horse is handicapped to win, he will bring it to peak fitness and then have a tilt at the ring. There is nothing wrong with that. It's common practice.

Prize money in racing is very poor and, until that is improved, owners need to land a gamble on their horses to cover the cost of their training fees. If a horse has to be stopped by running it over a distance, it can't possibly win at, isn't that stopping it in a way?

CHAPTER ELEVEN

Do you remember earlier at the start of this book when I wrote about my former father-in-law, inspector Jack Nightingale? Well, I have a little tale to add to that story. When Jack was a young man, he was a pretty fast runner and used to race for prize money at the big Powder Hall Sport's event. One year, having got through all the heats to the 200 yards final, Jack knew there was only one man to beat, the other four were not good enough. So, Jack got all the money he could muster and had his friend back the other chap at 5/2 to win the race. (Yes, there was bookmaker betting in the Powder Hall Sports with trail hound races the same day). Jack reasoned that he was on to a good bet. After all, he was favourite to win the race with the bookies, odds of 4/5 or evens.

When the race was run, so as not to make it too obvious that he was a non-trier, Jack went quickly to the front together with his intended winner. He told me that he only had to slow down a little to be beat and collect a good payout from the bookies. Twenty times more than the prize money, he reckoned. But, as they both approached the finishing line, poor Jack found he couldn't slow down and went and won the race. He shouldn't have. The moral of this true story is, if you can't stop yourself from winning when you're a non trier, it shows how difficult it can sometimes be for a jockey on orders of the owner or trainer not to win. Knowing the eyes of the race-track cameras and stewards are watching you..

Early in 1993, Kevin had marital problems. His sudden wealth seemed to be the main cause. His attitude and personality changed considerably and he suffered from delusions of grandeur. Whilst he became increasingly arrogant, I tended to side with Maureen.

His shift in attitude really started with the purchase of Charnwood Stables in early 1991 for £325,000 and then, later the same year, when we spent a further £150,000 on improvements. Kevin let everyone know that he was the master there - he even said the same to me, his partner.

Maureen finally left Kevin in March 1993 and, a few months later, we split up the partnership and I bought his quarter share of Charnwood. As part of the deal, I also paid our income tax for that year which was a total of £130,000. For me, it was purely business, nothing personal.

I realised that Kevin loved Maureen dearly and her departure was hard for him to bear. But, like the man he is, he got up, dusted himself down and went on to make his own fortune in the racing game. I feel that he received a good training with me as an apprentice. Plus, he is around 17 years younger than myself so has time on his side. (Today I would still call him my friend and we go for an Indian curry together when I'm in Newmarket).

Five months later on September 1st, 1993, Maureen returned to Charnwood. It was a day I would always remember. Of course, I was pleased she was back to Charnwood, her home. But sadly that day, my much loved 12 year old Jack Russell bitch, Meg died in my arms after I had nursed her all through the night. The vets could do nothing. She had been very heavily poisoned. I cried for a long time and buried my faithful dog under my favourite tree in my lovely garden. I was so dreadfully upset and was also dealing with all the months of turmoil in the stables and stress following Maureen and Kevin's personal problems, together with the further dilemma of my partnership with Kevin.

On September 2nd I suffered a heart attack and was fighting for my life in hospital where I remained for some weeks, visited daily without fail by Maureen.

When I returned home, weak, insecure and frightened which is normal for sufferers of heart attacks, Maureen and her daughter Kate moved into my house.

Stables House and Rose Garden at Charnwood 1995.

And my son Tim moved into Maureen's house. Maureen took care of me while I recovered.

As I recovered from my heart attack and felt better, I wanted to repay Maureen for all her loving tender care throughout my illness. And I needed a holiday. I had won a fair bit of cash that year and I wanted to spend it. After all, you never know when your next heart attack is coming. I knew now that I had experienced a very slight one in 1989. But didn't realise it then. Anyway, Maureen was for the adventure I was planning. She had only previously been abroad once to Italy with her mother when she was fourteen. Her daughter Kate went to stay with Maureen's mother. So I had the chance to show Maureen a bit of the world. First class. Why not? It was the bookies money I was going to spend. We were away for seven weeks.

I had always carried a torch for Maureen from the first day I saw her when she sat in my garden at Manderston Road and was crying and missing her past, lovely house and, by then, had moved into a council flat in Newmarket. A brave decision and, of course, Kevin had given up a secure and good job. I was just smitten by her. I can't tell you why, enough to say, I am doubly smitten these days.

I made India our first destination and took Maureen to see the Taj Mahal and many other sights of charm and history. We both thought India was very exotic and although we saw pitiful poverty and heart rendering sights, we will never forget that holiday for all the good things. I wanted to go on to Hong Kong to meet two Chinese punters of mine; big hitters in the game. They were expecting us and had booked us in at the Hong Kong Hilton as a way of saying; "Thank you" to me for services rendered that flat season. We were having a great time. The only downer was when we slipped over the water to the Portuguese colony of Macao where I dropped a £1,000 at the gaming tables. Not my day.

Maureen in New Zealand, a land of sheep, surrounded by horses,
as we tried to buy one.

Maureen being strapped into a harness
to go Para-Gliding, and on the waterfront
of our hotel "The Regent" in Fiji

Next day, surprise, surprise. We met Kevin Moorcroft in Hong Kong. It's a small world. He was staying at the world-renowned Mandarin Hotel and had flown there to be with his beautiful Chinese girlfriend, Mai Ling. We all had a meal together and talked about old times and future business, both keeping our cards close to the chest regarding the next flat racing season in England.

Maureen and Kevin got on very well which, in turn, made me feel more relaxed. Later, Kevin left us to go over to Kowloon to see his girlfriend's parents. We were off to the races at Sha-tin, having been given two horses to bet on by my Hong-Kong Chinese connections. Both won, one returned at shortish odds on the tote. The other a very good price indeed. I got my £1,000 back that I had dropped at the casino and was in front to the tune of six grand. Not bad, not bad at all.

We had soon had enough of Hong Kong and said our goodbyes to our friends at a floating Chinese restaurant with a memorable meal. Next day, on a whim, we were zooming to New Zealand. I had always fancied going there. In any case, I wanted to look at their horses and decided that I may even indulge in a jumper as they're supposed to be pretty high quality there - but the prices were high as well and I changed my mind.

New Zealand in early December was cold. We did a bit of exploring of Auckland and a couple of other places including Roturua to see the impressive geysers by luxury train, the Silver Fern Express.. Then we looked at our options - Bali or Fiji? We decided on Fiji and the next day we were staying at the glamorous Regent Hotel. Our room was right on the water's edge which was covered with palm trees. It was very hot though and, after a few days, I managed to hire a private yacht with a full crew in which we sailed around a few South Sea Islands. It cost me a packet. One thing for sure, my Hong Kong winnings wouldn't be going back home with me. We had a

Maureen in Fiji, posing with a couple of natives whose great grandfathers ate people!

Bula hour at the Regent Hotel in Fiji

holiday of a lifetime and then back to England for Christmas and my tipping business.

Early on, I realised that I was going to miss my partner, Kevin, and that I needed him more than he needed me. He was a tireless, conscientious worker, while I was more in the background; an ideas man. When you find a good partner in life, it is rare and you should do all you can to keep the partnership together. Maybe I should have done more?

At the same time, I had no intention of giving up on my original idea which was to give punters a good service. My business idea was still proving popular with those people who liked a bet. The difference now was that I had Charnwood to myself for my business and Kevin and I had spent over 1/4 million pounds on extra horse boxes and modernisation so it was quite a showpiece. Plus, after Kevin left, I spent a further £100,000 on new stable buildings. Maureen and I had planted over four hundred rose trees and a thousand conifers, so the landscaping alone was very impressive. I also had a full-time gardener and a manager to oversee everything.

Before I left for India, I clearly needed to hire a trainer - enter Gay Kelleway and a new chapter of my life. Gay was a young good-looking lady who came from a 'pedigree' family of racing folk and had plenty of style. Importantly, she had an impressive background in racing and her father, Paul was a successful trainer. From all accounts, I gave Gay the opportunity to start a serious career in horse racing. David O'Sullivan, the well-known porn king provided the Jockey Club with a letter of financial security for Gay and also gave her a few horses to train. Meanwhile, I rented her the trainer's bungalow at a cheap rent before I went away on holiday with Maureen, she was to be my new trainer and in charge of my horses.

Of course, I still had in my possession the greatest asset of all - the mailing list which I was ready to use

Surprise, surprise,
Kevin Moorcroft (tipster)
and
Ronnie Dawson (tipster)
meet up in Hong Kong.

My visit to the
Taj Majal, India,
with Maureen in 1993.

again. I suggested to Gay that I run all my horses under the 'Gay Kelleway Club' banner. And, in return for the use of her name, I would make sure that I supplied her with plenty of my own horses to train. In addition, she would receive a monthly cheque from the business and, of course, would bill me in full for the training of all my horses. She also had free water rates and other perks from me.

This deal appealed to Gay as it most certainly did to me. I can honestly say that, of all the trainers I had train for me, Gay was head and shoulders above the lot of them. The horses were always in tip-top condition and, furthermore, when she told me that one of my horses was going to win - it nearly always did, along with the 'Gay Kelleway Club' members, so everyone was happy and everyone was making money. Me more than most.

That winter when I went away on holiday having won thousands of pounds betting, I was feeling on top of the world. My one regret was that Kevin was no longer around to share my golden run. I'm not the kind of guy who seeks glory in any way. In fact, I am a person who never makes a fuss about anything unless I believe something is being done wrong or unfairly against another person. I learnt long ago in life that no one, apart from your family, really wants to hear if you're doing well. If anybody asks me how I am doing, I always make a point of saying that I'm having a bad time to make them feel better. Sadly, on the whole people do have a bad time, both financially and with their personal relationships. The last thing they want to hear is a smart ass bragging that he's won this and got that. Even when I became a millionaire, I was just one of the boys - or tried to be.

Upon my return to Newmarket, I found that Gay had been patiently getting one of my horses called *Castell Rossello* ready for a crack at winning the Lincoln Handicap. Once I had returned to Charnwood and spoke to

Two of a kind, racehorse trainer
Gay Kelleway who gave me a golden year in 1994.
Pictured here with her favourite horse called
'Backstabber'.

Gay about the horse's chances in the first big handicap of the season, I informed all our members to have a nice E/W bet when I saw, first-hand, what a superb shape Gay had got the horse in.

But when *Castell Rossello* ran in the Lincoln, he was drawn right on the stand rails. Notwithstanding, he was soon in front and finished clear on his side of the track. However, there was more pace on the other side of the track and the first three home were drawn on that side.

After this good run by *Castell Rossello*, we had backed E/W at 33/1 anti-post in this good handicap event. Fourth place was like a 8/1 winner. Gay was doing me proud. A few weeks earlier she had landed a good bet for the club members and myself. I was very impressed with her abilities, so much so that I decided that when Classic Bloodstock horses were bought, she would get the pick which involved horse purchases of a million pounds or more from my new project, Classic Bloodstock. But more of that particular saga later ....

With personal or business relationships, I had always imagined that, if you treated those around you with honesty and fairness, they would repay you in kind. That was a grave mistake. In my experience, it was the reverse; the more I gave to others, the more deceitful they became. Human nature was something you couldn't assess in my game of chess and this is often how I perceived my business to be.

I couldn't seem to see the wood for the trees, although I was starting to understand that I was not that lad of many years ago with my brolly and all my mates around. The difference was that now I was surrounded by deceit. It seemed that no one had self-respect - or was it just me? Was I expecting too much all the time from those around me?

When Gay Kelleway started training for me full steam in 1993, she made me a lot of money. In return, I gave her

David Sheckles buyer of the
Classic Bloodstock horses,
here with Classic Eagle 10th in the Derby

financial security and a chance to play a big part in my plans for the future. When you look at just a few of the major coups she landed for me with moderate horses, is it any wonder I had so much faith in her? As far as training horses to land a gamble, she was going to be a star. And in Classic Bloodstock I was hoping to buy her the horses that could put her firmly on the map for all to see her ability. I was hoping to make £1,000,000, plus available to her for making race horse purchases.

Gay started training my new horse *Castell Rossello* for me prior to running in the Lincoln to land a gamble at Southwall, where he was ridden by Alan Mackay at Southwell and won easily by five lengths at 9/2, (having been backed earlier in the betting at 20/1). As I said earlier, she then trained him specifically for the big Lincoln handicap at Doncaster where the draw beat him and he finished fourth, although we were all on E/W at 33/1 antipost. (If he had won that day, I would have cleared over £100,000).

Gay soon had us all swinging again when she landed a mega touch for us all (myself and club members) with *Castell Rossello* at Newbury winning at 6/1 s.p.(starting price) opening 10/1 with the bookies. Then she made a further sack full of money for us later that same day when another of my horses she had trained, *Lavender Cottage* won at 10/1 at the night meeting at Lingfield.

I was in a golden patch, it was as good as if I was printing my own money! The next big winning coup was *Aljaz* who was backed from 20/1 down to 7/2, then *Charlie Bigtime* was a winner twice, 12/1 to 6/1 and 6/1 to 7/2 at Wolverhampton. Every time I had a runner, the teletext on TV was writing about it and, of course, all the market betting moves were all noted there.

While all this was going on, other horses of mine were landing massive bets, like *Environmentalist* by an easy 8 lengths at Folkstone 12/1 to 9/2 and trained by Stuart

...at my stables 'Charnwood', before running 4th in the Lincoln Handicap, which would have won me £100,000, if he had won!

Williams. And there were other horses winning for me and landing big bets which, needless to say, my clients appreciated and enjoyed. I realised that my five year plan which I had drawn up in 1989 was at its pinnacle. It was checkmate all the way!

There was no doubt about it, this girl could certainly train racehorses and, more importantly, tell you when you could have a bet. I was going through a magic period I will never forget, yet I rarely went to a racecourse to lead my winners in. Instead, I would usually sat in my office with a calculator.

Classic Bloodstock plc, my new venture and a new five year plan, had attracted 6,500 new people into racing and I was planning to spend over a million pounds on new horses. Little was I to know then that Classic Bloodstock would play a part in my eventual life ban from racing.

Within a week, everything was thrown upside down; all my plans for the future with Gay and myself went down the drain over a filly called *Wardara*. It was a great pity. Me and my bloody principles! Of course, I realise now, too late, that principles and good intentions are for fools, just as horse racing is for conmen, cheats and liars..

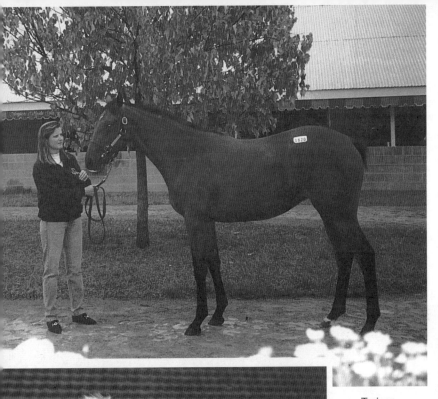

Trainer
Gay Kelleway
buys a horse at
Keenland Sales in
the U.S.A. named
Classic Coral
it turned out useless

Gay Kelleway
& David Sheckles at
Deauville Bloodstock
Sales, France. David
was later badly
criticised in the press
by Gay for buying
poor animals. This
was proven later not
to be the case.

137

Establishment 'Charnwood' Ronnie & Maureen
receiving a trophy presented by a national newspaper for
'Best Business Idea 1994' *Classic Bloodstock plc.*
Only for it all to go wrong later.

CHAPTER TWELVE

I want to mention here a little story which had a major impact on me and took place only days before I sacked Gay. At the prestigious Newmarket Houghton Sales in September '94, David Sheckells, my bloodstock buyer, and myself said to Gay that we had looked at this colt, *By Sharpo* and decided that we would bid up to 55,000 guineas for him on behalf of Classic Bloodstock shareholders. (I had launched the plc in February 1994 and, with £3 million pounds paid by shareholders, I was in the big league at the sales. So, as Gay would be the trainer, I let her in on all my discussions and my buying plans).

Later, Gay was sitting with some minor Arab owners in the sales ring right by the rostrum on the front row, practically in view of every one in the packed sales arena and was well-aware of our bidding intentions. She entered into the bidding at 30,000 guineas, either on behalf of the Arab owners or herself, but dropped out at 54,000 guineas, knowing full well that we were going to bid just a thousand guineas more up to David's valuation of 55,000 guineas. She won free mileage making herself look a big-shot in bidding up to 54,000 guineas, safe in the knowledge that David couldn't see her as he was standing right up the top of the sales ring on the opposite side, but behind a side panel, which is a usual practice when you want to keep your bids out of sight from any opposition. But I saw her and it left a bitter taste in my mouth. In fact, if I had been able to talk to David, I would have told him not to bid any further and drop out. Gay would have been left with egg on her face and with a horse that she really had no intention of buying. I most certainly don't think that her small time Arabs had the money and nor do I believe in playing games at other people's expense.

The losers here were the Classic Bloodstock plc shareholders because, when Gay came in the auction at around the 30,000 guineas mark, she and she alone, ran that price up to 54,000 guineas. I forgive Gay for all the nasty, spiteful, untrue things she got her press boys to write about me after I gave her the bullet. "Hell hath no fury like a woman scorned." I forgive her over *Wardara* episode, but I will never forget that incident at the Newmarket sales. Yes, she gave me a fabulous golden year. In fact, from those winners, I bought my villa in Spain and was able to buy a Rolls Royce. And with his winnings, my son Tim, who loves a good bet when the time is right, bought me my personal number plate: R.H.D. 1 for the roller for my birthday which stands for Ronald Herbert Dawson.

Herbert was my father's name and, although I never liked the name as a young lad, I use it now with pride. My Dad had the finest qualities any man could ever have and it makes me squirm to think of all the creeps who write untrue articles in the press which I am sure many people just like him believe. I know my parents always trusted unquestionably what they read in the papers. Working-class folk just did. Hypocrites have dogged my life and most of the time are supposedly well-educated and think they are above criticism when they are just little berks full of their own importance. Perhaps that's why I have tried to hold onto my working-class upbringing which I'm proud of. I never could, or would want to be a part of the establishment's hypocrisy.

But now let me explain how it all went wrong.

During August of 1994, Gay was at the sales in Deauville, France buying horses for her other owners and was a great help to me at looking at prospective purchases, though somewhat cold-shouldered by the main buyer for Classic Bloodstock plc, David Sheckles. However, I tried to make it up to Gay and, as she was planning to go to the States soon after to buy horses for some of her owners, I asked her to buy a couple of horses at the Keeneland Sales for Classic Bloodstock plc which she did. I had always had a high regard for Gay's judgement of horseflesh, but you need luck on your side as well and her Keeneland purchasing proved not up to the mark. They both turned out to be useless. *Classic Artiste* and *Classic Coral*. But that's racing, as they say!

Then, unfortunately, it all went wrong for Gay and I (me and my bloody principles were to cost me the best trainer I ever had as well as a great deal of money over the next two years). Whatever lies the sporting press have written about the affair, this is the true account of exactly what happened:

When Gay had returned from Keeneland and was back training for me at Charnwood, she had a runner at Newmarket. The horse ran in the head girl's name, Jo Crowley which is common practice in the racing world, (i.e. running horses in other peoples' names whatever the Jockey Club would have you believe). They know full well that I am not telling porkies - plenty of people do this for one reason or another, but mostly for the sake of a convenience at the time. Nothing underhand. I have yet to understand what difference does it make in anyway whose name a horse runs under. The Jockey Club makes such a song and dance about this. It's bloody ridiculous. Now back to Gay Kelleway and the truth about why we split up. At 10.00 a.m. on a Saturday morning, Gay called in at my house at Charnwood and I gave her the usual cheque from the Gay Kelleway Racing Club. I was about to put a message on the member's private phone for the punters to ring as we had a runner from the yard. Now, if this horse had belonged to a new owner who wanted things kept quiet, I could work with Gay to try and get around it. This was not the case right then, however and, as I have said, the horse ran in Gay's head girl's name, Jo Crowley. But Gay had just claimed it out of a claiming race. Just when it was being prepared by its previous connections for a tilt at the ring in its next race, it appeared that they were handicapping it to get its weight down and ready for its next race to land a gamble. A bit of bad luck because Gay bought it, not knowing that was the case. I suspect that the past owners had a word with Gay about their intended plan and told her the full story on the understanding that my members and myself were kept in the dark. If she had told me that - fair enough, she chose to lie.

"What should I tell them on the line?" I asked her that Saturday morning, referring to the message I would give to the members of our club about *Wardara*.

"Say it's got no chance. It's a non-trier," she replied.

"Okay Gay, thanks," I replied. "But I won't make it sound quite that brutal!"

What I said, in fact, was that we had a runner from the yard, but that it wasn't fancied.

I wasn't feeling too well that day, so I didn't go down to our local track at Newmarket but watched the race on TV instead.

And who should come on bawling as he does, but TV pundit, big John McCririck.

"There's been an almighty gamble on a Gay Kelleway trained horse," he said, rattling on and trying to get as much mileage out of it as he could - which was typical. What a fool! I thought. The trainer had told me that it had no chance and surely she knew best.

Surprise, surprise, the horse won easily and was very well-backed. As it turned out, I was the fool and my honest reputation to my club members was left in tatters. The next day the papers were praising Gay for landing a massive coup. One even claimed Gay had won a million pounds, bloody ridiculous that was. But it did me no good in the club members' eyes. I was left with two options.

Either I could let my clients and punters believe that I had misled and ripped them off and keep myself in with my excellent trainer, or sack my trainer for deceit and lose a lucrative business called 'The Gay Kelleway Racing Club'.

I chose the latter option and, looking back, it was an easy decision to make. If you lose your credibility with your punters and friends in the racing game, then you just become one of the conning pack to me. Nothing is worth that humiliation. Because I stuck to my principles of always putting the punter first, I had lost a brilliant business.

Gay Kelleway is the darling of the media, a glamorous TV racing personality who is often the guest on the racing channel. And as I have said, she is an excellent trainer. But, because of Gay's leanings, we were always concerned for the welfare of any new unsuspecting stable girl at Charnwood. For Gay's appetite for the ladies was legendary. There was a constant stream flowing into Gay's secluded bungalow: Swedish, Portuguese, Italian, etc. I always suspected these upper-class girlfriends of Gay's could take care of themselves. Indeed, on one occasion I personally witnessed Gay being physically beaten up in the winning enclosure at Lingfield Racecourse with an umbrella wielded by a dumped girlfriend; a hot headed Italian flame who, only a few days previously, had been proudly exhibited by Gay at a dinner party at my house.

But in late 1994, Gay introduced me to a very attractive Portuguese young lady. All the stable lads at Charwood fancied her which, in my opinion, was obviously a waste of time! She and Gay made a very glamorous pair. And I understand the relationship is still strong and I am pleased about that. Gay had confided in me that this girl was special. I also found that, besides being a good looker, she was articulate, clever and very feminine. "A classy bit" who had a lot of obvious charm.

Life at Charnwood was never dull that's for sure. Occasionally Gay would invite Maureen and me to one of her many parties. All harmless fun. Plenty of girls, booze and a bit of "wacky backy" being smoked. Gay was always a generous hostess and the best champagne flowed freely, especially following a winning week with the horses. But many of the best looking girls were not on the menu for the boys - which was irritating to say the least! And it was rare for a stag to get fixed up. In any case most were legless or in a trance before the clock struck midnight.

Racing is a scabby business underneath its cloak of public respectability. Again, we have the media reporting the dawn arrests of two more famous jockeys to add to the trio who have recently had their collars felt. A few top trainers have also entered the supposed plot. This latest bombshell in the 'race fixing' rumours or allegations was the arrests by the "organised crime squad" of household name jockeys, Graham Bradley and Derby winner, rider Ray Cochrane, who has also ridden for me. I don't know if the lads have committed any crime. Personally, I would be surprised if they had. But when well-known trainers are also hauled in, or make trips to the police station with their solicitors, it must give the public some concern. But the statement from Jockey Club executive director, Christopher Foster was: "The licensing committee considered that the fact of implication for the integrity of horse racing did not pose a sufficient threat to the public confidence. However, the matter will be kept under review and allow licences to be kept at present." As I said, I don't know if the jockey lads are culprits or not. That's for the organised crime squad. But Foster of the Jockey Club is a mouthpiece supposedly to soothe our concerns. But I can imagine the Jockey Club braves dancing and whooping round the Portman Square totem pole because, since they took a couple of easy scalps off Tim and me for a minor infringement, the Portman Square war party will be well painted up with sharpened tomahawks to snare any conspirators (or rumoured ones for that matter ...). At least, that's my opinion.

More of the Jockey Club later in the book. Bookmakers must take a share of the blame in racing for a lot of the hanky panky that goes on. I will give you one instance here that gives me grave concern. Take Victor Chandler, a top respectable racetrack bookmaker. He offers a very interesting package to my ex-trainer Gay Kelleway. She can bet with him tax-free. She can also have the very best price available! Then the icing on the cake - if the horse loses, she does not have to pay. It's this very bookmaker stuff that is a problem. For example, look at this scenario. You may have a horse in Gay's stable; you want to land a gamble with and keep it quiet. But you could have Gay ringing up Victor and saying, I will have £2000 on Ivory Dildo in the 3-0'clock race at Doncaster. She has warned the bookie about your intentions. And, to cap it all, if it gets beat, she has had a free bet. And it if wins, the bookie aware of the intended gamble has got himself a sack full of money out of your horse. But this sort of business could open a whole can of worms. For instance, a phone call could go like this.

"Hi Victor, Gay here. I want £2000 on Ivory Dildo."

"Okay Gay. How about your other three runners this afternoon."

"No Victor. I don't expect them to win."

And you see dear reader, if, as a bookmaker, you are giving out favours such as you don't pay him for your bets, if they lose, then it's logical to suspect that, the bookies, want something in return. Now, if Victor Chandler has other trainers on the same terms, it could be assumed that he knows about many horses that are not expected to win that day. Perhaps many in the same race, and then me "old punter" you have a big, big problem.

However this kind of free betting should not really be treated as a bit of a laugh. There are many trainers like Gay who are not blessed with family money and struggle to make training racehorses pay as a business. This sort could be easy prey for bookmakers seeking special information. To my mind what I am saying could prove the answer to a lot of questions being asked over certain horses which should be hot favourites but are easy to back.

I was horrified to receive a compromising letter, from bookmaker Victor Chandler to my trainer Gay Kelleway. It arrived in my letter-box during the night, I suspect as an act of spite from one of Gays' rejected lovers.

This letter set the alarm bells ringing for me, because it asked Gay if she was prepared to carry on with the *same financial arrangements as the previous year*.

Now the penny dropped with me, and it could be that Gays cosy arrangement with Victor explained why a few of my gambles were attracting money before anyone should have known about them, and before I had got my own money on. Also when I had a horse not expected to win, known only by Gay and myself, why it 'drifted' in the market, as though bookmakers knew it wouldn't win.

If bookmakers are dangling carrots to trainers for stable secrets, I suspect those same carrots are also on the menu for jockeys. Many jockeys struggle to make a living. Bookmakers have been caught in the past paying jocks for information. But the Jockey Club have been lenient in their sentences to guilty parties, compared to Tims and mine minor indiscretions.

Victor Chandler it seems is so intent of doing business with trainer Gay Kelleway that he supplies her with no less than three different telephone numbers for her to contact him on. His private office, mobile and his home number, which in my opinion is extremely odd for a top bookmaker to do. I most certainly have never before heard of such cosy arrangements.

Could this free bets business be rife in racing? Could bookmakers have certain trainers and jockeys in their pocket?

In my opinion, most struggling trainers and jockeys would welcome the Victor Chandler-Gay Kelleway arrangement. Also in my opinion, few trainers are loyal to their owners - and vice versa. Surely the Jockey Club don't condone these sort of business arrangements? Or do they? Knowing the Jockey Club ostriches like I do now, I wouldn't be surprised at anything from them.

Like I said, the Jockey Club lads at Portman Square have their head in the sand. So I will leave them with this one. The dope van is at the racecourse to dope test jockeys. They all know what it looks like. So, if any jockey turns up at the racetrack as 'high as a kite', or has flown the night before, he sees the dope box parked up ready for testing, he turns round, then goes back home saying he doesn't feel well. Oh I could tell some stories!

This is yet another true racing story. And it is a story of another real bookmaker sting, and this sting was masterminded by a close friend of mine.

Indeed, he masterminded, not only for the big pay out, but to satisfy himself it could be done. And for the first time ever, he had a hot one. But he never told me, although we had always exchanged jobs (bets).

But I must start at the beginning. My friend has owned so many horses he would have a job remembering most of them. Here, I will only give one example of his disappointment to demonstrate why he did what he did. But first the disappointment. This friend of mine, we will give him the alias of Kevin. He bought a filly at the Irish sales for just 2,000 guineas. Within a few months, this filly was showing that at this price she was an inspirational purchase indeed. On the trial gallops she was slamming all the other much more pricey two year olds in her trainer's yard.

Now, our lad, Kevin liked a bet and he knew he had got one here to 'mortgage the house for' so to speak for a tilt on the ring. But he made a mistake. He let a certain well-known jockey sit on her in her final trial gallop, to give our Kevin his opinion. In the gallop was this good handicapper which had won previously at Kempton. And this bit of work showed Kevin that, indeed, he had a knocking bet. But what my friend had not taken into account was the jockey who rode his horse in the trial gallop had more private punters than is strictly fair. In other words, he had a sackful and, consequently, although our Kevin's horse won its race at a canter, the odds were so cramped there was no meat on the bone. Yet, on the morning of the race, the sporting press had her odds in double figures: 20/1.

Now as I have said, my friend liked a bet and although his horse won, the icing on the cake had gone. And he was taught a lesson he would never forget. Next time you get a nice little horse for a touch, only mention it in your prayers. That way, the information doesn't get back to a living soul.

Well, now in our Kevin's life "lightening did, indeed, strike twice" and someone above - up on high, looked down on our Kev and gave him the tool to have another crack at those cigar puffing bookies with their jockey informants with their "mettle mickeys" (mobile phones). This is what happened.

Kev, the lad was in Ireland to try and buy another bargain and this ex-trainer of mine bought one for a punter (in this case, an owner) who could not come up with the money. So our gallant bookie, bashing hero, ends up with the nag in a roundabout way.

The horse was sent to the breeze up sales (horses run three furlongs to show something) because, as I say, the original owner cannot find the money. So the trainer has to sell it. A bit of hanky panky. A few quid dropped in the right grubby hand and this horse breezes up like it has only got three legs. So our lad, Kev steps into bid for it and gets a bargain. For, unknown to all but three, "sworn into secrecy like the three musketeers". This little filly is a flyer and because she was bought out of the breeze up sales for buttons, it qualified her for median auction races at a low weight (poor races were the cost of the horse at the sales determines its weight to carry in a race).

Now, our Kev writes to me in Spain with the story, after the deed was done and the filly had won its race.

"Ron, that affair at Catterick when I should have 20/1 my money not a 5/4 fav. learnt me a lesson. You know that a horse like that comes along once in a blue moon. And here's me know with another blue moon horse. So I set out my stall this time, good and proper like.

"If you put your horse with a Cecil, Stout or Cumani, etc forget it, because if it's got a wooden leg, the press will make it a favourite. So, what I did was give this filly to a trainer to train who last had a winner when they were ration coupons. He was a muppet trainer whose whole family as trainers had only trained three winners between them since the Titanic sank!

I did my homework. Precision galloping and no jockey ever sat on her until the day of the race. Only three of us in it, the trainer, me and a work jockey who was so silent he only spoke to his mother on her birthday. Well, you know the rest. Four grand on the horse all over the country in bits at 33/1 which gave me 132 grand in cash. And that is the way to do it. Incidentally, I put a monkey (500) on for you. 20/1 so find enclosed ten grand inside the package of the box of your favourite cigars. (Whoops! There was no room so I had to smoke them all).

"You know Ron, I would have told you but I was sworn to secrecy. I know you will understand." said Kev. "It was like Sinatra's song: I Did It My Way." I looked at the money and smiled to myself. That's what you call a true racing friend, I thought.

But hang on, Kev, if you had told me what you were up to, my bet would also have been four grand at 33/1, not a monkey (500) at twenties!

Have you heard this one? Two Irish lads decide to go to the pictures for the afternoon because racing is off at The Curragh. Apparently, the course was waterlogged.

The film being shown was Ben Hur. In the chariot race "Paddy" says to "Mick".

"Do you wanna bet, Mick?"

Mick replied. "Yes I do, I'll have twenty pounds on the white team."

Paddy says: "I'll have twenty pounds with you on the black horses."

Anyway, Ben Hur's white team won by a few inches.

Paddy says to Mick.

"I don't know how you pick 'em Mick."

"I just follow the form Paddy. The white team won last week at the Odeon!"

This here's another true story. I've had lots of people ring my stables out of the blue for racing tips. And the calls I never objected to were from one of the Kray twins. I always felt that they had paid for their crimes and an example had to be made in their case while others as violent or cruel had got off with a lighter sentence. I like to think that he was only after racing information and had no other motive in mind. Surprising isn't it who likes a bet on the horses?

When I was at the pinnacle of my betting coups in 1994, there must have been someone who was jealous. Maureen and I were disturbed from watching our Sunday afternoon film on the telly with the noise of several cars roaring into the stable's car park. The next thing we knew about thirty plain clothes police officers surrounded both my house, as well as Tim's which was also within my stable complex. I couldn't believe it. "a visit" from 'the Sweeny'. For three hours, my usual relaxing

Sunday was turned into a 'Carry On ...' farce while cops ran a fine toothcomb all over my estate. They didn't find a thing, not even a bent nail and left red faced several hours later. I wonder who sent them on such a wild goose chase, wasting tax payers' money (yet again!).

And it got worse, I had an income tax investigation by the big squad. They went through all my business dealing with a nit comb. It cost me over £10,000 in extra accountancy fees. For over two years of the investigation, there was a big cloud hanging over me. Nearly everyone around me knew about it. Even my brother, Richard was later roped in. They left no stone unturned. All I ever got from them was that they were acting on a series of tip off's. Naturally, there were no apologies.

Well the sun came out, the clouds blew away and everything was clear. What a waste of time, effort and government money. My £10,000 accountancy fees were no problem - they were tax deductible.

A few years ago, I discovered by accident a fantastic source of racing information. My youngest son, David was staying at Charnwood with me for a few days and was fiddling around with a contraption called a phone scanner. I became very curious when I heard a well-known trainer's voice through it, telling an owner he didn't think this particular horse would win that day. I couldn't believe it. David showed me how to use the scanner and every morning, between 7 a.m. and 9 a.m. I would listen in as the trainers from all around the Newmarket training ground had conversations with owners or jockeys on their mobile phones. I got some very good betting information from this, as well as advice as to which horses I shouldn't bet on. It just shows that there are lots of ways to skin a cat.

Up until this period of my life, I was in a very secure financial position having made the biggest money in my life in the shortest period of time, 1990-1994.

The original concept for Classic Bloodstock plc which I was promoting, followed a lunch I was invited to at the Jockey Club in Newmarket in 1993 by Peter Amos, the Jockey Club's Newmarket Estate Manager. I remember that there were about seven or eight guests; all successful in their chosen profession. It was a wonderful experience for me. We ate in a magnificent dining-room, full of antiques, including some masterpiece paintings, such as works by Stubbs who, for obvious reasons, was an artist much sought-after in the high echelons of racing society. We enjoyed gin and tonics served by the butler, followed by an excellent lunch accompanied by a fine wine, culminating with port and cigars and plenty of lively debate.

My bank manager from the National Westminster Bank was among the guests and, as I had been told beforehand before I accepted the lunch invitation, the main topic of the conversation was how could the Jockey Club interest more race horse owners into racing? Apparently, they had done some research and tried various schools of thought and schemes, all of which, I would say, were unsuccessful. There could be little doubt that race horse ownership was dropping fast and had been since the financial and housing market had crashed in 1987. Peter Amos, like many of the Jockey Club staff, was an ex-army officer. He was a splendid host and we were all at ease, exchanging points of view. However, what did strike me at the time was how naive everyone was about this problem of dwindling ownership. They could provide very little input, only vague suggestions, some of which were plain daft.

I understood the problem and I knew full well how difficult the task of attracting new owners into racing could be. But I also knew that, because of my long business association with horse racing and the way racing punters thought, if I set my mind to it, I could come up with a solution. Furthermore, as I wrote earlier, I had the biggest and best mailing list of racing punters and enthusiasts in the country.

My putting together a plc in racing had started following my lunch at the Jockey Club room's in Newmarket to explore ways of introducing more people into the love of my life; the wonderful world of the thoroughbred. Racing had not only made me a rich man by my standards, but had also made my life interesting and exciting for more than thirty years. I felt I owed a debt to racing and was determined to put something back into the game.

One thing I understood in racing or selling anything by direct mail was that, if the mailing list was a genuine one of people interested in your product then, providing your spiel was fair and honest, you could post out 5000 trial mail shot letters and expect a percentage of returns of say 3%. So, if you sent out 5 million letters you could expect the same 3% return, providing you wrote to the same type of person you used in the trial mail shot.

Eventually, I conceived the idea of Classic Bloodstock plc. I knew that if I could get my idea across to the public and stimulate enough interest to raise sufficient money, it could be very successful. I reasoned that if I could reach a certain type of person then, if he or she were keen, I could offer them a lot of pleasure in return for a minimal investment. Furthermore, with a little bit of luck, they could possibly also make a profit. And, one thing for sure, if I could raise the money we wouldn't have to be paying the ridiculous high prices for young horses that Classic Thoroughbreds had paid in the eighties which I felt was the main reason for their failure and losing 12 million pounds along with thousands of small investors who lost their money.

I had set certain conditions myself before I did my mail shot, especially pointing out that this investment was primarily just for fun.

Sporting Life reporter, Andrew Sim, a villain of the piece, in my opinion a liar and disgrace to his profession.

CHAPTER THIRTEEN

When Classic Bloodstock was launched, I threw my own racing stables open to all investors, twenty-four hours a day. I also provided a cottage at the stables which shareholders could use for overnight stays and from which I made no profit. Neither did I take any sort of salary. I didn't need to. I was (and still am) a giver in life, not a taker. I made mistakes, but I tried hard to make Classic Bloodstock work. I dearly wanted it to succeed.

But the knockers were on the march, The Sporting Life being the most damaging with their nasty, vindictive reporting, wagging the tail of The Racing Post who followed up with the same stupid scaremongering which, in turn, started off a chain reaction in the world of horse racing. Why did The Sporting Life, hate Classic Bloodstock so much?. They didn't, it was me and the Classic plc directors they hated. They wanted to get back at us, believing we were responsible for the PPS exposures. I can think of no other reason. This is a typical piece of vindictive journalism. They tried so hard to convince their readers that the Dawsons had stolen money from Classic Bloodstock plc.

The hostile press was very harmful to Classic Bloodstock and myself as Chairman of that company. The Racing Post and The Sporting Life were all out to cause mischief. I will give you a sample of what I mean here, and it is an extract that The Sporting Life have repeated periodically which states: (In Gay Kelleway's opinion) "It's all very well buying by pedigree, but some of the horses they bought! I'm thinking in particular of the three they bought in France. They had things wrong with their legs and could not stand training. One had two legs coming out of the same hole!" (I can just picture the smirk on Sim's face every time he writes this piece) or The Racing Post who like to get the boot in.

So, please let me tell you the truth, because the press won't. The three horses Gay refers to are *Classic Moonlight* (she was bought for breeding, she has a wonderful pedigree and now has a foal to be sold; a very valuable foal indeed by all accounts). The other two fillies are *Classic Ballet* and *Classic Affair* and have run 40 times between them winning or being placed in nineteen races (five victories) so that puts the record straight 'wouldn't stand up to training?' Have The Racing Post or The Sporting Life ever apologised or retracted the grossly offensive words? No pigs might fly first. (The Racing Post is owned by Arabs and those in editorial power are so two-faced and dishonest. I understand The Racing Post has just been purchased by Mirror Group plc. In my opinion, they deserve each other).

To my mind, its reckless reporting and they, the papers, should be charged by the Jockey Club for bringing racing into disrepute. It's also a slur on David Shekells, the buyer, and a slur on the directors of Deauville Select Sales, as the compilers and vendors of the French sales catalogue. Those silly comments by Gay Kelleway were from a woman twisted by jealousy. You must remember I gave her the boot and threw her out of my stable's kicking and screaming. Previously, in 1994, when she thought she would be training the plc's horses, she wrote the following:

"I fully support the business principles of Classic Bloodstock plc. My father, trainer Paul Kelleway, has had several notable successes in making large profits from shrewdly bought yearlings. One who comes to mind readily was Madam Gay, who cost only £8,000 guineas as a yearling but won the fantastic amount of over £235,000 in prize money in one year alone. She was then sold in a private deal to a famous French millionaire owner breeder at a huge profit."

That's racing folk for you.

They couldn't lie straight in bed.

I received a fax from Alan Byrne, editor of The Racing Post on 31st March, warning me not to write or copy anything in my book that The Racing Post had written about me or Classic Bloodstock. Such hypocrisy. What are they afraid of? The public knowing the real facts?

The following is typical of what I was having to contend with, with the newspapers in trying to get the truth over to the public. This is just one sample of correspondence.

Classic Bloodstock plc
Newmarket

PRESS RELEASE

From: Ron Dawson MD
Date: 13 January 1996
Classic Bloodstock plc

Subj: Open letter to the Editors of The Sporting Life and The Racing Post

Sir,

Following your months of detrimental reporting on Classic Bloodstock plc 1, especially The Sporting Life, I would welcome the opportunity to put the record straight and stop all the nonsense your newspapers seem to enjoy writing. This seemingly infantile reporting, with unfounded hysterical outbursts, appears to indicate that, unless something is "rubber stamped" by you as journalists, racing cannot possibly benefit from it.

I wish to answer a few of your queries here, for while the Press have run around trying to dig up dirt on Classic Bloodstock, all they have managed to succeed with is scaremongering. Not once has either of our only two racing papers been able to bring themselves to say anything positive about Classic Bloodstock. I have learnt one lesson from this, and I will not make the same mistake again, never do anything philanthropic for racing, for the more you do the less you are thought of, and have to suffer snide remarks (which, of course, have never been backed up with any proof whatsoever) and innuendoes which probably make good reading for those who cannot think for themselves.

When I first had the idea for Classic Bloodstock plc, bloodstock prices were low. In the past, The Sporting Life and Racing Post have made heroes out of people like Sheikh Mohammed, Robert

Sangster, Vincent O'Brian who had spent millions and millions of pounds on horses that couldn't run downhill on wheels. Two of these great heroes were leaders in a plc which lost all their shareholders' money when they bought horses costing millions each which were disappointing considering the huge sums of money they paid for them - more than I have every done. My record will stand up against anyone's. Mr Minton and Charlie Gordon Watson (leading bloodstock agents) will tell you that they have bought more bad horses than successful ones.

So, what is it all about? 'Classic ' spends £1.25 million on 25 horses (not £5 million or £10 million on one horse). Our buying plan was well thought out, for we had seven 2 year old winners in 1995, though the majority were bought to make 3 and 4 years old. Still, the so-called racing journalists do not understand racing. A trainer who has any sense does not wind up a horse, bred to win at 1 1/2 miles, to win a 5 furlong sprint and ruin the animal!

Now, let's get down on paper the facts of the journalist's complaints, along with those of a very few shareholders.

Tim Richards writes in The Racing Post on 8th January 1996 that Classic Bloodstock shareholders want an Action Group. He mentions two names, Bill Ryan, an assistant in a publishing firm and Robert Carson, a semi-retired lecturer.

Mr. Ryan's bone of contention is lack of newsletters. Okay, 6,500 shareholders in plc 1 equals 6,500 newsletters. Okay, let's do two a month. With typesetting, printing and mail-shots, each one costs 80 pence that's £10,400 per month, nearly £125,000 per year. I am not sure the shareholders would like to see £250,000 spent in two years on newsletters, double that again for plc 11 and your are talking of half a million, which is a waste of shareholders' money. But if it's what they want, that's fine by me.

However, I never get paid for writing them, so perhaps Bill would like to volunteer his free time. Thanks, Bill, give me a ring.

Mr. Robert Carson just wants an Action Group. Good idea! We'll meet at the stables every morning at 7 am to discuss the plans for each horse's following day. We can speak to the vet, go through the entry book, ring round various trainers and ask them if they are running their horse in a particular race as we might not beat them if they do, watch the work, make the entries, etc. etc. Then Robert can make us all tea or coffee. Oh yes, of course, each day, come hail, rain or whatever, one of us volunteers will show the usual dozen or so shareholders round the yard and house. This takes about 2 hours and it is unpaid work. So it would not be appropriate for any of the Action Group to claim expenses.

Tim Richards of The Racing Post phoned my brother Rick regarding a rumour that Classic Bloodstock directors "have made a killing". How gullible can a man be? he should know that the DTI check out everything very thoroughly and when they did check, following some anonymous mischief making to my certain knowledge they found nothing at all untoward. I myself, have invested plenty of my own money in shares in plc 1 and have spent probably a further £5,000 out of my own pocket for the benefit of shareholders. I have also given the company hours upon hours of my time without thought of any remuneration. I am no martyr. Just enjoying the pleasure of others.

Where has the money gone? Every penny is accounted for. Attend the AGM's and listen to the Company Accountant's report. It appears that Mr Sims of The Sporting Life wouldn't know a horse if it kicked him and doesn't appreciate the difference between a 2 year old and a 3 year old. He has, however, done his utmost to run the company down, even retorting to untrue personal writings about me and my family.

Another shout from the shareholders was "Get rid of the Company Secretary". Well, Maureen has resigned and was glad to do so. Now, instead of her free services, the shareholders can have someone with letters after his name who will probably not be any better but will certainly not do it for free. Unfortunately, Maureen's departure means that we also lose the use of her lovely cottage at Charnwood for shareholders where she provided free Bed and Breakfast for visiting shareholders. Perhaps, we could ask for a volunteer from the Action Group to provide this service but, sorry, it doesn't carry a salary or expenses.

Mr Sims reported in The Sporting Life that a Mr Cottam, a fish and chip man, criticised my son Tim for his lack of experience in conducting an A.G.M. This does not surprise me as it was his first and his lack of experience was bound to show. However, as I was unable to take the chair myself due to ill health. I thought the shareholders would prefer to have a chairman who knew all about the horses. I wanted someone in my place I could trust to tell the truth about the horses rather than someone who covered up his lack of knowledge with bullshit. With the company accountants

*giving out the financial details. Perhaps Mr Cottam will join the
Action Group. I can see his suggestions for Public Relations Officers and Non-Executive Directors adding absolutely nothing to
what counts in the end of the performance and value of the
bloodstock purchased on behalf of the shareholders.*

*Could I now draw your attention to the following plc's below
which were all very large advertisers in the sporting press and,
obviously, raised a great deal of money from shareholders and I
could ask a good question: " What happened to the money?" I
personally joined two of the under-mentioned plc's and I never received anything back at all. I believe I know the reason why these
plc's fronted with high profile names and finished up with little or no
assets for their shareholders (or none worth mentioning).*

*All I ask the press is to give the Classic horses a chance to
prove themselves for the purpose for which they were purchased,
as 3 and 4 year olds. Then, if they fail, I deserve all the criticism
your journalists can throw at me. The buck stops with me. I will
take the responsibility for any failure. But let's stop all this missing
millions nonsense which the press are trying to promote.*

Some past plc's records below:

1. Pipe Scudamore
> Pipe Scudamore Racing plc   *(unsuccessful)*
> Pipe Scudamore Racing 11 plc

2. Gordon Holmes - M Easterby
> Gymcrack Thoroughbred Racing plc *(unsuccessful)*
> Gymcrack Thoroughbred Racing 11 plc
> Gymcrack Thoroughbred Racing 111 plc

3. Toby Balding - T. Kelly
> British Thoroughbreds Racing plc *(unsuccessful)*

4. O'Brian-Sangster
> Classic Thoroughbreds plc *(very unsuccessful)*

5. Colin Tinkler
> Full Circle Thoroughbreds A plc *(all six unsuccessful)*
> Full Circle Thoroughbreds B plc
> Full Circle Thoroughbreds C plc
> Full Circle Thoroughbreds D plc
> Full Circle Thoroughbreds E plc 1988
> Full Circle Thoroughbreds F plc 1989
> Full Circle Thoroughbreds G plc 1990

Surely these plc's are not a hard act to follow and I am pleased to say I was not part of any of the management of these companies.

Sims of The Sporting Life goes on incessantly about Classic being monitored by the Jockey Club to make shareholders believe there is something amiss. I can report that not once have I had any word of criticism or otherwise from the Jockey Club. It is obvious to me that the two most important papers to us as shareholders i.e. The Sporting Life and The Racing Post are determined by these actions, to devalue your investment. They have even brought to notice that an ex-conservative MP, Tom Benyon, is to investigate Classic Bloodstock. He has an open invitation to attend my meeting with The Sporting Life and Racing Post journalists at Charnwood on 29th or 30th January, though I doubt very much if he or they will turn up. Could I therefore ask shareholders to express their disgust at these newspapers' actions by writing to their Editors asking for an explanation of the biased and untrue reporting which will no doubt affect your financial investment.

Personally, I am looking forward to the next AGM when I will hopefully be in the chair myself. By then, perhaps, the supposed "missing millions" will have turned up on the moon and Mr Sims and his other mischief makers have gone to collect the evidence.

In the meantime, I feel it is my duty as MD of Classic Bloodstock plc to answer back on behalf of the shareholders to the vindictiveness of the press. Perhaps, Mr. A. Sims and one other Sporting Life journalist and Tim Richards and other Racing Post journalists would care to visit and question me at my stables at Charnwood on 30th January, the day before I go into hospital, on any matters that are still concerning them over PLC1. Should we say 11 p.m. Regarding plc 11 let's not prejudge that company in the press until after the EGM.

Ron Dawson - Managing Director, Classic Bloodstock PLC.
"Did the sporting press print any of this press release? Did they hell. It's not their way to reveal true fact to their readers" What The Racing Post did do though was alter my letter and write a pack of lies.

The press reports were so bad that I had to sue one national paper for substantial damages. The Daily Telegraph and their reporter, Dominic Prince settled out of court. The following year, Prince got his own back like the child he is by writing a nasty bit on Classic Bloodstock in a racing periodical. I know that The Sporting Life have never forgiven me over the support I had provided for PPS and the exposure of their unethical advertisers. However, even I was shocked at the depths they would stoop to, with venom and lies in a string of articles, right up to the latest garbage which was published on 23rd February, 1998. To quote journalist Andrew Sims: *"The scandal of Classic Bloodstock plc which relieved mostly small first time owners of more than 5 million pounds and enriched the Dawsons beyond their wildest dreams."*

Now, if that is a true statement and Classic Bloodstock has enriched me and Tin beyond our wildest dreams, well I am rightly exposed as a conman, cheat and liar and should go to prison. If this is not true, however, then these words are libellous to myself and my family. Furthermore, who is Sims in this article in The Sporting Life referring to when he says 'The Dawsons'. He is obviously referring to my son, Tim? But he never had any part in Classic Bloodstock until much later when he was made a director only because of my illness. He took over showing shareholders around Charnwood Stables and meeting them at the racecourses when Classic Bloodstock had a runner. He was never paid a salary. Nobody was who was on the board. In Sims' latest article, he calls the Dawsons: *"The Family from Hell"*. My Mum was upset by that one.

It is little wonder that, after three years of this type of untrue garbage written by newspaper reporters, that the Jockey Club look upon me as some evil bastard that must be expelled from racing all together and as soon as possible. But, once again, I am racing ahead of the field, so will take a pull and return to the beginning.

I had my mind set. I would go for a plc investment in racing. I had my solicitors draw up all the legal documents and, because it was a plc, all the associated criteria legally applied. This was done and I believe to the satisfaction of the Department of Trade and Industry (DTI) but first and, most importantly, would it work? I wasn't sure so bought only 10,000 names and addresses from the largest data base company of specialised addresses in England and mailed the lot of them. And, yes, my returns showed that it would, indeed work.

Those addresses I purchased were of people who had invested in shares in the past, ranging from British Airways to North Sea Gas.

Now, this is the problem I had to solve. If you buy horses at the cheap end of the market, you may well buy winning horses. Indeed, you are just as likely to buy a winner of sorts for peanuts, as you would for millions of pounds. However, what you won't get is a good family pedigree but, very likely, a racehorse that can only run and win in low class races.

I worked out that as we received one and a half percent returns from a 10,000 trial mail shot averaging £485 per investor, that equals just 66 subscribers paying approximately £32,000 which would buy a horse for only £10,000 as the balance of £22,000 would be easily swallowed up in training fees. In other words, it can't work and is a total waste of time. It's small time racing club thinking. To give all shareholders a chance of making a profit, you had to get into the big league, that's where the big money is, but you also need luck. I really wanted the Classic plc to be a success and with those percentages I got from the 10,000 mail shot test, I knew I had a winner if I had a big enough mailing list to use.

As I said earlier in my story, Sheikh Mohammed paid over $10m for only one horse and that was useless. The average price for buying a champion nowadays is in the range of £50,000 and £150,000. If you are paying that amount, you are undoubtedly paying for a good pedigree.

Of course, you need luck, but before you can try your lucky dip you need money of the right sort - say £1 million plus.

I knew, as sure as night follows day, that if I mailed my prospectus to 1,000,000 people of the same mode as my trial shot that, of 10,000 then the amount of money into the company would be about £3.2 million and attract approximately 6,600 small investors averaging under £500 per person. If Martin Pipe or Elite Racing Club charged, say, £500 per person to join for a year, the VAT man takes about £80 of that, leaving you with £420 invested in your chosen racing club for one year. At the end of the term, if you're lucky you might get 10 pence in the pound back and you will hopefully have enjoyed watching your horse racing on TV, received a few newsletters, a couple of stable visits and, if very fortunate, had a day out at the races when one of your club's horses have ran.

The bottom line is that you had a bit of fun for your money, but with only the remotest chance of ever having a good horse. Why? Because there was never enough money in the racing club to buy one. I don't know of one racing club ever in this country having a runner in the Derby. I can't even think of any plc for that matter and there's been quite a few having done so, aside from Classic Bloodstock plc.

Now, anyone with any brains should be able to recognise the fact that, if you are able to play in the top half of the market, you are more likely to buy a winner with a pedigree. Look at it this way. If a horse wins an English Derby and its pedigree is top drawer, it could be worth up to £10 million. Yet if another horse wins an English Derby which has no sound family pedigree, it is worth a fraction compared to the other horse, perhaps as low as £1 million - but they have both won the English Derby.

I had a dream and that dream was to do something big for racing. I was not interested in earning money from the dream for myself. I had enough money already for everything I needed in life; I had made my wedge in racing.

So, I put the idea into practice, I did the mailing shot and raised £3.2 million. The investor now had a chance. But I wanted to be extra safe, so decided that we would buy more fillies than colts. That way, if the colts failed, we could continue to safeguard our investment for a few years until we could breed and sell our own foals which would be all well-bred from our own good pedigree mares.

Of course, as I write this, it sounds all too easy. But why shouldn't it work? The only one thing we needed was a good share of luck with our purchases. The champions of the future are for sale at one sale or another every year (or they were until the mega rich Arabs with their oil money came along and bought just about everything decent on offer). Thankfully, there were still a few that escaped their trawl nets. And, today, as they breed a lot of their own horses, they are not the big buyers that they were.

Anyway, we had £2.6 million in the pot after all expenses and, as Chairman and Managing Director, I decided to spend £1.3 million on 24 thoroughbred yearlings. I was well-aware of the wastage rate in racing so knew that, if we could end up with a couple of decent horses from our initial purchases we would have done well, we were par for the course in racing terms. Obviously, in the first year you can start cutting down and sorting out the wheat from the chaff and, of course, you will always lose a few with leg or breathing problems, etc. But yes, you need one champion horse from the twenty-four bought and I failed to get one. That's part of the racing game.

We had £1 million in the bank for training fees (which I knew would fluctuate initially as I sold on horses which couldn't make the grade). I was ready to make a careful selection of fillies, some of which I knew would retain their value because of their pedigree.

Another point I had to consider was the following: If the £1.3 million I was spending on bloodstock was my own money, I would have relied solely on my own expertise. However, it wasn't, so I brought in professional advice. David Shekells had managed a successful stud for years. He knew the conformation of a horse as well as anyone I had ever met - and better than most.

I personally had also carried out a considerable amount of research regarding pedigree and, as I wrote earlier, had also asked Gay Kelleway to buy a couple of horses in America at a sale that she was planning to attend. I was very conscious of the fact that I was spending the shareholders' money and, while I would have loved a trip to the Keeneland Sales in the U.S.A. myself in order to oversee the purchase of the horses, I couldn't justify in my own mind spending the shareholders' money for that purpose. My intention was never to line my pockets although I fully realise that some Classic Bloodstock shareholders may be sceptical of this statement and think that I am trying to worm my way out of a tight corner. We shall see....

Before you point that accusatory finger though, let's take a long hard look at the figures. Remember that £2.6 million in the pot equals just £1.3 million actually spent on horses with £1.3 million left in the bank under the control of Robin Ronnie as the press would have you believe. The training fees for 24 horses during the first two years costs approximately £600,000, including veterinarian fees, etc.

Everyone had given their best, David Shekells was pleased with all his purchases on behalf of the plc and Stuart Williams was a well-respected trainer who was chosen to train half the horses at his own yard at Trillium Place. I would have preferred them all to be trained at my own stables at Charnwood but, if the horses caught a virus, for example, we could have been totally wiped out of action. So, I didn't want to put all my eggs in one basket, so to speak.

David and I shared the same opinion regarding the horses purchased. They were a grand lot to look at, but we would only know over the ensuing two years, whether any would prove to be champions, or not. Our trainer, Stuart Williams wrote the following in 1995:

"With around forty-five horses already in training under my care, the twelve Classic Bloodstock plc horses I train represent a tremendous opportunity for me. These are high class horses that have cost Classic Bloodstock plc over £840.000 (on average £70,000 each horse) - that's quality in my book. I had sixteen winners in 1994 so you can see why I am looking forward to the 1995 flat season with great expectations.

"My ambition now is to train a classic winner and I would love to do it for Classic Bloodstock plc. They have given me the chance and have shown faith in me, so you can be sure I will be doing my best for their shareholders.

"I believe in really getting to know and understand each horse. You rarely get a nasty horse. I believe that if you're fair to them, they will be fair to you. I don't believe in bullying them, that only brings problems. I love my horses and they repay me on the track."

So if Stuart was telling the truth, (and I certainly think he was on this occasion), shareholders could be accordingly optimistic at this stage. I had the same positive impression of Stuart Williams.

The other trainer we chose was Brian McMath. He would be given the other twelve Classic Bloodstock horses to train at Charnwood. He obviously had not had a successful career in training so far but, if the horse is good enough, the trainer should be up to the job. No trainer in the world can train slow horses to be champions. All the top yard's Cecil's, Gosden's Cumanies and a great many others, have their share of dead ducks. I wanted Brian to have his chance. We all need a helping hand in life at some time or other in order to climb that ladder of success.

In 1995, Brian McMath wrote:

"Classic Bloodstock is a wonderful idea - it provides a whole new possibility and outlook for owners. It's not just a club where you buy a share for a year. Shareholders can feel involved in the whole process of racing - in the breeding side of it, as well as the actual racing with top-of-the-range horses that have a great chance of winning good races - it's a great idea for all kinds of people. It's ingenious and very simple but it has taken someone like Mr Dawson to think it through and have the courage as well as the knowledge to make it work."

"Of course, it's also fabulous for me, too! We are going to have the sort of horses we can take to the Ascot and Newmarket top meetings with solid chances of winning. The string of twelve Classic Bloodstock plc horses which I train has given me a tremendous chance."

Is Brian telling the truth? I think he is.

Now, let's see what the ultra-respectable David Shekells wrote in 1995.

"For many years I have run a profitable business breeding and selling bloodstock. Even during the latest economic recession my business has continued to thrive and I have no hesitation in agreeing with the objectives of Classic Bloodstock buying yearling fillies with correct conformation and proven bloodlines."

Is David telling the truth? I think he is..

As the captain of Classic Bloodstock plc I will sink or float with her. Well, the company started taking water aboard and The Sporting Life was out to destroy the Captain. They obviously thought that this 'Jack the lad' just can't be allowed to succeed, especially when all the others who have gone before him have failed. We will put a shot or two across his bows and then send in the torpedoes. We will do as much damage as we possibly can to the company, but blaming Dawson all the time. We, The Sporting Life will stand up for the ordinary man in the street (as Tom Clark, The Sporting Life editor stated on Sky TV news in February, 1998 after his paper lost a libel case against Jack Ramsden and champion jockey, Keiran Fallon, inferring they had cheated punters by stopping a horse in a race only to win with it easily next time it ran). As I said, The Sporting Life lost the libel action and with only £195,000 damages and an estimated cost of half a million pounds and got off very light, in my opinion. "We, at The Sporting Life, look after the punters' interests." Yet they let their advertisers rob punters blind and have done so for years.

I wrote to Tom Clark following his interview on Sky TV and said: "If you tell porkies in 'life' you get spanked?" - if you get the pun! This man made me want to be sick. He was so two-faced in my opinion.

Returning to ClassicBloodstock plc, we had ten individual winning horses out of twenty-four. Some of the others were only placed second or third while four couldn't race through death or injury. But I would say that's not a bad record or, rather, it's not good and it's not bad - it's merely average. And, despite the continued poisoning of the company, it survived, and still does to this day. But I was hurt, hurt enough not to go with *Classic Eagle* to run in the Derby, which was a once in a lifetime opportunity. The press had won. They had managed to sour my life and, of course, in doing so, put the seeds of poison in the minds of the shareholders. *Classic Eagle* ran his best race in his life when finishing tenth in the Derby. If the ground had been in his favour that day he would have finished a lot closer, although he still beat other horses that were very highly thought of by their connections.

Tim was assistant trainer at the time and was responsible for training the horse. Didn't he do a good job of it? Other trainers had failed to get the best from *Classic Eagle*. So I suppose Tim's highlight of his life would be training a horse to run well in the Derby and, of course, saddling *Classic Eagle* was a great thrill for him.

But the destruction of Tim's life and future by a biased and hostile Jockey Club combined with a dishonest and spiteful press leads me to believe that a great many so called respectable people should hang their heads in shame. Another of the original gang of trouble-makers towards Classic Bloodstock in the initial stages was Jockey Club Estates Manager, Peter Amos. Despite his early charm to me and my wife, Maureen, he turned out to be a turncoat, in our opinion. But that's par for the course for many people in the horse racing industry.

CHAPTER FOURTEEN

The press rattled on like a disgruntled general, trying to rally his troops. Headlines screamed: "Classic Watch Formed to Oversee Classic Bloodstock by M.P. Tom Benyon." One of those M.P.'s that come and go in a flash," DTI Investigates Classic Bloodstock plc." "Classic 5 Million Pound Mystery. Classic Inquiry Rests With The DTI Members Target Classic ," "Classic Under New Scrutiny," "Classic Forced To Call EGM." "Shareholder Slams Classic Bloodstock," "Second DTI Probe For Classic Affairs."

(A little bit of humour here from me. *Classic Affair* was the name of one of our horses that won at 25/1 for shareholders "You're losing your grip, Sims")

More 'Classic ' headlines. The press went on the rampage, there was no stopping the flow of reporting, all aimed at stirring up the shareholders and myself.

"Williams Ends Classic Partnership"

"More Classic Woe"

"More Disquiet in Classic Camp"

"Classic In New Furore"

"Classic Shareholders Want Action Group"

"Classic Boss Asks For Time"

"Classic Venture Trouble"

"Classic Concerns Flood Line"

"Classic Under Fire Again"

"Classic In New Losses"

"Dawson Likely To Come Into Fire At AGM"

"DTI to Investigate Bloodstock Group"

"DTI To Investigate Again Bloodstock Group"

"Classic Pair Under Further Investigation"

"Classic £1M Loss"

"Huge Classic Losses"

"Williams Ends The Classic Connection"

"DTI Again To Probe Two Founders Over Classic Bloodstock"

"Classic Under Fire Yet Again"

"Classic Will Go Into Liquidation"

"£6M Spent On The Horses And Not One Penny Back"

"£8.5M Spent On The Horses And Not One Penny Back"

(that's the press for you, £2.5 million extra!)

"Members Target Classic "

"Classic Enquiry Rests On DTI"

"Classic New Losses"

"Classic Clear Out"

"Classic In Lines Row"

"Williams: My Classic Row"

"Dawson Under Fire"

I particularly like this one:

"Classic Bosses Shut Out Press"

And then the real painful headline:

"Classic Founders Warned Off For 10 years"

"Ten Years' Ban For Race King"

Now, most of these headlines can be laid at the same door. It just goes to show how much P.P.S. troubled Sims. The press boys are dogs. No that's an insult to the canine species! It's also an insult to good honest journalists. I have been reading The Daily Mail for years. It's a wonderful newspaper. Why can't other papers be the same. 'Honesty and quality'.

Has anyone ever before been subjected to so much adverse publicity? Yes, the government, but no one private individual, I am sure. And, of course, this is not all. I could continue virtually ad infinitum spouting off all the rubbish those racing hacks have written. The above headlines all had stories with thousands of words. It is little wonder that the Jockey Club was growing uncomfortable under the collar over me. I've been reading newspapers for forty years and I can never remember such a consistently venomous onslaught by the press. My Mum said that Hitler got a bad press back in 1941 - good memory my Mum!

All these continual innuendoes in the press over Tim and I were getting to me. A constant flow of a cynical press. Rumours abounded all over Newmarket and the missing millions of pounds was the talk of the town. Tim felt so uncomfortable. It's not nice, people pointing at you over press reports, of which you are not at all guilty of what they want their readers to believe.

I decided to take the bull by the horns so to speak, and write this letter to the DTI.

Mr. D. I. Granger

4th September, 1996

Department of Trade and Industry

Dear Mr. Granger,

Your letter dated 29th August has just come to my attention, the delay no doubt due to the postal dispute.

Before we proceed further with your enquiries, I must protest at the way the DTI have conducted the investigation so far. You have caused myself and fellow Directors acute embarrassment, to say the least.

Firstly, Robert Miller in The Times informs the world of the DTI investigation, then The Racing Post and also The Sporting Life with a quote allegedly from ex-MP Tom Benyon and his 'Classic Watch' team to say the DTI are to come knocking on shareholders doors to gather statements. That finished my days in racing good and proper - knocking on doors is similar to Gestapo tactics in the night. I am guilty in the eyes of whoever reads that article. Little wonder all those you have interviewed so far have been frightened out of their wits.

And I naively thought the DTI operated investigations in secret, not through the press. However, it would seem the whole world and their dogs know about your investigations, excluding myself. Of course, I had dozens of shareholders very concerned and all I could answer was the truth, that I know of no new DTI investigation. Where does that now put me as M.D. of Classic Bloodstock? I will make a big issue of this later in what would appear as deliberate manipulation by the DTI, the press and Classic Watch against myself.

I have also read the press reports with the heading - Classic £5 Million Mystery. The rumoured missing millions and a Bermuda bank account are a source of continual gossip at Newmarket. I suppose that is because I have paid off my one million pounds racing stables, bought a top-of-the-range Rolls Royce with a £20,000 RHD 1 number plate, a tasty villa in Spain and some racehorses for myself, a Porsche for my son, a business for my other son in Thailand, etc and all since I started Classic Bloodstock.

As your latest letter referring to myself being interviewed in accordance with the Police and Criminal Evidence Act, 1984. I suggest they would be better used investigating serious leakage from your department.

While on this subject, I am continually harassed by a Mr. J.M. Spackman from the DTI offices who has written me, sometimes on DTI headed notepaper. He writes pages upon pages of drivel, and I would really like to know whether these letters are part of the DTI investigations? Perhaps you would like to clarify this point.

Referring back to the subject of rumours, I would also point out that it has been said that thousands of Classic shareholders have not received share certificates. Don't be so bloody stupid and believe that.

Finally, of course I have to assist you - I have no choice. Despite your methods which are very traumatic to myself and many members of my family who have accounts at the local Nat West Bank. I myself am on first name terms with the Manager there so surely a personal letter from me, giving the DTI authority to have access to and full co-operation in all plc matters to my bank should suffice? Do I really need to be forced to sign forms that look very discriminating to me and others when a simple authority will suffice?

The DTI have already ruined my reputation with revealed press articles. Until you have proof of any wrongdoing, please shut up.
I await your reply.
Yours sincerely,

Ron Dawson

I wrote that letter in 1996. I have since flown to England to be interviewed. The DTI, I understand, do not believe any money is missing.

For now, we shall put Classic Bloodstock plc to one side, long it may survive. It was four years old in February 1998. Now let's bring on a real villain of the piece, namely Classic Bloodstock plc 11.

But first, a little tale....

One of the press kids on the block was Robert Miller.

He was a reporter on The Times who was another journalist who liked to stir the pot up with Classic Bloodstock. His articles were usually just plain silly. I rang him once to speak to him about C.B. He was both ignorant and arrogant. It made me wonder how those lads get these jobs. I will give you here just one of Miller's reports in The Times and you will see why I call him Max Miller.

JOCKEY CLUB INQUIRY INTO MISSING 'PASSPORTS'

by Robert Miller

The Jockey Club racing's governing body, yesterday confirmed that it has launched an official investigation into the mysterious disappearance of vital passports belonging to eight racehorses.

The horses are owned by Classic Bloodstock, which last year raised in excess of £3 million from more than 6,500 private investors. Some £1.3 million of the money has been used to buy 24 racehorses.

The equine passports, which all horses must have to race, went missing from the Newmarket stables of Brian McMath, the trainer, this month. Ten fillies, including the eight without passports, were removed from Mr McMath's yard after the three directors of Classic Bloodstock placed the horses with another trainer.

the directors, listed at Companies House, are Ron Dawson and his wife Maureen Moorcroft. Last month, Mr Dawson's son Tim was also appointed a director of Classic Bloodstock, said the company's auditor Stephenson Davies.

David Pipe, a director of the powerful Jockey Club, said: "I can confirm that we are looking into these allegations which involve irregularities over the handling of passports relating to these horses." The Newmarket police have also been informed. Newmarket CID said: "An incident in which some passports disappeared did take place and was reported to us."

Newmarket C.I.D.? I am surprised the flying squad was not put on this one! Any minute we could have a Sherlock Holmes look-alike wearing the whole outfit. Although I can assure Miller, he would only need fingerprint powder. What Miller doesn't seem to grasp is the passports were of no use to anyone else other than the trainer of the horses. i.e. In this case, Mr Williams, I cracked the "mysterious disappearance of the vital passports" - wearing my pyjamas. I leaned out of my bedroom window as ex-C.B. trainer, Brian McMath was riding past my house into my yard on a horse, and shouted: "Brian, when the passports are found, come over to the house and I will pay your wages. Not until then!" I went back to bed for a lie-in and the passports turned up in Brian's office, 20 minutes later, discovered under a Sporting Life. Brian came to the house for his wages. "Sherlock in his pyjamas cracking the case!"

This is how I imagine these fairy tales get started in the press. Here are two reporters in a pub frequented by the newspaper hacks, Arnie (Sporting Lie) and Gary (Racing Boast) in conversation...

Gary: "I went up to Newmarket last week. My best contact bar lady, Madge in the Golden Ball told me its rumoured around the town that Dawson nicked a million quid from Classic ."

Arnie: "Oh, my mate, Basil behind the bar in The Black Dog reckons it's two million. Lucky bastards - I mean, poor shareholders."

Gary: "Stuff the shareholders. It's the Dawsons. Bloody uneducated working-class bastards. All that money. It makes me sick to think of it. It wouldn't be so bad but I got nothing out of it.

Arnie: "Listen, I drove down the High Street in New-market the other day and saw his son, Tim in a flash new Porsche. Got a photograph of Tim and the car for the paper. Printed it in full colour. The editor thought it best to leave the number plate in the photo, so if anyone wants to find the lad and give him a good kicking he's easily iden-tified. Must have made a right few quid out of Classic, deserves all he gets."

Gary: "Who's this Tim bloke you're always raving on about?"

Arnie: "Oh, some young kid. His Dad nicked the mil-lions, put his son on the board two years later because he's in a wheelchair now and needed someone to show the shareholders round the sta-bles and meet them at the racecourse when they have a runner.

Gary: "Well I never! I bet he's selling a few of the horses out of the stable back door. Twenty-four horses. Shareholders wouldn't miss a few."

Arnie: "What the hell does Tim know about horses? He's only been in racing 10 years."

Gary: "I see his old man has just bought a new roller. Madge said it cost 140,000 quid."

Arnie: "No bloody good to him at the moment in a wheel-chair. Ha, ha, ha..."

Gary: "Lucky we have these crooks to write about. I don't know what I'd do if the editor ever asked me to write about horse-racing. Anyway, Arnie,

you must have a lot on Tim, the way you always
go on about him. What's he done really. Go on,
tell me?"

Arnie: "Nothing that I know of, but when did that ever
count for anything. It's the way I write it. Ha,
ha, ha"

Gary: "Another shandy, Arnie?"

Arnie: "Thanks Gary. You ever tipped a winner, Gary?"

Gary: "What tip a winner? You must be joking. I
couldn't tip over."

Arnie: "You do when you're pissed, Gary!"

And I think that's how all the bad press started the
tittle tattle and rumours. If only I hadn't tried to make a
success of Classic plc with all the time and effort I put
into it. What a lovely, carefree, easy life I could have
had. I've never met anyone in racing who gives better
racing information than me. So, I should have just carried on doing just that, after all, it has made me a millionaire and, without all the hassle. But no, I am a bit of
an entrepreneur, and so put into practice single-handed
something I believed would be good for racing.

In the Sporting Life, Simm's aparent vendetta against
Tim and I reached an all time low in dishonest journalism, when following another good week of winning tips
on my premium tipping line, when I gave five winning
bets from only six selections, including a 10/1 winner.
Simm's wrote the following week refering to my phone
service; "and Dawson is still tipping loser after loser"

What Simm's was doing, in writing those lies in the
sporting press, was deliberately misleading his readers,
and in doing so, he was misusing his position as a 'journalist' to try and damage my business by writing lies.

This once again proved to me just how much my success at tipping was eating him away.

But his editor Tommie Clark obviously sanctioned
these lies of Simms.

CHAPTER FIFTEEN

Today, looking back at Classic Bloodstock plc 1, I re-alise that I made mistakes. For example, I know that I should have bought ten yearlings, averaging £100,000 + each. Okay, they cost about the same as the twenty-four plc horses to buy, but that way you have a slightly better chance of buying a prospective champion. But the other important thing is that ten cost only £230,000 to keep for two years, instead of the £600,000 pounds plus, for the twenty-four CB horses' keep. At least that is what I think now.

In my prospectus, plc 11, I said that bloodstock prices were at the lowest they had been for years and, as I have said in my previous prospectus, now they are starting to rise again, just as I forecast. Meanwhile, the Arabs are breeding a lot of their own horses, having spent many millions of pounds in the bloodstock business. Good horses at the very top of the bloodstock market are still there but are no longer being sold at inflationary prices. Any one doing a plc in racing should remember this advice.

The following are some examples of the type of horse I was hoping to purchase at the time: These are just true examples. What could have happened for Classic Bloodstock if we were fortunate (obviously we were not).
"Generous"

"Sold in the sales ring as a foal for IR80,000 gns, his initial price was to prove a bargain. He won four Group 1 races, including both the English and Irish Derbys, the King George VI and Queen Elizabeth Stakes at Ascot and the Dewhurst at Newmarket at the betting odds of 50/1 His total prize money earnings were £1,119,944, which made his original price look cheap. In addition, as a stallion he should make his owner another fortune at stud."

"Assert"

"Sold as a yearling for only £16,000. *Assert* was a wonderful inspirational buy, winning two races as a 2 year old. His connections could hardly have known what lay ahead for him as a 3 year old, winning no less than four Group 1 races, the Benson and Hedges Gold Cup at York, Irish Sweeps Derby at the Curragh, Joe McGrath Memorial Stakes at Leopardstown and the Prix du Jockey Club in France. His winnings totalled £353,739. The syndication valuation placed on him to stand at stud in America was $24 million." Yes $24 million!

"Urban Sea"

"Bought at the Yearling Sales in Deauville for less than 50,000 French francs. Three years later, she had won nearly $2 million in prize money and has given her Hong-Kong owner David Tsui the unique thrill of winning the Prix de l'Arc de Triomphe. Her owner can now look forward to many years of excellent further profits as her foals will command very high prices in the sales ring."

"Alleged"

"Cost only $34,000 as a yearling and proved to be one of the most outstanding buys in the history of bloodstock. Winning not one but two Prix de l'Arc de Triomphes, Europe's richest race, he became the biggest money earner of 1st prize money of all time on the turf. His nine victories made him the target of the American market where he went off to stud, sold for $16 million." Yes $16 million!

"Stormbird"

"Here is a horse that should be mentioned not for his price in the sales ring, when bought in America to race in England, but for the fact that he won only one Group 1 race, the Dewhurst for 2 year olds at Newmarket. He promised everything to come as a 3 year old but ran only once more and could not be brought back to his best. He was retired to stand at stud in America for $30 million, as he was superbly bred for stallion duties and has since become a successful sire. Well now dear reader, that's not a bad profit is it - $30 million dollars.

Just read those figures again and rub your eyes; they're true, I promise you.

These samples represent only a few of the lucky strikes, the pot of gold and let's face it the fantastic profits to be made by those lucky owners. In fact, I can't think of anything you could invest in to surpass those kind of possible gains when you consider the amount(s) invested in each case.

Can you? Can anyone? Like one of the press knocker boys. How about Robert (Max) Miller of The Times. He's a clever clogs. The self styled know it all "but know nowt". He's spouted enough rubbish already in The Times belittling the idea of a fun investment with C.B. Come on Robbie Boy, the ace investment advisor in his paper. How about the Channel tunnel? Should we buy shares in that company? We could all get taken for a ride - at least a train ride. That could be classed as fun for some.

I know full well how difficult it is to buy a champion for £50,000, even £500,000 is no guarantee of success, but if you're not in the game, you can't have a winner. By far the majority of people who invested in Classic plc have only shelled out a comparatively modest £250. Four years later, the company is still in the business. It's cost them about £60 a year, say £1.15 pence a week for a lot of fun. Not bad is it? Which is what I told those who took the trouble to ring me to ask how much they should invest. In my view, £250 was about right. Those spending more were obviously hoping we would get a good horse and that they would make a big profit. I had clowns ringing me up saying they wanted to put in say £10,000, I told them the truth: "you're nuts!" Perhaps one of those callers was Miller or Sims. I wouldn't be surprised. But really a £1 a week cost, on average, for a bit of fun. Miller and Sims can't see value for money.

In the largest type right across the centre pages in my Classic 11 prospectus were the words. *"For investors with a sense of fun in a rich man's game. We can all afford to join in."* Sorry you press berks but nearly everyone could afford to join in at £250. Well, if that's not clear, I'm sorry. I realise that I've referred to plc 11 as the villain in the piece, but the number one main culprits were the people who sold me the mailing list, I.C.D. Marketing.

Remember how I bought one million names and addresses to use for the first plc from them? All those people were registered shareholders in one company or more, and sorted out and categorised via the data-base which meant that their names and addresses were only printed out once. Therefore, if one million mail shots raised £3.2 million, I only had to raise the similar addressees and the 'sky's the limit', as they say.

After six months of negotiation, I was informed by our top London mailing list distribution company, I.C.D. Marketing that they have compiled a list of 5.5 million individual shareholders' names and addresses on file. If that's true, and there was no reason to believe otherwise, obviously if I mailed out to the lot of them, Classic 11 would take a total of around £18 million. I expected perhaps £20 million and, equally importantly, it could encourage 35,000 new people into racing for the first time. So, forget the money for the moment, and think how, out of 35,000 new people, there would undoubtedly be a percentage who would buy The Sporting Life or Racing Post, (poor buggers) while thousands more would be tempted to have a day at the races when we had a horse racing. Could be a bloody knighthood in this, Ronnie boy.

Instead, my reward was a nightmare of torment induced by the press. Perhaps I had no education and was belittled for it by Sims in The Sporting Life in his article this February. I wish I had been educated and, if Sims wants to make fun out of that at my expense, so be it. But to be unable to grasp the possibilities there are in a plc for a small investor shows me his naivetè in such matters.

One thing is crystal clear to me, the racing establishment doesn't deserve to have a person who tries his best to do something for racing for the good of the sport, without being paid any salary. Like myself, Maureen Moorcroft or my son, Tim. Your good intentions are pulverised by the know it alls, the 'know nowt' boys. Earlier in my book, I wrote of bad apples. Surely to any decent person, it is obvious where the most rotten apple of all is. The Jockey Club is also certainly a true villain of the piece. They had to act, but not overact. Not be judge and jury. On the evidence of hearsay by Sims of The Sporting Life. It was those lies of his, I believe, that contributed to my and Tim's heavy warning-off sentence.

Also, I place much of the responsibility of Classic's failure firmly on the shoulders of the sporting press editors. Ably assisted by their Neolithic hacks. The rumour is out, both sports editors are jockeying for any vacancy in the editorial position for The News of the World or David Sullivan's Daily Sport; a position they are certainly qualified for. But whinging shareholders with a weak Jockey Club must also share some blame, although Ronnie Dawson, I admit, should take his share of blame.

Before I launched the ill-fated plc 11, I did all the research, £18 million is a fair whack of money. Shareholders might want their own stud or their own stables, at least. But this time we would do it differently; we would buy around ten horses, paying for the very best perhaps £200,000 each, perhaps half a million pounds for the buy of the year and more if we had to go for a really special one. That's what the Sangster team tried to do with the ill-fated Classic Thoroughbreds. The right idea - the wrong time. Bloodstock prices were too inflated and, of course, in those days you had the rich Arab sheikhs to contend with.

In other words, whatever we wanted would not be out of our reach and, at the finest bloodstock sales in the world, we could spend £3 million on horses, plus training fees for two years. After this, we would still have around £14.5 million which would earn bank interest in the interim and which we could use the following year to buy the champagne slip of the pen (or champions). And you would get one or two in the end, for sure.

I will now run a few figures past you again. During and after January 1980, world bloodstock prices reached their peak. Sheikh Mohammed's madness, namely buying a yearling for $10.2 million, only made the underbidder pool's magnate Robert Sangster a length behind him in the 'Silly Stakes'. A race run for those mega wealthy people who supposedly couldn't fail with their top advisors giving bloodstock advice of such quality. But they did and more fool them. And, it wasn't because they bought a few pigs in the poke, they bought a sty full. It was because they were those very people whose vanity was such, they couldn't stop bidding against each other.

My mother bought a wardrobe once at Ossie Wood's Second-Hand Sale Room in Barrow for £3. I asked her why she had paid £3 for it. She replied: "Because I thought it was worth £3." My Mum has a lot of common-sense.

The moral of this story is that if she had lost it to another bidder at £3.6d, another one just as good would be along shortly at the price she wanted to pay.

CHAPTER SIXTEEN

Now I have always admired mega-rich Robert Sangster. After all, for all his millions, he was only a lowly private doing his national service, like me at one time. He could have taken the easy way out or at least got a commission. He talks a lot of sense when interviewed on TV these days. He is a true gentleman and a pleasure to listen to. He doesn't suffer fools gladly, methinks.

Sheikh Mohammed, I suspect, is also a splendid chap. But in that £10.2 million fiasco both came out of it with no credit. A bit like one of my favourite films: 'A Bridge Too Far'. Valuing bloodstock had gone haywire. The 1982 Keeneland sales started a madness in the price of thoroughbred horse flesh. The scene was set early in the sale in Lot 30; a good-looking colt by the sire and triple crown winner, *Nijinski* was put in the sales ring. The bidding started low, $50,000 - first bid, but didn't finish until it reached a final bid by Robert Sangster's group of $4 million, 80 times more than the first bid of $50,000 and the underbidder, Sheikh Mohammed at $3.8 million.

Another lot went through the sales ring out of a mare called *Masked Lady*. This time it was knocked down to Sheikh Mohammed at $2.2 million, thus outbidding the Robert Sangster team. Now, if you look at this surge in bloodstock prices, the previous nine foals of *Masked Lady* had never fetched $200,000 before, never mind $2 million. Then, Robert Sangster steamed in and bought a couple more for around $4 million the pair.

Sheikh Mohammed and his brothers brought their spending at the sales to around $43 million. But one must remember that, at around this time, Robert Sangster's team syndicated four stallions for stud for just under $100 million, so it seems hard to criticise those who would spend up to $10 million for a yearling of the successful

North American sire, *Northern Dancer* who, without doubt, has since proved the greatest sire of all time.

Thus, by having some choice lots by him in the Keeneland 1983 sales, a few fireworks could be expected between the 'almighty' Robert Sangster and Sheikh Mohammed. The Sheikh was in full flow early on in the sales. Two nice colts for around $6 million the pair and two fillies for about $4 million. Lot number 308 was to make history.

The first bid from the floor was $1 million and neither the Sheikh nor Sangster would give way. It was a dual with money as the weapon. From the opening million dollars bid, the chase was on and up went the price. When it reached $10 million, everyone thought that Sangster had won. But this time the Sheikh would not give in and, with a final nod of $10.2 million, Sangster was duly disposed of.

Vincent O'Brian, the great trainer and judge of horseflesh and a main man in the Sangster team was supposed to have said, upon seeing this yearling: "My word, he is the most beautiful mover." Even the king fails at times and, for the underbidder, Robert Sangster? Was he fortunate - what a let off!

From the $10.2 million dollar purchase at Keeneland, the sales madness of high spending by the world's high rollers continued unabated. I won't bore you here with the full details of the countless millions spent at these prestigious sales. If anything, 1984 and 1985 saw even more money spent as the mega-rich battled against each other for what some would say the world's finest young bloodstock. In what I call the final race in the 'Silly Stakes', Robert Sangster paid a world record price of $13.1 million dollars for a yearling by the sire, *Seattle Slew* but, unlike Sheikh Mohammed's $10.2 million fiasco, this horse was named *Seattle Dancer* and proved a decent racehorse, though not a champion by any means.

Finally, in 1986 the madness was over and we witnessed the biggest crash in bloodstock prices for two decades.

I personally felt that in 1994/95, horses were sold at around their true value. And, yes, they were bargains to be got all right, inspirational buys - which has always been the case in racing.

When I put my plan together for plc 11, the time was right, but the mailing list was wrong and I was cheated by the marketing company, ICD. The five and a half million names and addresses were not genuine, it's as simple as that. Of course, I blame myself for plc 11 not being a success. The captain sinks or swims with his ship. I sunk but the negative publicity which had dogged the plc's was also to blame and resulted in the impending disaster. But this has little to do with the duff mailing list. In short, I was gutted. One recipient of the brochure received no less than nineteen separate copies at his home, while dozens of others rang me to say that they had never bought shares in their life. I was well and truly ripped off by a supposedly respected London mailing company. Yes, the accountants got compensation of around £75,000, but that could in no way compensate for the damage done.

Once I realised how badly the returns were coming in, I tried to save an unmitigated disaster by selling my own mailing list to the company. The brochure was then sent to over 100,000 people and, from this racing mailing list of my own, we received a high percentage of replies. I charged Classic Bloodstock £100,000 for the list, no cash changed hands and I bought shares in the company with the same paying about £40,000 in capital gains tax. So, obviously, by far and away I am the biggest loser in plc 11. Funny isn't it? According to the press, it's made me rich beyond my wildest dreams. But those reports damaged Tim and I. In the racing world, we were finished, no matter how much we tried to protest our innocence we were branded crooks.

In trying to rescue plc 11, I prostituted my very own successful business. In the Gay Kelleway Club and the Inner Circle in 1993, I had 2,000 clients. In 1995, after using my mailing list for Classic plc 11, I had 1,000. This was to cost me a great deal of money for many years to come.

Essentially, in racing, the ordinary man only has so much to spend on his hobby. Sometimes, I asked for £375, sometimes, say £250 to join my own business, the Gay Kelleway Club, Newmarket Racing or the Inner Circle. In return, you received betting information on around a dozen horses running in my name, at any one time. But, now, for £250 you could get betting information access to the twenty-four Classic plc horses and it seemed like another twenty-four was on the cards. So, where would any punter with commonsense put his hobby money? Well, the best value for a punter for his £250 pounds was obvious. So the loss to me in personal subscriptions to my inner circle business was about £250,000 in 1995. All this is documented in my financial accounts and can easily be proven. But nothing can compensate me for how bad I feel and how sorry I am that so many people lost money in my Classic plc venture. I never thought that some day in my life I could cause so much anger. The poison pen letters I still receive are a constant reminder.

Indeed, my mailing lists were the finest in the country and of much more value than any other of my substantial assets. Meanwhile, as I said, my own business never recovered from the loss of my own clients that joined the Classic Bloodstock plc 11. If you look at the shareholders' list which is obtainable from Companies House in London or Cardiff on microfilm and check those names and addresses against my private clients, you will quickly discover that what I say is true. I try not to lie. I did once, years ago, when I was arrested at my home in

Newmarket while having breakfast with my family. It was over the Barbara Mayo AI murder. I was taken to Nottingham police station in handcuffs and held in the cells. All because I had bought a car in good faith which, it turned out, that the police were looking for. A most unpleasant experience. No blankets and prison cell lights running all night to keep you awake and make you crack up (they hope). Now that was a nightmare.

The problem was that I had been with someone I shouldn't have been with in that car on that same day and I thought it best to keep my mouth shut for the time being or at least until my partner at that time knew the predicament I was in. At that time, The Sunday Mirror, God Bless them, got a barrister up from London to Nottingham and before the beaks (the magistrates) got my release. I received damages and costs from the police for this dreadful experience. But it taught me a lesson in life. "If you tell porkies, you get spanked". If I had not tried to cover up for another in the first place, I could have avoided the worry, a few gentle police enquiries, a peep in the hotel register; loyalty has always been a part of my upbringing. "You never spilt the beans." Sorry about the deviation here, I wandered off course.

As I am writing this down, I am interrupted by my young son, David clasping the Sunday newspaper (yes, now you can get the English papers on the same day in Spain).

"Dad, hell Dad! Have you seen today's Sunday People and The News of the World?" he shouts.

"Steady on son," I reply. "What on earth are you saying?"

I looked at the one paper he was holding. The headline in The Sunday People screamed out in large bold letters: "Race Punters Are Taken For A £3 million Ride" written by Brian Radford. There is a nice picture of me (if I say so myself!; a copy taken from my plc prospectus along with two supposedly old-age pensioners with that sick looked obviously induced by The Sunday People's slick photographer. And then there was the caption: 'Roy and Ann Howe lost cash. They put a £1,000 investment into Classic Bloodstock plc 11' (more about Classic later...). Howe is the man who instigated all the trouble at the Jockey Club for me finishing with my 10 years warning off." After all the nice things my family did for them, I even let him and his wife lead in my own race-horse winners many times. A true creep of a man. Another person in your life is not very nice when you see his true side.

What the newspaper forgot to mention was how Mr. Howe still owed Classic Bloodstock for goods supplied. But then that wouldn't have made such a good story, as slamming me by that conning, lying newspaper: The Sunday People.

Anyway, to stop boring you completely, this particular newspaper is well-known in the racing world for its scaremongering tactics of journalism. It's to be expected with such a downmarket publication I suppose.

The last part of the article I actually found distressing. It read: "The Sunday People tracked Dawson down to his villa in the Costa Blanca, sipping a cold drink by the swimming pool, he callously boasted, "I've made millions from racing, it is full of mugs." Those words are dreadful lies. I have never even been visited by The Sunday People, let alone Brian Radford. I hereafter enclose the article in its entirety:

RACE PUNTERS ARE TAKEN FOR £3 MILLION RIDE

by Brian Radford

Thousands of race fans have lost their life savings after investing 3 million pounds with a businessman who branded them "mugs".

Punters handed over millions to racing syndicate boss Ron Dawson, only to discover their shares were as worthless as the horses he backed.

Brash millionaire Dawson was banned from every racecourse in Britain over a separate scam after a Jockey Club inquiry last month. He is currently sunning himself at his luxury Spanish villa.

He is also being probed by the Department of Trade and Industry in a bid to discover what happened to £3 million of investors' cash.

Dawson set up two racing syndicates, Classic Bloodstock 1 and Classic Bloodstock 11.

Glossy brochures detailed how punters could win thousands backing his team of winning racehorses. They even boasted how 1981 Grand National winner, Bob Champion had been recruited as a trainer. But Champion told The Sunday People he had NEVER worked for Ron Dawson.

"I have acted neither as an advisor nor trainer for Ron Dawson. I have never been involved," he said.

Former welder, Dawson 59, advertised his scheme in the racing press and watched the cash roll in.

Leading trainer, Gay Kelleway who worked briefly at Dawson's stables, said cheques totalling £250,000 arrived in one day alone.

She turned down an offer to train some fillies after he laid out his business plan.

"I didn't get involved because it just didn't feel right," she said. "One of the horses that was bought looked like it had two legs coming out of one hole. They just didn't have what it takes to race."

Roy Howe, 58 of Worksop, Notts who invested £1,000 of his pension cash said: "It makes my blood boil to think he is enjoying himself while people are scratching for their money."

"I got involved because my wife Ann has always dreamed of owning a racehorse. But this has brought her nothing but heartache."

Dawson is believed to have attracted more than £5 million from 6,500 investors for his schemes.

But Classic Bloodstock 11 went into liquidation after it was discovered that six racehorses made just £7,933 pounds in winnings.

The Sunday People tracked Dawson down to his villa in Alicante on the Costa Blanca.

Sipping a cold drink by the swimming pool, he callously boasted: "I've made millions from racing. It's full of mugs."

The Sunday People are liars. This is newspaper reporting at its lowest. How many more untrue articles do they print, I wonder?

So, in future, anyone who reads this paper (and other similar tabloids) should be well-aware that they are full of blatant untruths. Furthermore, if what I say is untrue, then I am sure The Sunday People 'Mirror Group' will sue me but I'm equally sure there will be nothing but silence on their part.

Another sad note: journalists like Radford are very deceitful liars. I rang him up to complain about his article in the paper. The ace investigative reporter said he never wrote it, it was written by a Barry Gardner. The Sunday People should not con their readers like this. It's a disgraceful practice when the newspaper is read by millions and they are making money by writing such devious lies. No less than six of his bold statements are totally untrue.

The following is a copy of the letter I wrote to the Editor of The Sunday People.:

13th March, 1998

The Sport's Editor
The Sunday People

Dear Sir,
I refer to your article on Sunday 8th March which, according to the by-line, was written by Brian Radford. However, when I telephoned Mr. Radford he denied the same and told me that the article was in fact written by a Barry Gardner. I have this conversation on tape.

What I would like you to explain to me is why you told your readers in that article that (I quote) "The Sunday People tracked Dawson down to his villa in Alicante on the Costa Blanca," when you know that this is a downright lie as I have never been visited by anyone representing your newspaper. You also state that my plc brochures detailed how punters could win thousands backing his team of winning racehorses. You are lying again. I never wrote that.

Also to use the expression that I "callously boasted..." is extremely offensive to both my wife and myself.

You also say thousands of race fans have lost their life savings. That's news to me! Name one, never mind the thousands.

Your paper also insinuates that punters handed over millions of pounds to myself. How and when exactly did this happen?

I await your comments with interest.
Yours faithfully,

Ron Dawson

p.s. Please don't fob me off, just reply to my questions honestly.

Yes, their solicitors replied. Yes, it was a fob off.

And as for the other newspaper, the ' News of the Screws', sorry News of the World, there is a similar article to muse over. Even my house which I paid only £95,000 for three years ago is now a £1m pound villa according to ace sleuth reporter Colin Cooper. I've heard that there has been a property price boom lately on the Costa Blanca but this is ridiculous! For those readers who don't mind reading some typical News of the World tripe, I have enclosed the full text. Some is true, most is not. First of all, there is the provocative headline: "We Track Down The Most Wanted Man in Racing!" Hereafter I am taking the liberty of reproducing the News of The World article. It is so misleading, I just have to include it.

FOUND. WE TRACK DOWN MOST WANTED MAN IN RACING

Exclusive by Colin Cooper, Racing Editor

"This is horse racing's most wanted man. Infamous Ron Dawson has been BANNED by the Jockey Club from going anywhere near a racecourse or stables for 10 YEARS after his controversial syndicate scheme Classic Bloodstock went spectacularly bust.

We set off in pursuit of Dawson and tracked him down to Spain where he's busy enjoying the champagne lifestyle only millionaires can afford - while thousands of punters who trusted him are left penniless back home in England.

They accuse Dawson of ruthlessly ripping them off in an apparently sorry tale of deceit and mismanagement.

We found Dawson on the sun-soaked Costa Blanca and on behalf of the hordes of hapless investors who burnt their fingers when Classic Bloodstock went belly-up, we demanded to know: What happened to the £5 million Dawson raised after flooding Britain with brochures promising a spectacular profit from the sport of kings?

How can he justify living as a tax exile when the punters who pinned their faith in him have been left penniless?

Why, if he is innocent, won't Dawson come back home to face them?

We confronted the elusive Dawson and his glamorous wife Maureen at their luxury £1m villa outside Alicante.

The villa has its own sauna and swimming pool. A Rolls-Royce with personalised number plates is parked in the drive.

But Dawson, a former welder from Barrow-in-Furness who made his fortune as a Newmarket-based tipster, remains unrepentant.

He claims to be the victim of a Jockey Club plot to run him out of racing.

He says: "I've been hounded out of the game by the Jockey Club and The Sporting Life, who have waged a campaign of hate against me. I can account for every penny raised by the Classic Bloodstock share issues - my conscience is clear.

"I cried when I realised that my punters were going down the pan.

"The only reason I am in Spain is because of three heart attacks.

"My jockeys were always under orders - either to win or to finish down the field.

"I cleaned up and I soon had some big punters in tow. They all wanted my tips. And the rewards were more than just cash.

Prostitutes

"There were always parties after a big win. I had punters all round the world, but my Irish connections were the best.

"They would fly me out to Dublin and lay on girls - well, prostitutes, but real lookers. We just helped ourselves.

"But we never broke any rules and now being warned off for 10 years on a technicality is more than I can bear."

Dawson, currently the subject of an investigation by the Department of Trade and Industry, is writing a book which he claims will reveal all about racing's seamy underside.

He will tell how trainers fixed races; how he paid bent jockeys and stable lads for inside information; and how they were rewarded with cash handed out at sex parties.

He says: "The fact is, my face never did fit in racing. The nobs didn't like me. I was from the wrong side of the track."

Dawson made his fortune in the 1980's out of persuading punters to join his successful tipping syndicate. He wrote a racing column. But he was up to every trick in the book.

He says: "The Jockey Club are hypocrites. Of course, you lay out horses to do a job. Sometimes they are trying, sometimes not.

"Jockeys are always told the score just before the race."

Then, in 1994, father-of-four Dawson hit on the idea of launching a racing-related PLC rather than a conventional racing club.

His mailshot for Classic Bloodstock 1 attracted 6,500 investors who between them put up £3,146,093.

But his plan to raise £ 20m with Classic Bloodstock 11 went wrong.

He says: "I thought I could revolutionise racing by bringing in thousands of new investors.

"I spent a fortune on a mailshot list that turned out to be a dud. I was ripped off."

Of the £5m raised from the two mailshots, only £1.3m was used to buy racehorses.

Classic Bloodstock 1 made a net loss of nearly £1.5m in its first two years. The 24 horses Dawson bought on behalf of shareholders won only £12,000 pounds in prize money the next season.

Worse still, the Jockey Club's security department investigated claims that an electric cattle prod was being used to make Classic Bloodstock 1 horses go faster on the gallops.

Dawson says: "I was appalled to hear this. I was naive - I didn't realise that this is common practice in racing when a horse is not keen to gallop.

"They insert the prod up its backside and switch it on. The thing runs for its life. I couldn't believe such cruelty."

To complete the dismal picture, Roger Harris, the trainer for Classic Bloodstock 11, is behind bars after pleading guilty to importing a ton of cannabis resin (street value nearly £5m pounds) stuffed into a horse box.

Dawson says: "I have never made a penny. The DTI have looked at all the figures for the first issue and have cleared me. They are now looking at the figures for Classic Bloodstock 11 but I've got nothing to hide."

Last month, Dawson and his son Tim were both barred from any involvement in racing for 10 years by the Jockey Club.

Racing's rulers decided they had broken every rule when it emerged that horses bought by Classic Gold, Dawson's latest venture, were registered as belonging to his son.

Dawson rages: "They were out to get me and made it more or less impossible for me to register the Classic Gold horses.

"The horses were crying out for a run and I put them in Tim's name. I'll appeal."

However, Jockey Club spokesman John Maxse said; "The Dawsons displayed a blatant disregard for the interests of the investors of Classic Gold. **(note: Bloody rubbish Mr. Maxse, it was just the opposite. What could I have gained?)**

"In doing so, they've damaged the reputation of racing."

(note: John Maxse would have made a good sheriff. Hang 'em High John!)

The truth of the matter is that I actually invited the Racing Editor, Colin Cooper to come to Spain and meet my family and myself as I wanted a chance to state my side of this mystery Classic Bloodstock millions missing case and get the truth across to the British public. I even went to a lot of trouble getting Colin into a hotel. He couldn't track one down.

Like it or not, The News of the World is by far Britain's largest selling Sunday newspaper and they wanted my story, even offering me a four figure sum for the exclusive rights - which they have yet to pay me. However, to make it look good, they had to exaggerate and say that they had 'tracked me down', (Sherlock Holmes style; the full works, the spyglass, fingerprints powder, the deerstalker hat, pipe ... the lot! You can get the whole outfit at your local toy shop for a fiver).

What really happened was that I phoned Mike Dunn at The News of the World Sports Desk who is the main man and said, "Fly Colin out, I will collect him at Alicante Airport. It's just down the road from my place."

Evidently, my picking up, their reporter like this was not challenging enough for The News of the World. Their readers would like the story better if they told lies. In Colin's words 'glossed over'. So they put poor Colin on a plane to Malaga, hundreds of miles away from Alicante. Then he travelled in the opposite direction from Malaga to Madrid by train which takes eight hours, next he continued back on track from Madrid to Alicante, also by train, which is a further eight hours. Finally he travelled from Alicante to Calpe on the Lemon Express which takes an hour and a half. Note the word, lemon.

Here I picked up a, by now, exhausted, bleary-eyed Colin Cooper at my local station - Calpe. I put his hat and Sherlock Holmes cape and bag in the back of the car and drove to my house where Maureen was waiting with tea and sandwiches. Now this is the truth - not the downright lies of The News of the World headline. However, The News of the World weren't finished yet. In true Sherlock Holmes fashion, they decided Holmes (Colin Cooper) needed Watson to come along, as a photographer to take some photographs of my villa to make it look like a million pound mansion which would make the article sound better and, of course, The News of the World treats its readers like fools, believing that the more lies they tell their readers, the more they like it. As the saying goes: "The truth never sells newspapers." It's too boring, bullshit sells newspapers obviously, written by so-called journalists like Cooper, Sims and Green who kow-tow to their editors.

So into the plot comes Watson and his assistant, who turn out to be a nice couple really called Richard and Louise, photographers from Marbella, an eight hour drive away. Snap, snap, then an eight hour drive back. By now, everyone around me is exhausted which is hardly surprising. Colin Cooper's done a trip of 4,000 miles instead of 2,000 and it's warm, far too warm for a Sherlock cape and deerstalker. So there you go, folks. Life for the press boys is one deceit after another.

When I worked for The Sunday Mirror; the top sports' writer was known as 'World Wide Wilson', his pen name. How I used to envy his international travels. The truth is that, quite possibly, he never left Baker Street. But one thing was true about Peter, he was a true gentleman and a credit to his profession.

"Old world wide" Peter Wilson's son, Julian is now a racing commentator for the BBC, but the first time I met his father, Peter, he was, indeed, wearing a Sherlock Holmes cape and deerstalker! It was at a boxing match,

Cooper versus Bugner for the British Heavyweight Crown. Four free tickets supplied courtesy of The Sunday Mirror for me and my pals.

Apologies for the slight detour here, we'll return to the main story in a minute.

But first I just want to leave the reader in no doubt about the media. I had been avidly following the big court case in racing every day. Jack Ramsden and jockey, Keiron Fallon bringing a libel action against The Sporting Life. I was pretty sure all along that the paper was going to lose this case, I knew from my own experience just how rash The Sporting Life could be in its articles. It was losing circulation with the real racing public. It was during this case that my mind was finally made up to try and do something about their never-ending slurs of me and Classic Bloodstock. But what could I do?

Well previously, I had invited the Radio 4 programme producer, John Waite of the popular programme, 'Face the Facts' to come to Charnwood to record an interview with me. This he did. He had about 20 or 30 prepared questions. I answered them all except the one about P.P.S. I couldn't help with that, but I thought it was an odd thing, why they seemed so interested in that.

The producer was very surprised I had granted him this interview. People in the public eye apparently don't do so, especially if they have had a smearing press. I explained to him I was pleased to have been given a chance to put my side of the story over to his listeners. Sadly even Mr Waite and his sidekick, Mr. Herbert turned out unethical. Just a pair of the usual media creeps that dog my life.

On the night of the programme, I listened to my interview, and believe it or not, they had edited out parts of it I wanted the public to hear (the facts as I knew them) and concentrated on those parts of my interview that were ambiguous and, surprise, surprise who was in the studio sitting on the 'Face the Facts' panel? Yes, you got it in one, Sims of The Sporting Life, and surprise, surprise, I found out later from my mole on that paper, that Sims was the person who gave the producer of 'Face the Facts', the list of questions to ask. That's how P.P.S. was brought up. It must be burning a hole in Sims' brain!

How underhand can journalists get? Well, let's see, I had previously written to The Racing Post with a nice positive letter (press release) for publication in its entirety, signed the chairman of C.B., plc which stated some of my decisions regarding Classic Bloodstock. To my utter amazement and disgust, they turned the letter into an article and twisted everything I had said in my letter. I would like to try and find words to describe how I felt about that - deceitful liars is one that comes easy to mind.

Later, believe it or not, I had a letter from their editor threatening to sue me for something I said about that paper. They were eavesdropping on a private telephone line which I was using to speak to Classic shareholders. Apparently, they rang this private members' number every day. After I received this threatening letter from that paper, I wrote back and told them that they were idiots. I heard nothing further, so I reckon they got the message. They are nothing but press bullies. They feel they can write anything they like, but put the boot on the other foot and they are screaming foul, like small boys. I have more respect for The Sunday Sport than The Racing Post. At least The Sunday Sport shows its true colours. The task in hand is how do I get the media to report the truth?

I want to pause here for a second for, while I am in the process of amending my book for its second re-print, I have just received a fax from England with a copy of an article in today's Racing Post. Wednesday, the 22nd of July, 1998. Despite threats from The Racing Post's editor not to print anything they write about me. "Bollocks

- I will!" What grieves me about this article is that it contains the same ambiguous claptrap I have had to contend with before. Graham Green refers to my versions of various letters to and from the Jockey Club disciplinary department, together with several press reports. These are not my versions Mr Green, they are factual faxes, letters and reports. The bloody truth, you silly, silly man. Ask the Jockey Club for copies!

Hereafter is a copy of The Racing Post's latest effort on Dawson:

DAWSON FINDS A PLATFORM FOR HIS GRIEVANCES

by Graham Green

Millionaire, Ron Dawson who, along with his son Tim, was warned off for 10 years by the Jockey Club in February has come up with yet another intended money-making scheme.

Dawson senior, the brains behind the disastrous Classic Bloodstock 1 and 11 syndicates, has now written and published his autobiography, called 'Conmen, Cheats and Liars'.

Not surprisingly, the title does not refer to the Dawson family but instead is aimed at the press, Jockey Club, rival tipsters and others in the racing industry.

Among the first to receive a courtesy copy of the book which Dawson is set to market at £10 a throw after publishing it in Malaga, was Nigel McFarlane, Secretary to the Disciplinary Committee.

Within its covers, Dawson, who now lives in Spain brags about how he made a fortune out of betting and tipping. But he insists there was no wrongdoing associated with the Classic Bloodstock syndicates which together raised over £5 million from investors, predominately small shareholders.

He even paints himself in a favourable light over the running of horses owned by Classic Gold in the name of Tim Dawson, the offence which primarily resulted in the pair being warned off and branded as having "damaged the reputation of British racing".

In the book, Dawson reproduces the letter he sent to the three stewards who sat at the inquiry (he calls them 'The Motley Crew') in which he demands to know if adverse newspaper coverage of Classic Bloodstock had been a factor in the length of the sentence.

He also prints his versions of various letters to and from the disciplinary department, together with several press reports, frequently commenting on them in derogatory fashion.

The Jockey Club at this stage has no plans to take any action over the book.

Dawson also claims to have put the wheels in motion to have a new team of horses put in training. "Okay, they can't run in my name but that's never impressed me," he says. "I will control them their careers and their programme for my betting activities."

True to form, the final paragraph plugs his daily premium rate tipping service which costs 50p per minute.

Why can't The Racing Post by honest with its dwindling band of disgruntled readers. I have just tried to phone Green at The Racing Post, only to be told he doesn't have a contactable phone number. It's hilarious, so Mickey Mouse!

I wrote back to The Racing Post editor and the author of the article, Graham Green. Of course, I am still awaiting a reply....

23rd July, 1998
Racing Post

For the attention of:
The Editor and Graham Green
Dear Sirs,

I refer to your article about me on July 22nd.

Please note that, despite your attempt to lead your readers to believe I may not be telling the truth, ie. "His version of various letters ..." Surely, a quick phone call to the Jockey Club would establish that every letter from me, or fax, or letter, or fax from them were all word perfect "exact copies". Unlike the Racing Post, I don't change words to suit myself.

The other piece I found funny:

"The Jockey Club, at this stage, have no plans to take action over the book." You can't very well do much, can you - about truthful events?

My only wish is that the Racing Post would stop writing its innuendoes about me.

Why don't you try and find out why, in 1996, my son was refused a permit to train? Now that would make a good story.

If I can ever fill in any gaps, please ask Graham Green to fax me, and I will phone him back. The second edition of my book out in October is a good read, with some startling facts of a press conspiracy. And, of course, details of my DTI interview, among other things.

Yours faithfully,

Ron Dawson

Now back to my story - and how you persuade the media to tell the truth.... Okay, I thought. I will try The Sun, at least they have never written anything derogatory about me. So, I rang the Sport's Desk and asked to speak to their racing man, Claude Duval. He wasn't in then, but later returned my call. I spoke with Claude for some time. I was trying to explain that I wanted a newspaper to write a true story on the Classic Bloodstock saga. After about 10 minutes of conversation with Claude, I told him as kindly as I could that he wouldn't be good enough for the job. He was too weak. I wanted a hard hitter to get at the truth, not the romance of a bloke supposedly running off to Spain with a sack full of money. I know, I thought, I will try The Sunday People, they will be interested.

So I'm put into contact with their ace sleaze reporter, Brian Radford. "Brian," I said. "I am writing a book about racing, but first I want to get this missing millions embezzlement story of Classic Bloodstock over to the public.

"Right," he replied. "I will fax you over questions." I include here an exact copy of his first fax:

February 21, 1998
From Brian Radford (01635-47040)

Dear Ron,
    Thank you very much for telephoning me this morning. I'm sorry I wasn't here to take your call. My moles tell me you're happily soaking up the sun these days. Well done! Enjoy it!
    After last week's Jockey Club ban, and all the bad publicity. I thought you might like to put the record straight by giving your side of the story.
    What actually did go wrong?
    You've taken the rap - but was justice really done?
    What is the truth?
    These are the types of questions I would like to chat about. How do you feel?
    I could do it over the telephone, or maybe fly out to meet you. It's high time we met, anyway.
    It is now 5.15 p.m. in chilly Berkshire. I shall be at home all evening, and all day Monday except from 6.30 p.m. to 10.15 p.m. Should we do a story together - which I hope will be the case - I guarantee that you will see a copy, via the fax, before it leaves me to be published.
    I look forward to hearing from you.
    Best wishes,
    Brian Radford

I phoned Brian back and said, send me all your questions by fax, including all you want to know about Classic . I also told him the following:

"But Brian, I have to say to you that, in the past, I have found the press very dishonest and guilty of trying to manipulate its readers. Things like Sims of The Sporting Life taking a colour photograph of my son, Tim getting into his Porsche car in Newmarket High Street, printing that large colour photograph in that despicable paper, The Sporting Lie with the car number plate for all to see and with a story which led one to believe that car somehow was bought out of Classic Bloodstock plc money. Tim was so upset by the innuendo that he called to see Peter Amos at the Jockey

Club office in Newmarket with documents confirming the car was purchased completely by his father's racing business. Just to try and show he had nothing or any benefits from the plc, it was humiliating for the lad, and so unfair. He was not guilty of any wrongdoing. Why the hell would the press want so hard to destroy an innocent person?"

"It's bizarre!" Radford replied "But look Ron, trust me. I am not like that. I am a genuine person and an honest reporter."

"Well, Brian, we shall see!" I replied.

His second fax reads as follows:

February 23, 1998
From Brian Radford (01635-47840)

Dear Ron,

Thanks again for yesterday's frank chat. I know we arranged that I should ring you on Wednesday - which I will - but I thought it might be helpful if I faxed a few questions in advance so that you could have time to put things together.

Pleased to say that it has now stopped raining, the sun is peeping through, and it's a great deal milder than yesterday.

Best wishes,

Brian

P.S. I shall speak to The Sunday People Sport's Editor early on Tuesday and tell him that I can do a story. Then I'll call you on Wednesday, as arranged.

Now this is it, I thought. Now the true Classic Bloodstock saga can be put to rest. At the same time, I thought, funny - this paper is going to tell the truth about Classic Bloodstock at last. Yet, it's owned by the Mirror Group who also own The Sporting Life and therefore are employers, in a way, of Sims. Anyway, I'll just answer the questions from Brian Radford of The People with honesty about Classic Bloodstock. Back comes the third fax:

March 1, 1998
From: Brian Radford (01635-47840)

Dear Ron,
*I am delighted to see that Barry Gardner's story did not ap-
pear in today's Sunday People. He obviously took the sensible
view - after my chat with him - that your story is the one that they
should be publishing.. Having told the News Editor that you are
willing to speak, he will certainly be in touch with me first thing on
Monday morning, having taken the decision to pull Gardner's investigation.*

*To speed things up, can you please fax to me today all that
you have already written so that I can be fully prepared for the
News Editor's call tomorrow?*
What would be your grounds for appeal?
*A ten-year ban for a technical offence seems severe and unjust,
especially when the trainer is fined a mere £750 ... so why did
they do this to you?*
*You're a self-made millionaire. You rose from living in a council
house (correct?) to a magnificent stable with luxury home, and
lavish villa (presumably) in Spain. How did you do so well?*
When and where did it all begin?
*When you stopped your horses. Was this done to obtain the best
odds for your clients and shareholders at a later date?*
Was it also done to beat the bookies?
Were you good at beating the bookies?
Have you ever stopped more than one horse in a race?
Did you give instructions direct to the jockey or through the trainer?
*You also landed some enormous gambles ... Castell Rossello,
Charlie Bigtime, Aljaz, Environmentalist, etc. How much did you
win on the biggest of them?*
Were there others?
How well were these coups planned and executed?
How could you be sure of getting your money on?
Did you ever place bets overseas?
Did you know jockeys who bet?
Would they be household names?
Still riding?
Would they be rewarded with gifts and cash?

You had horses with many trainers ... Stuart Williams, Colin Williams, Ian Campbell, Paul Kelleway, Gay Kelleway, Brian McMath. Dave Thom... Were there others?
Who was the best of this lot - and the worst?
Did you look after them well?
Were there any spectacular fall-outs?
Were drugs being taken by jockeys, trainers, stable staff, drug parties? Heavy drugs - cocaine, heroin? Household names? Sex parties?
Attended by household names (jockeys, trainers, owners, bookies)?
Any good examples?
Are you aware of any drugs being given to horses in races - stoppers, stimulants?

Well, I read this fax from Radford of The Sunday People ten times. I was absolutely speechless. He couldn't care a damn about the truth of Classic Bloodstock. That would obviously not go down well at all, because it would contradict The Sporting Life's ace investigator reporter, Sims for years of hysterical biased, without facts, reporting.

Needless to say, I never contacted The Sunday People or Radford again. Despicable people. Yet the same paper writes an article in which they lie to their readers and say they visited my home to interview me in Spain. And that article is printed here in this book in full. That paper fits one true saying that Kevin used to say to me, "Today's news is tomorrow's fish and chip paper." The Sunday People tell big lies to their readers and it's only fit for wrapping-up fish and chips.

I was snookered. I was never going to get the true story of Classic's mystery missing millions over to the public, but I thought of an idea, the last throw of the dice. I rang up The News of the World. "Look, I have a story about all the truth over Classic's missing millions. Get your reporter out here and I will spill the beans. Enter a villain of the piece and investigative reporter and Sherlock Holmes lookalike with all the gear, the ace smear reporter, Colin Cooper and folks, as you read in this book, the rest is history.

For Cooper was not interested in Classic Bloodstock because there was no story. No missing money and I suppose he couldn't go back to England and his editor to say: "Hi Ed., there's nothing in that story I just went 4000 miles for, but I can write one in its place..." And that's what he did.

Now, I know better than anyone that I'm no angel. Sure, I've pulled more strokes than the Oxford and Cambridge Rowing Club. I've had to go close to the edge on many occasions to survive. If you want a life - and a good one, you have to go and get it with the best of the abilities you were born with. I'm just 'Jack the Lad', I'm not smart or clever enough to have been anything else. I made a million out of racing, it's no big deal. But the fun is a big deal I've had in my life, ups and downs like a seesaw, not sat in an office in a dead end job. I've had a life.

Why are journalists called 'hacks'? Hacks are kindly horses, not given to nastiness. I always remember faxing the Editor of The Sporting Life, Andrew Sims (or was it Tom Clark?), I can't be sure. Anyway, they printed only part of my fax to try and make me look a berk. But not the part of the fax they didn't like - the truth. My brother was so upset about what he read, he screamed abuse at me down the phone. I can't blame him, Sims is always referring to the Dawsons. In his latest article, he refers to us as "the family from hell". My brother, Dave is a local well-known businessman and it's not fair on him when Sims says awful things in the press about the Dawsons. He is not involved. The problem is that the press can practically screw you into the ground. And it may befall you, gentle reader one day ... it can happen to any one.

Just always remember that certain newspapers don't want to know the truth about anything. The truth doesn't sell those kind of newspapers. I hope that, at least, I have got this message across in this book. When The Sporting Life lost a libel case against them this year for writing untruths, the penalty against the paper was £195,000 pounds damages, plus costs reputed to be around half a million pounds, I wrote to Clark supposedly the main man on the paper and said: "If you tell porkies in life you get spanked," and, if I have told a lie in my book, I would expect the same.

But I doubt that I would ever have anyone try to sue me because I only write the truth. However, if my book sells only three copies (one for me, one for my wife and a copy for the dogs to share) or a thousand, it can never be read by the multitude who are served up a daily dose of crap by the press. That's how newspapers beat you, they cater to the masses.

Look at the face of Sims in the photo section when given an explanation about the Classic Bloodstock position. Is he going to believe the truth? Look at him; a paragon of virtue. My sympathies go out to the late Princess Diana who was so misquoted by the press, it made her severely depressed.

Then I had trainers like John Gosden writing in The Times about Classic Bloodstock plc. Gosden's a fool. What does he know about it? Nothing. Just because he trains for the Arabs, doesn't give him a God given right to put the boot into others business trying to get a few decent horses. In my opinion, another hypocrite is the millionaire racehorse owner, Peter Saville, a Cayman Island tax exile and the biggest British owner, after Sangster. He also criticised me in The Sporting Life for giving my trainer, Stuart Williams the boot. He wants to keep his nose out of other peoples' business. By his own admission, he has had up to fifty horses in training with eighteen different trainers. Why did he give many of those the boot? And, why won't he let champion jockey, Keiron Fallon ride any of his horses. The truth is, it's none of my business. Likewise, Classic Bloodstock plc is none of his.

I will just say one other thing that springs to mind. I believe Gosden trains about 200 horses for the Arabs at his stables. Why don't the press ask him how many of those beautifully bred thoroughbreds couldn't run fast enough downhill on roller skates? The truth is all stables have a fair share of bad horses.

CHAPTER SEVENTEEN

After The Sporting Life libel case evidence was over, I rang Jack Ramsden, the man who had been libelled. It was about 9.15 a.m. on Saturday morning and he said: "I'm watching TV's Channel 4's racing programme, 'The Morning Line' about the court case yesterday. "Everyone in that court knows that Derek Thompson was lying," Jack Ramsden told me. (For those readers who never followed the case, is was basically about non-triers in racing - which are horses stopped from winning by the jockey). If I had been in court, I would certainly not have thought that Derek was lying. I knew Derek, a top TV racing commentator, and his lovely wife Julie, a little and found them to be a very nice, hard-working down-to-earth couple. They lived next door to me at my stables in Newmarket. They came to supper with Maureen and me a couple of evenings at my home at Charnwood. In our eyes, Derek Thompson was an honest, truthful man. How can I say that? Let's just say that I have a "gut feeling". The judge in the case thought differently in his summing-up. What people forget is that those in racing are sometimes economical with the truth. Poor Derek, the repercussions in racing will be with him for ever. Sometimes life is just so unfair. I just hope Derek picks himself up, dusts himself down and gets on with it. I am sure he can take it in his stride.

So let me here try to make a little impression on the dogmatic press boys at the newspaper offices who try to influence the gullible with their reports. Classic plc1 is doing okay at the moment, according to the ace reporter, Graham Green of the Racing Post. Is that penny dropping now, Graham? And you want to back-peddle a bit, perhaps? Not one penny piece is missing from plc 1. To the best of my knowledge, the DTI have done a too thorough investigation on the books and furthermore, I doubt if anyone would have happily replaced me as Managing Director or Maureen as Company Secretary if there were skeletons in the cupboard. The truth of the matter, Graham, is that the horses weren't good enough. It's that simple, you twerp.

Now, for some big facts for little-minded Sims of The Sporting Life. His favourite subject is inferring that I've robbed those plc companies. It's little wonder that, because of his scare-mongering, the Jockey Club cowards got cold feet and my shareholders thought I had lined my pockets with their money. It's a true fact in plc11 that I never saw one penny of the money that was paid for shares. It went straight to the accountants. Also, thankfully I can say that, to the best of my knowledge, I never wrote a cheque out from plc 11 for anything and neither did Maureen, I am sure. It was all done by the accountants. So where are these missing millions that have enriched the Dawsons beyond their wildest dreams? (As Sims wrote in The Sporting Life. Well, someone is lying? It's Sims or it's me. We will let the courts decide when the time comes. The newspaper clans are having a field day at present. But every dog has its day and my day is coming soon.

But the sad thing for me and especially for my son, Tim, is that it's too late, his career in racing is over on the strength of Sims' reports before it's begun and it's all down to his cruel pieces of unfounded journalism and editors who allow their hacks to write these stories. I think The Mirror Group plc should sack The Sporting Life's editor, Tom Clarke, for disgraceful conduct and bringing his once respectable paper into disrepute.

I realise that one thing that does stand out in my book is my feeling of disgust for the Editor, Tom Clark of the failed paper, The Sporting Life and his side-kick reporter, Sims. His personal attacks on me and my family have been misinformed and despicable journalism.

My son Tim,
Tipster, Chess player
and an up and coming
'Jack the Lad'
Tims alias is:
'The Captain"

Tim, listening to jockey
Alan Mackay on how his
horse 'Charlie Bigtime' ran.

Nobody wanted Classic Bloodstock to succeed more than I did. Maureen, Tim and myself willingly worked long hours for no pay. We all gave it our best shot. In fact, nobody came within a mile of losing the £40,000 I lost through that company. As I have said before, most people only put in £250 with the overall average well under £400. It makes The Sunday People (of the same newspaper group as The Sporting Life) claim that thousands lost their life savings, so bizarre. Such wicked and reckless journalistic quotes can only come out of the mouths of fools.

As for Classic Gold, Sims hasn't got the brains to grasp it. We all worked so hard for it to succeed. Tim and I are paying a penalty for putting those 852 people first. They were deliberately being denied their rights to run their racehorses by a hostile Jockey Club, I suspect brought on by irresponsible press reports.

The trainer decided that those two Classic Gold two year olds were ready to run. The Jockey Club had me in an arm lock. But I just had to put the welfare of Classic Gold and the investors first. A fine of a few thousand pounds, I could live with - no problem. I also knew that, once we got a couple of the horses in races, the Jockey Club would be satisfied they could make a case against Tim and I and would let the Classic Gold horses be registered - which they did. But I didn't think they would put us in irons and throw away the key. And I apologise here to readers because of parts of my next chapters show my bitterness and contempt for the Jockey Club.

Sims 56th article appeared on February 23rd, 1998 and is reproduced word for word overleaf under the heading of: RACING CLASSIC CLEAR-OUT

RACING CLASSIC CLEAR-OUT

"Just before the egregious Ron Dawson sailed into the sunset on a one-way ticket to Spain, Classic Bloodstock's founder vowed to make a comeback.

With no sense of shame and little compunction about the small investors whose interests he had disregarded and whose naiveté he had exploited, Dawson would be born again.

Dawson's comeback vehicle was to be called Classic Gold. After the 'disaster' (his words) of Classic Bloodstock, Gold would restore his reputation in racing.

Well, in the event, Classic Gold turned out to be his downfall.

This time round, the Jockey Club was watching Dawson's every self-aggrandising move.

In case anybody has failed to notice, the Jockey Club is having something of a clearance sale at the moment and Ron Dawson and his son, Tim, were marked down as damaged goods well past their sell-by date some time ago. The misdemeanours with Classic Gold for which the pair were warned off last week, were bad, but they were nothing compared with the scandal of Classic Bloodstock plc which relieved mostly small first-time owners of more than £5 million and enriched the Dawsons beyond their wildest dreams.

The fault for this debacle lay not at the feet of the Jockey Club but the British Horse-Racing Board which, in its eagerness to attract new owners to the sport, made multi-ownership schemes far too easy to set up and far too simple to manipulate.

The loopholes have now been closed by not before many - perhaps hundreds - of small investors were allowed to experience their first taste of owning racehorses at the hands of scamsters like Ron and Tim Dawson.

Ten years might seem like a long time in the sin bin for wrongly registering half a dozen horses, but the manner in which it was done spoke volumes for the exploitative contempt in which the Dawsons held the naive souls they duped.

Nailing them has been a long and exhausting trail."

(I bet it has Sims, but what are you saying you have nailed us for? Surely the public have a right to know and, of course, Tim and I. Come on Sims, how about some wonderful explanation of what crime you want everyone to believe we have committed that has bugged you for four years? "We are waiting"). And I see now you have the two horses in question as six. Can't you add up? Let me help: one and one is two - not half-a-dozen.

Then Sims goes on to write:

THE CREW OF THE GOOD SHIP DAWSON

"Ron and Tim may have gone, but their awful legacy lives on. Classic Bloodstock continues to this day, well-scrubbed down of course, but there are some stains you just can't get out. Andrew Irish, the Dawson's close friend, who acted as Classic Bloodstock's accountant, advisor, auditor and chief bottle-washer is still, curiously, very much in charge.

Another Irish claim to racing fame is his business relationship with Roger Harris, the trainer who has pleaded guilty to importing vast quantities of illegal substances into this country in a horsebox. Irish is not doing well with his choice of associates, is he?

And then there is Ian Campbell who was fined £750 for doing the Dawson's dirty work over the dodgy registrations of the Classic Gold horses. Last year, a court was told he issued a bogus invoice to a tipster - another of his illustrious band of owners - maintaining that he was being paid for tips."

Now, what really pisses me off about all the newspaper claptrap by the Racing Post and The Sporting Life is their total lack of race horse knowledge. They are so stupid they begger belief. I have found dozens of instances why they are fools - I will give you just one. *Classic Form*, a filly bought as a yearling for Classic Bloodstock plc on my recommendation, pedigree-wise cost only 50,000 Irish guineas. She ran second one time and was then injured. In 1998, a filly from the same sire, *Alzao* and *Dam*, *Formulate* called *Shartouch* won the Oaks at Epson. So, what is the winner's full sister *Classic Form* worth for breeding? Perhaps £350,000, perhaps more.

I know one thing, if the press clowns hadn't caused me, the Chairman, or Tim, a Director, to abandon Classic Bloodstock plc, I never would have allowed the filly to be sold, especially for the idiotic low price the new directors sold her for. But there you go. Press boys again in their ivory towers dispelling their wisdom to the world. I suspect none of them would know a horse if it kicked them in the face!

So, whoever bought *Classic Form* for peanuts has made a killing for every foal off her for the next ten years which they could sell for a lot of money in the sales ring. The Racing Post and Sporting Life should change their title to 'Only Fools and Horses'...

But can you all now see, after reading Sims article, why I feel so disgruntled? Because a low-life parasite like Sims, who has done nothing for racing, or even ever tried to, yet continues with this spiteful claptrap. He should be charged by the Jockey Club of bringing racing into disrepute. People like Sims who continue to put the boot in when you're on the floor have no feelings of honesty. It could be something that he was deprived of in his childhood. And probably still is! If that is the case, I feel sorry for him. But there is a place for his kind in life. His bosses at the Mirror Group of Newspapers will, I suspect, promote him to writing his muck for The Sunday People. If not, I am sure if he buys a Sherlock Holmes outfit, there could be a place for him on The News of the World.

Now, let's have some serious fun. That well-known couple, Fester and Lurch. Sorry, Tommy Clark and Andy Sims. Can they give me one good reason (only one will do) justifying their pitiful attacks on my son, Tim in The Sporting Life over Classic Bloodstock plc? Like taking a picture of him getting into his Porsche on the Newmarket High Street and printing it, with number plates, in full colour in that same paper. What do they have against him? Aside from jealousy and spiteful revenge over P.P.S. exposures.

Now, the serious bit, I will pay £50,000 to any charity of the couple's choice, if they can justify these absurd attacks in their articles against my son related to Classic Bloodstock plc. So, for you, Tommy and Andy, how about a little kiddies nursery rhyme: "Clap handies for Tommy to come, to give little Andy a cake and a bung! Sorry - bun. And a gee gee to ride on." And the silence from these two pricks will be deafening.

About seven years ago, Tim was only a young lad and, because of the case outlined hereafter, the Jockey Club banned him for a year from racing, I will leave you, the reader, to decide upon the fairness of the Jockey Club in this case. Tim has had to live with this one smear from The Sporting Life and Racing Post for years. Every so often they dig it up again for their readers.

In this instance, I won't go as far as to say that this smearing was totally without due cause as I do think that my son, Tim, acted unwisely.

What happened was that my business, Newmarket Racing Club, had a runner in a claiming race, *Lambton Lad*. Tim used to drive trainer, Eric Eldin to the races. However, on this occasion, Eric didn't go to the track. There was no need to, *Lambton Lad* was not going to win. However, Tim was instructed by Eric to put in a friendly claim for Kevin and myself, as was the norm in those day. Tim did as instructed by the trainer and filled in a bank letter provided by the racecourse clerk. Then, for reasons we have never been able to understand, Eric said: "Don't pay. I'll sort it out. Your Dad owns the horse anyway." So I cancelled the bank letter authorising payment.

It was my own horse owned by Newmarket Racing and run in the name of my partner, Kevin Moorcroft. The horse came back to its own stable with its passport from the racecourse. So what was the problem? I have never got a straight answer from the Jockey Club, only waffle. They warned my son off for twelve months. Why couldn't they have just said to the young lad: "Look son, it has to be done this way," instead of the heavy-handed, over the top job they did on Tim. In short, they handled it wrongly. On the 14th August 1998, I wrote a letter to a main man of the Stewards called Malcome Wallace, I reprint part of it below;

Now, Mr. Wallace, I will go onto another matter. One I am finding painful and with much misgivings.

Mr. Wallace, it gives me no satisfaction. In my second edition of Conmen, Cheats and Liars, I have focused on the Jockey Club and its stewards. In my cause to get justice for my son. For over 30 years, I dreamt of the day my son would be a trainer. That dream is finished and all I have worked for is now in shreds. Because you are weak, you have, I suspect, allowed newspapers to influence you. Pity you could not be strong and believe in innocent until proven guilty .

The love of my life has been horse-racing and it has never been my intention to damage the sport I loved. What I consider unjust against my son is the conspiracy of some sorts within the Jockey Club. And I find it a shame that this highly prestigious club with so many distinguished members is to play their part in Tim's libel action against the press. Those distinguished members, I believe, do not deserve the ensuing bad publicity your good office will undoubtedly receive, unless I am totally mistaken in my assumptions. We shall see.

I will say here that, until your brutal offhand dismissal of Tim's letter for a permit, I had always admired the Jockey Club and their members for their integrity and honour. Now, however, the stewards' actions have vastly changed my outlook and I suspect that I am not alone in this viewpoint. I trust that you, Mr. Wallace, have read or are aware of all the correspondence between myself and Lyn Williams and R.L. Smith over the past years. Or do your secretaries act on their own initiative?

I will no doubt get some satisfaction from seeing those very stewards, who took a worthless decision over a young man's life, subpoenaed in court, then Tim will doubtless be given the courtesy of an opportunity to respond to the Jockey Club's stigma against him. Surely, regarding all the three subpoenas, the stewards of the Disciplinary Committee will testify honestly and attempt to demonstrate why they ruined my son's future.

We shall see though, I suspect, that the reasons go far deeper than first imagined, compounded by all the bad press we "the family from Hell" have received. Trainer, Brian McMath and his mentor, Peter Amos (both ex-army) may have conspired together, on the lies and bitterness of McMath who I sacked - perfectly justifiably. They, in turn, I suspect could have persuaded, the stewards that Tim Dawson was some evil bastard who is not worthy of a permit to train. I also suspect that Peter Amos will be subpoenaed in court to put these suspected allegations of mine to the test. Like the stewards, he should make an excellent witness. But I am confident it was mostly the press article that sealed Tim's fate.

Now you may ask, Mr Wallace, why am I writing all this? Well, in the Racehorse Owners magazine, it stated that McMath had tried to sell the story of Classic Bloodstock plc to the press. Obviously, there was no story to tell and no financial wrongdoing. But that statement had very serious implications. Especially as I understand that McMath and Peter Amos had a meeting or could we say a friendly chat before that article was published. And we all know of Peter Amos' hostility to Tim and the Classic Bloodstock venture....

So, both these men - Amos and McMath hate Tim Dawson and both these men could have some influence on the Jockey Club. The question is: was there a conspiracy? We shall see. The only fly in the ointment is that I was assured by David Pipe that the stewards of the Jockey Club would not be influenced by anything other than facts. So obviously, we will no doubt all wait (well, Tim will) with bated breath to learn what these facts are.

Tim suspects that, because of his personal fractions with Peter Amos and his apparent lack of respect of McMath, that possibly the stewards have been misled by these two mens' personal vendettas towards him.

Now I have one further request which I am sure you will provide me with.

I require, as soon as possible, the names of the three stewards who made the decision that my son would not get a permit in the foreseeable future. I would hope you will oblige me with this information, by return.

I trust you are aware of the long fax outlining Tim's grievances sent to Mr R.L. Smith on 12th August? Copies of letters are also in the post.

Yours faithfully,   Ron Dawson

Here follows another true another true story concerning stewards of the Jockey Club.

I was at Doncaster Races with my trainer who held the training licence in name only, Roger Harris and his assistant trainer (but the real trainer) - Tim. Our horse, *Old Provence* was running and was well-beaten (as we expected it to be). Just after the race, Roger and Tim noticed a horse that was looking in a bad way. There was no trainer with the horse, just the lad. "Keep him walking," Tim suggested. The lad did not take any heed and the horse proceeded to drop dead of a heart attack. Next thing, over the racecourse loudspeaker, the stewards ask for Roger and Tim. "Must be the way *Old Provence* ran," Tim surmised, looking worried. So, next thing, Roger and Tim are on the mat in front of the stewards.

"What happened to *Old Provence* Harris?" asked one.

"Nothing Sir, he just didn't run too well today, sir. We've hosed him down, put him in the horse-box and he's on his way home to Newmarket, Sir,"

"Don't tell us lies Harris. The horse is dead."

Tim burst out laughing. "I don't know what he's on, but I wouldn't mind some!" he whispered to Roger.

Obviously, the buffoons had seen Tim near the dead horse and that was enough for them to jump to the wrong conclusion. What a pantomime! And starring stewards of the Jockey Club. I am now convinced someone has poisoned Tim's name there.

Those in racing used to call the Jockey Club estate manager, Peter Amos, 'Old Shiny Shoes'. Over the years, he has had a few barneys with my son, Tim. Peter does the finest job possible for just about all the trainers in Newmarket, especially the younger and poorer ones. But he just didn't like Tim. It may be because our stable was over the road from the Jockey Club's Pheasant Hatchery and Shoot, and the number of birds decreased after we moved to Charnwood. Tim could have been the culprit or it could have been Tim's lack of respect for unnecessary bloody-mindedness of authority. Come to think of it, I wasn't a novice poacher either. My poor little Jack Russell had been poisoned and then Maureen's Jack Russell, Nell went missing; she was always chasing rabbits or pheasants. We searched for days all over the Jockey Club's shooting land. Peering down rabbit warrens, checking out traps. Maureen was distraught. She had had Nell since she was just a pup. I remembered that I had heard a shotgun go off around the time the dog went missing and confronted the Jockey Club's gamekeeper. "Have you seen our Jack Russell?" I asked.

He wouldn't look me in the eye. "No," he replied and walked away.

But I will add one remark here, Nell had been out with my other dog, Jack that day. Jack returned distressed. And if a bang, say from a firework or gun goes off these days, he is in a dreadful state.

It makes you wonder. But then I can't prove anything.

However, I can tell you that those Jockey Club boys didn't blast as many pheasants that year as they usually did on their annual shoot next to my stables. But then I have never believed in killing for killing's sake. To breed pheasants only to blast them out of the sky for sport is not my cup of tea. They should take up clay pigeon shooting, that's my advice.

CHAPTER EIGHTEEN

My 10 Years Ban From Racing

Classic Gold was a business I really didn't want to be a part of. I was getting cheesed off doing my bit for racing, especially given all the bad press publicity that Classic Bloodstock had received. Although most of the plc shareholders were happy enough, we hadn't budgeted to purchase any more yearlings the following year. Some plc shareholders obviously felt like they were missing out with no two year olds to race. So, in 1996, I was pressured to take action. I wrote to Classic shareholders in their newsletter and told them that, if they wanted, I would run an offshoot for their benefit and call it Classic Gold and, for £250, they could have some fun.

To ensure that we received sufficient replies, I also used about 20,000 names from my own mailing lists. The outcome was 850 people sent me £250 which equalled about £212,500. Tim bought five yearlings at the sales. The cheapest, 9,400 guineas, the dearest 63,000 guineas, all with Tattersall's documentation. So, a total of 166,000 guineas leaving £46,000 pounds for the training fees. The five horses are all named by the 852 investors by asking for suggestions and drawing five names out of the hat: *Charlies Gold, Pursuit of Gold, Gift of Gold, Elsie's Gold* and *Emperor's Gold.*

On the 31st October, 1996, I received a letter from the Jockey Club stating that, because Classic Bloodstock plc 11 may go into liquidation the following year, any application to register Classic Gold will not be automatic. And it rattles on, making it obvious that they will do everything in their power to cause me as much difficulty as they can to register Classic Gold. The letter was dated 31st October, signed Richard L. Smith, Secretary to the Licensing Committee. I just replied to them with the truth, four days later on the 4th November. Both letters are reproduced hereafter:

The Jockey Club

31st October, 1998

Classic Gold Racing Club

Dear Mr. Dawson,

The Licensing Committee's attention has been draw to the Newsletter of Classic Bloodstock plc, Summer 1996 in which mention is made of 'Classic Gold'.

The Licensing Committee has been advised that Classic Bloodstock 11 may go into voluntary liquidation early next year and in view of your connection with that company, which is registered as a recognised company under the Rules of Racing, I have been asked to inform you that acceptance of any future application to register 'Classi Gold' will not be automatic.

I suggest you furnish the Licensing Committee with full particulars of any new venture you may wish to register under the Rules of Racing at the earliest opportunity and I remind you that the Stewards of the Jockey Club have complete discretion under those Rules whether or not to register any person or entity as an owner.

Please also bear in mind that the Licensing Committee may wish to meet with you and/or the Directors and Company Secretary, should any application for registration be received.

Yours sincerely,

Richard L. Smith
Secretary to the Licensing Committee

I replied four days later.

4th November, 1996

Mr R.I. Smith
Dear Sir,

Enough is enough. I suggest you and your committee members stop reading press reports which are mostly nothing but lies and get a grip of the situation regarding plc1 and plc11.

All the rubbish again in the Racing Post about the DTI where it states "we understand Dawson has been interviewed" - I never have and don't expect if I ever was that there could be any wrong-

doing. The whole situation is making me ill. Instead of the Jockey Club supporting my own good intentions, you are showing your- selves to be biased about me. Furthermore, I told the whole truth about plc 1 and plc 11 on Radio 4 'Face the Facts' programme but, of course, they edited out the good things from the recording. That's the media.

Classic Gold - No, I have not registered it yet, because I am not happy at the way racing clubs are conducting themselves in their advertising for new members. Take Elite Racing Club or Martin Pipe Racing Club - £250, but no reference in their advertising to say that £35 of that is VAT. I have been informed they may be acting illegally by not informing their members that 17.5% of their money is going to the VAT man. I am therefore looking at a way around this problem and am writing to my Classic Gold investors to find the best way to register ourselves under the Rules of Rac- ing.

May I just add one further point, it is the Classic Bloodstock plc 11 shareholders who decide the policy of the company. It does not concern any other body.

Yours faithfully,

Ron Dawson

I just want to add a short note here from Carol Pipe. It shows their concern also about paying VAT on mem- bers' subscriptions.

Mr. Ron Dawson
Dear Sir,

The Custom and Excise insist that we pay VAT on our sub- scriptions. We have taken this up with them and the matter is still under review. But in the meantime, we have paid the VAT and hope one day we shall have a refund.

Sorry that I cannot be any more help.

Carol Pipe
Martin Pipe
Pond House
Nicholashayne
Wellington, Somerset TA21 9QY

Because I now had to get a new trainer into my stables and grovel to the Jockey Club, I sent the following letter to them. But I was on thin ice. I knew the Jockey Club boys were out to cause me problems.

6th November, 1996
The Secretary
The Licensing Committee
Dear Sirs,

May I be allowed to put forward my views on my proposed new trainer, Ian Campbell. I can assure you he will have total and complete control over all the plc horses and those registered by my family trained at Charnwood Stables and, of course, his own owner's horses. I have reason to believe he will give the job one hundred percent.

He will be living on the premises in what was my main home until I moved to Spain, though I will use one of my other properties in Newmarket when I am in England.

The very difficult problem of a trainer for Classic plc is that the majority of shareholders want to see their horses, and it is not unusual to have twenty or more people turn up on any day or every day at Charnwood. That unlimited access any time is important to the shareholders. Unfortunately, it stops us farming our horses out to other trainers, because though they want the horses, they do not want a large body of shareholders trampling around their stables every day including weekends.

Sadly for me also, because of difficult circumstances, I have not been able to keep the good trainers here at Charnwood. i.e. Miss Kelleway and Stuart Williams, both excellent trainers.

I am probably the most loyal of any owner in racing. I have a standard and I can assure you I would never dismiss a trainer without exceptional good reason. I just want to be allowed to get on with my business without all the silly media humbug distractions.

If you, like the bigoted press, want me out of racing, give me one good reason and I will go. You will throw many out of employment. You should give me and my shareholders your backing for Classic Bloodstock and not be seen to be against me and against them. You do need more people in racing. The press and others have to stop this persecution and be less deceitful. I see the lat-

est gossip now in The Sporting Life is yachts. Drugs will be next. Isn't it all rather pathetic?

I just hope Mr. Ian Campbell will be to the Jockey Club's satisfaction. I will have his draft lease drawn up before his interview at Portman Square.
Yours faithfully,

Ron Dawson

At first, I just couldn't fathom out why Sims of The Sporting Life was doing all he could to blacken my and Tim's name without any proof whatsoever of any financial wrongdoing over the Classic plc.

Now the plot is becoming much clearer. I suspect the Jockey Club felt they had to act because of the dreadful press reports. As Mr. Williams said to me on the phone, my ten year sentence was unprecedented in the history of the Jockey Club for such a minor offence. But all these missing millions: "We don't know if you're guilty or not, but the press does" So see what Sims has accomplished? He will be proud of this if you read this faxed letter which follows, written to my brother Richard from R.L. Smith of the Jockey Club on 23rd July 1997:.

Racing Partnership - Classic Gold

Dear Mr Dawson

I refer to your application to register the Racing Partnership and the Partnership Name of 'Classic Gold'.

In view of my previous correspondence with your brother, Mr. Ron Dawson, the Committee might look more favourably upon the application if neither he, nor members of his immediate family such as yourself, have any involvement in the control, administration or management of the Racing Partnership. Therefore, I suggest you consider obtaining written confirmation from your brother and his son, Tim that they will have no such involvement.

With regard to your own involvement in the Racing Partnership, it appears you have replaced your brother and/or nephew and therefore the Committee will wish to establish how you intend

to manage the Partnership and what experience you have of such matters. Will you need to rely on any involvement by your brother and nephew to manage the Partnership?
Yours sincerely,

Richard L. Smith
Secretary to the Licensing Committee

Obviously, the Jockey Club have Tim and I marked down as crooks, without any proof at all. I faxed the following back to Richard Smith the next day:

24th July, 1997

Dear Mr. Smith,

Thanks for your letter dated 23rd July to my brother Richard, I will deal with the answers to your questions in the order as set out in your letter.

To save expense on postage to our 850 Classic Gold investors, I put a telephone message on our private line for three days outlining our proposals and inviting any objections to Richard Dawson, managing the Classic Gold affairs, and asking for any other nominees. There were none. Mr Kettle, a racing enthusiast, was asked and he accepted. Of our 850 Classic Gold investors, none other it seems than Richard Dawson has the experience required and I take umbrage to your comments.

Richard, with a long career in the RAF and a well-noted poet, is a person who had not one blemish on his 55 years and is the obvious person if you don't want me to run Classic Gold. He is at the stable office every day to show any of the 850 investors around their horses. All the accounts are done by him, lads wages, racing and trainers' expenses, blacksmiths, hay straw, etc. are all paid promptly and efficiently. It would be ridiculous to expect anyone else to give all that time and work involved and be here for the investors, not to mention all the daily phone calls, racing badges, etc. unless they were paid. Rick does it all for no charge. I believe by far the majority of Classic Gold investors very much appreciate this, not to mention the continuous updates of the news line.

If the Jockey Club for their own reasons, have treated me differently from others registering their horse syndicates, etc., by some how deeming me not to be a fit and proper person and by their continuous and what would appear deliberate vendetta to stop the Classic Gold horses from racing or delaying as long as possible the outcome, I must protect the quarter of a million pounds invested by Classic Gold people and also your comments about my family are grossly discourteous.

Yours sincerely,

Ron Dawson

PS Classic Gold investors present training and heath fees are running at £1,000 per week. Four weeks after we asked for your urgent help, we have not progressed forward one inch. If you work at the same urgency it will be the year 2000 at the earliest before we run a two year old "all ready to race now", hardly justice to 850 people who have faith in you and racing. It would deem cheaper to stick them all in a field, for I do not believe you are doing all you can for them. You obviously have a "bee in your bonnet". It may sting you some day. Be careful.

It's true for me to say that, following that letter the Jockey Club were so unhelpful, it's hard to believe. How grown men out of some spiteful, uncalled for revenge, can act the way they did, yet trying to make me a "villain of the piece". They knew from day one of Classic Gold's full history. If they want to deny that fact then, they are not gentlemen. I will even go so far as to charge them with conspiracy.

It is now obvious that the Jockey Club didn't want Tim and myself in racing. In other words, they would never have let us register Classic Gold. They even told my brother Richard, that they wanted it in writing that neither Tim nor I would be involved in registering Classic Gold. Justice dealt out on press rumours and silly inside tittle-tattle by troublemakers.

So, obviously, when I received the letter below on 4th December, 1996 from the Jockey Club, they had already made up their minds. What the Jockey Club is guilty of is that, despite Tim and I not having a hearing in their court of our case, they have punished us first. In other words, if they were judging a murder trial, "hang 'em first, then listen to the evidence."

The next letter from the Jockey Club is, I suspect, no more than a delaying tactic by them.

4th December, 1996

Dear Mr Dawson,

I refer to your letter dated 4th November 1996. The Jockey Club does not have specimen rules for the different types of owning entities to which you refer, but, if you merely wish to know what Rules of Racing or Orders of the British Horse-Racing Board apply, I would draw your attention to Part 4 headed "Owners" and in particular Rules 41-45, 47B and 47C. I also enclose "The Promotion of Racehorse Ownership - Advertising Guidelines" issued by the Jockey Club and which you may need to discuss with your advisers if you intend to proceed. I would reiterate, however, that in the light of current problems with your other ventures the Stewards of the Jockey Club may wish to exercise their power under the Rules of Racing to refuse to register your new venture and you may wish to bear that in mind before incurring any significant expenditure.
Yours sincerely,
Richard L. Smith
Secretary to the Licensing Committee

Previous to this letter, I had suspected that the Jockey Club were being dishonest with Tim when he applied for a training licence. It was a good application better than most, a financial guarantee. I even promised that he could have my stables, a top-class establishment on a free rent, 5 year lease. He also had fifteen horses of his own and I promised to buy him a further six two year olds. On top of that, we had several owners (five) who would put horses with Tim as soon as he was granted his licence. His was an experienced assistant trainer who had worked for two and a half years (and three years in a stud farm), plus five years in our racing stables. It should have been a formality for a licence being granted. References were also provided from trainers and others. To my knowledge, no one in the history of the Jockey Club has ever been refused a licence with all those criteria in place. Tim was refused. Why? Then to rub salt into the wound, he asked for a permit only to train some national hunt horses, (of which he already owned six). He also had all the top class facilities anyone could wish for. This should have been a certain formality, but he was refused again. Why?

So, by this time, I was most perplexed. Have we murdered someone or committed some other crime? Can I get a reason for the Jockey Club's stance? You must be joking! It's a bit like the Lord Soames blackballing incident (to be explained later...). All they would say was the same as the letter, i.e. that "with regards to your son's application for a licence or a permit to train. I remind you that each application is considered individually upon its merits" - liars! The truth is, they are spineless and I will tell you that Tim has done absolutely nothing to justify their double standards. How about this reference he got from one racehorse trainer?

July, 1996
The Jockey Club
Licensing Department

Dear Sirs,
Mr Timothy Dawson
  This letter is to be regarded as a reference for Mr. Timothy Dawson in connection with his application for a Trainer's Licence.
  I have known Mr. T. Dawson for a number of years and since January 1996 he has been employed as my Assistant Trainer. In my opinion, he is very capable and able to train thoroughbred flat horses. He has gained experience in training, yard management, making entries and expert knowledge of horses' health problems

and veterinary procedures. He has a very pleasant manner with owners and adheres strictly to all the Jockey Club rules and regulations, of which he is fully aware.

I have no doubt he will become a top-class trainer.

Yours faithfully,

R. Harris

Now that letter was genuine and a true account of how high Tim was thought of in racing.

Next I will turn back to more Portman Square jiggerpokery.

On Monday morning, March 16th, I rang the Jockey Club to ask about appealing against this ridiculous ten year ban. "No you can't appeal," the Secretary of the Disciplinary Committee, Mr Lyn Williams told me. "You have to lodge an appeal within seven days."

"But I wasn't told that procedure when you wrote to me immediately with my life sentence!" I protested.

"We don't have to tell you, it's written in the rules somewhere," I was informed.

Game, set and match to the Jockey Club. They must be proud of that.

"Okay," I said, containing my anger as best I could. "Then why has the Jockey Club been so vindictive in its verdict and why was Tim refused a permit to train, never mind a full licence?"

"Well, it's the press you see and all the publicity about the millions of pounds stolen."

"Well, if those reports are true, Mr Williams, I should be in prison!" I protested.

"We're not bothered whether they are true or not," he replied. "It's just the press saying all those allegations."

"Okay, Mr Williams," I replied, trying very, very hard to contain my anger. "So, what on earth has all this to do with my son, Tim? He had no part whatsoever in forming Classic Bloodstock plc 1 or plc 11."

"Well, he is your son, isn't he?" I put the phone down. One more second and I would have exploded and had another heart attack.

So, that's all they have on Tim, he's my son and if he was involved in Classic Gold, it would or could not be registered. (What the hell has he done to anyone, please, please someone explain?)

Now, surely any decent folk must ask themselves, can this really happen in 1998. I know my son is no angel. Who wants a boy who is? But he has no criminal record. He is a decent lad, extremely well-liked in the racing fraternity and wanted to make his career in racing some day. Now that can never happen. The Jockey Club committee conducted a small minded inquisition took place where justice was dealt out, not on facts but hearsay. Destroying a young man's life is obviously of no consequence to them.

This is important and it's all true. As I've explained a few pages ago, I wrote seven times to the Jockey Club in 1996 and 1997 trying to register Classic Gold and they tried as hard as they could to delay the registration, sometimes taking a month to reply. They finally gave way in the summer of 1997 when they had no other choice.

In the meantime, Classic Gold's trainer, Ian Campbell tried to register the horses with Wetherby's, but they wouldn't accept the registration. This put my trainer in a bad position. Two of these two year olds were ready to race, they were at their peak. Any more delay and it could have been too late. Tim was a registered owner and a member of the Classic Gold syndicate. So what's the big deal?

So we ran the two yearlings for the benefit of Classic Gold in Tim's name. It was a deliberate mistake. It was because of the Jockey Club's that we couldn't register the horses. I wrote to the Jockey Club and apologised for breaking a petty rule. To my mind, it was no big thing, it happens all the time.

Neither Tim nor myself could benefit from this. Only the Classic Gold investors could benefit. At least their horses were racing and not lying idle and wasted in their stable boxes. The Jockey Club know that this is a true fact. Who entered those horses? The trainer, Ian Campbell and, as aforementioned, they were registered in Tim's name. The trainer is fined £750. Tim, his assistant trainer, is banned for ten years. It doesn't make any sense. Little wonder Tim thinks he's been victimised, wouldn't you?

This is a copy of the letter I sent to the Jockey Club on 7th December, 1997. I could just picture it in my mind - the inquisition waiting to try us. Words are hard to find to say what I feel about the Jockey Club toads trying to make a mountain out of a mole hill

Ref: Hearing of the case 8th January 1998

To the Disciplinary Committee

7th December, 1997

Dear Sirs,

I apologise for not being able to attend on the 8th January at Portman Square. I am not well enough to travel to England. My son, Tim also sends his apologies. He is abroad at the moment.

We both plead guilty to the charge of running two horses in the name of Tim Dawson, instead of Classic Gold which we have tried to register with the Jockey Club. It's my fault. I should have sorted it out, but didn't. We have nothing to gain from this offence, only the Classic Gold investors benefited. Their horses had to run. One member from a total of 852 investors complained. If you look at my record as an owner since 1963, it's a clean slate. Only the adverse press reports have not looked good for Tim and I.

Tim and I have committed an offence and broken the rules. We both apologise. It will not happen again. We ask you to fine us on this occasion. A warning off over this matter would be just too much for us to bear.

Yours faithfully,

Ron Dawson.

Their reply was to give my son Tim and I a ten year ban from our beloved sport. I hate to think what our sentence would have been had we pleaded not guilty. Deportation to Antartica in chains, I suspect.

I have now sent a copy of this book to the Jockey Club with a letter of appeal. I want to be given the opportunity to stand on the mat with "The Committee" in no doubt of my contempt for them.

I truly believe that I was set up by the Jockey Club in a way that would do justice to the Mafia or bent coppers.

I want the reader here to be in no doubt about my guilt in trying to get round a way to run the two Classic Gold horses: Gift of Gold and Emperor's Gold. But what could I do? The Jockey Club was determined not to let them run. If I had anything to do with Classic Gold. Why? Well, obviously they felt I had made a mess over Classic Bloodstock plc and I suspect that if The Sporting Life was making a big song and dance over missing millions of pounds, it was a case of "no smoke without fire". So, to their shame, they went along with those reports.

The fact was that neither Tim nor I were guilty of any wrongdoing over Classic Bloodstock plc but was not the real issue. Someone had to be blamed for the bad publicity. So they jumped on us. Put the bastards in irons was on their agenda and that's what they did.

Now, in their defence, they say I deliberately misled the Jockey Club. Yet, right from the beginning of the Classic Gold purchase at the sales they had full documentation from me. To contradict that fact they would be lying. Now whatever my faults and God forbid, I probably have more than most, lying is not one of them. They, the Jockey Club, lay in wait like a 'praying mantis', waiting for the one opportunity to squash me. They found a weak spot - my honesty and straight dealing. With underhandedness that is typical of a schoolboy sneak, they led me on, knowing full well that the two horses were indeed owned by

Classic Gold and because I am a fool and would put the welfare of others before my own interests, they let me register and run the two horses in the name of my son, Tim who was a current registered owner.

Their trap was sprung, back slaps all round. I am trapped like a spider in a web, they have got their man and to fill their greed they are going to eat Tim as well. "Jockey Club spider pie," wrap them up to be devoured later. Okay, but what if these two food parcels have a fair and just case for acting the way they did, say. For the benefit of the Classic Gold people to get their horses running. After all, it was costing those people £2,000 a month to leave those horses idle while the Jockey Club were dishonest in their dealing with Classic Gold.

You see, dear reader, the truth of the matter is, that to commit a crime you must have a motive, or be a lunatic. So what possible benefit could I gain from instructing the horses to race for the time being in any name. Okay then I am a lunatic, but I have not deceived the Jockey Club in order to gain any personal benefit. And that's their problem for they have no answer to that question.

The Jockey Club are unable to shown any sound reason for their actions. Only their 'pie in the sky' waffle, waffle. For the bottom line is, yes Tim and Ronnie Dawson committed an offence, but it hurt no one. Naughty boys.

What harm did they do to anyone? Come think of it, what harm did they do to racing? And that's the stupidity of it all. All the adverse bad publicity that they, the Jockey Club have brought upon themselves. Every jockey, trainer or owner I have spoken to thinks its hilarious. Schoolboy stuff. Wouldn't the Jockey Club's time be better spent in trying to get out of racing the crooks, the dishonest trainers, the bent jockeys, the dopers, etc. etc. instead of running around like headless chickens trying to make mountains out of mole hills to try and justify their jobs at Portman Square.

CHAPTER NINETEEN

My bone of contention with the Jockey Club is mine and Tim's ten year sentence. It's a fact that I was a first time ever offender in over thirty years as a registered owner. And, if I was warned off for my minor infringement for a year, say - fine! I agree that I should have possibly done things differently.

What Tim and I find so bloody ridiculous over this ten year ban is that they, the Jockey Club, have forbidden any of our life long friends in racing, who are trainers or jockeys from speaking to us for ten years. For instance, say there is a jockey who is godfather to my daughter (and one is), he can no longer ask me about her welfare. It is so stupid it is the law of imbeciles. For example, if I am in a restaurant dining with a jockey friend, I can say to him, "pass the salt, Maximillian, but he cannot say the same to me. I am not sure if hand signals are allowed. I must ask the Jockey Club for a ruling. In fact, dining out in a foursome can be a nightmare. The jockey and his wife can speak to my wife, Maureen. But he cannot converse with me. What we do at present when having dinner with a jockey friend is that he writes notes to me on a paper napkin or a cigarette packet. I then pass him back a scribbled message. But if we think we are under observation by the Jockey Club snoops, one wanders off to the toilet and leaves a message in the loo; then I sneak off and read it (it can be messy) and replace it with my message. The only real drawback here is that dinner can take ten hours instead of two, with all the comings and goings to the loo.

I can see the Jockey Club's point. Hell, you could have a jockey pal trying to say to me which wine should be chosen from the menu, or discussing that day's weather. He might even want to enquire about my health (that is, inside information).

It is all so bloody childish. But as the Jockey Club mouthpiece, Johnny Maxse said in the press over our ten year sentence: "All jockeys and trainers will be informed of their responsibilities to observing the rules towards a warned-off person".

In my racing years I have only had twelve different trainers, unlike Peter (Sack-um) Saville, who has had a bus load. I've often been asked who was the best trainer and most honest. And, so I give you my list in alphabetical order. These are solely my opinions, other owners will no doubt have other opinions.

Trainer	Training Ability	Honesty
Ian Campbell *(Never had much luck in racing, Ian lacks personality to attract owners, but is a genuine article)*	3	9
Eric Eldin *(Couldn't attract enough owners and eventually went out of the game, but got me a few winners)*	6	6
Arthur (Fidler) Goodwill *(Wonderful character, good card player, dealt from the top in life also)*	6	10
Roger Harris *(Sadly in prison for a long time for a major drug bust, importing a huge cannabis haul in a horse box from Spain instead of his usual cargo)*	3	8
Barry Hills *(You could say I got him going, got on a bit in life since the good, old bad old days, ex-stable lad who has done well)*	9	10

Paul Kelleway	9	10
(Sadly recently passed away from a sudden illness. Never got the horses to train that his talent deserved)		
Gay Kelleway	9	5
(This lady is a shrewd cookie, but burns her owners now and again. A prodigy of her father, Paul. May God bless her)		
Colin Williams	9	10
(A useful jockey before he started training. If I had to pick a top job training, he would be top of my list).		
Brian McMath	3	5
(Poor Brian, he must forget his days as a sergeant in the boys army, he has to work in a mans world now. I hope he wins the lottery)		
Jeff Pierce	7	7
(I have had my differences with Jeff. When Kevin and I split up he nailed his colours to Kevin's mast. But the mast soon broke. Fair trainer)		
Dave Thom	7	10
(A true real gentleman. But never got enough of the right horses to train. If he had he would have done well, I'm sure)		
Stuart Williams	7	0
(Conscientious, thoughtful trainer, but has a lot to learn to satisfy small owners. Looking for a big break. Stuart told serious lies once, but I bet odds that he regrets it)		

Best trainers at fighting? It would be a long list. So I will just mark Luca Cumani, 7; Frankie Durr, 7. Their famous set to on the Newmarket Heath put the Tyson-Holmes fight in the shade. Entertainment value - 10!

Now back to my 10 year ban. And I would ask the Jockey Club this - what would be the sentences for any of the following?

1. Bookmakers found paying jockeys for information.

2. Doping horses to stop them winning.

3. Doping horses to make them win.

4. Running a better horse in place of another that looks the same to pull off a scam (a ringer as it's called in the trade).

5. Registering a business with the Jockey Club, like the Palacegate Corporation, using different false names to the trainers, Jockey Club and shareholders.

6. Trainers found guilty of stopping horses deliberately to cheat. I could go on with dozens of examples.

Now, the question I want to ask the stewards of the disciplinary committee is, where do I fit in with this lot? Because you have put me on top of the pile of offenders. Why?

What you have done to me and my son Tim is to punish us like those prisoners of the 1820's who were deported via a prison ship to the penal colony of Australia, just for stealing a sheep.

In 1998, everyone should expect fairness of sentence to fit the crime, not have to suffer the judgement of some upper class twits who have a set of rules for themselves and another for the ordinary man.

What right do these people think they have to play God? Oh yes, I forgot of course they do. They were born with a silver spoon in their mouths. Sorry, gentlemen!

Here follows my fax to Mr Williams dated the 19th March

Lyn Williams   Thursday 19th March
Secretary to the Disciplinary Committee
Dear Mr. Williams,

Thank you for your prompt reply to the fax I sent yesterday. I was trying desperately to register Classic Gold with The Jockey Club and specifically asked Mr R.I. Smith of the Licensing Committee for an urgent response, having already had the experience of waiting more than a month for replies in the past. Now, mysteriously, replies from the Jockey Club are very much faster.

I anxiously await your answer to the following question and trust that it will be as similarly speedy as yesterday's.

Are the gentlemen, Mr. Hall, Mr. Rose and Mr. Motley (all of whom sat on my disciplinary enquiry) stewards of the Jockey Club or members of the Jockey Club? If neither, then in what capacity are they acting in order to try my case?

I feel I should mention here, my confusion over an earlier fax sent to you. Yesterday, my solicitors informed me that I do, indeed, still own Charnwood Stables which has been placed in a trust - Chappel Ltd. by my legal advisors in order to avoid inheritance tax. I own the Virgin Island's based trust company.

However, I have now requested for the deeds to be transferred back into my name alone. I can confirm that the Directors of my trust were instructed to lease part of my stables and that the lease to Mr Kelleway is binding. I have no intention of interfering with his business activities.

When the weather in England warms up, perhaps after Easter, I will return to the UK and plan to reside at my main house on the Charnwood Racing Stable complex where I intend to continue my established tipping business.

I would appreciate a prompt reply to this letter, via fax, to Spain. Any correspondence from the Jockey Club via mail should be directed to Charnwood. My son, Tim will also be in residence there for the entire racing season. Please note, I have nothing to do with the Classic Gold horses which I understand belong to a trust and are trained by Mr Anthony Kelleway. He has the second main house at my stables.

My son, Tim will live on my training complex in my ex-trainer's bungalow.
Yours sincerely,

Ron Dawson.

The reply from the Jockey Club was quick.

Dear Mr Dawson

Thank you for your fax of yesterday's date.

All three gentlemen are members of The Jockey Club and Christopher Hall, in his capacity as Chairman of the Disciplinary Committee, is also a Steward of The Jockey Club.

Yours sincerely,

Lyn Williams

Here follows a copy of the letter I sent individually to the three gentlemen of the Jockey Club Disciplinary Committee. These were my judge and jury. Up to the date of publishing this book, neither of these people have had the decency to explain to me my unprecedented sentence of a ten year ban in the history of the Jockey Club for such a minor offence.

I think it is only fair for this case to be known in racing circles as the motley crew case. The Motley Crew are: Time Motley, Christopher Hunt and, John Rose

20th March, 1998

Dear Sir,

I understand you sat on my Disciplinary Enquiry. Would you be so kind as to reply to the following questions with honesty.

1. *Were you persuaded by my involvement in Classic Bloodstock when warning me off for ten years?*

2. *Were you persuaded by my continuous adverse newspaper publicity when warning me off for ten years?*

As I was a first time offender in breaking a Jockey Club rule, and have been an owner for over thirty years, it is a mystery to me and many others why you have in your judgement seen fit to give me and Tim a warning-off for life, ten years.

Did you take into consideration my sincere letter of apology over this minor infringement, by allowing my son, Tim as a registered owner to make entries for Classic Gold Horses?

If you did take into consideration my sincere letter of apology when handing down my sentence, would my sentence therefore have been greater without my admission of guilt?

I would ask you to answer this letter personally, without conferring with the other two gentlemen who sat on my enquiry. I must also warn you that I intend to print your reply in my forthcoming book or, alternatively, if you decline to answer my request, that will be confirmed in my book with a copy of this letter.

I believe it is in the public interest that you, the Jockey Club are seen to act fairly and without malice at all times and judge each case before you on merit, without any victimisation. I consider the warning-off sentence of ten years bestowed on me and Tim, so pathetic for a quite minor offence in comparison to other very much more serious offences, to be a ridiculous erroneous decision on your part. I await your reply.
Yours sincerely,

Ron Dawson

No reply has been received from any of these gentlemen prior to the publication of my book. But Mr. Williams said to me during a phone conversation that the Disciplinary Committee do not reply to warned off persons. No, I replied, because they are bloody ostriches.

Then, on the 30th March, 1998, my son, Tim wrote this letter to the Jockey Club.

30th March, 1998
The Secretary to the Licensing Committee
Dear Sir,

I am writing this letter to give you the opportunity, once again, to reply to the request of why the Licensing Committee refused to issue me a training licence, or even consider a permit to train.

Of the last twenty training licences issued, no less than five did not have the qualifications required equal to myself, and very few of those twenty indeed did not have the financial security I was able to provide. Don't you think feed merchants, blacksmiths, vets, horse transporters, etc are sick up the teeth chasing broke trainers. They all want to do business with my father because he is a good payer

In case you are once again going to fob my father and I off with your past comments ("we do not have to give a reason"), I believe you do. If only to show the public you require certain standards for ALL applicants, without favour, as it does not appear in this case. Of course, I realise my warning off for ten years does now effectively put me out of racing for the rest of my life - why you have treated me so harshly is extremely difficult to understand.

I do intend to put in writing an appeal to this sentence in due course, but first I want you all at the Jockey Club to be aware or have read my father's book, 'Conmen, Cheats and Liars' which puts the Jockey Club in a very bad light indeed. (Nothing more than you all deserve in my opinion).

So obviously, following my ensuing letter of my appeal, if granted by the Disciplinary Committee of course - but due to the exceptional circumstances the racing public may feel you are obliged to grant, my father and I will attend Portman Square. At present, though, I demand an explanation from you over why my trainer's licence application was refused. No reply may be seen by the racing public that you at Portman Square have something to hide.

Yours faithfully,

Tim J. Dawson

I want readers to put themselves in the place of Tim. And following is a copy of the letter Tim sent to the Jockey Club on the 23rd September, 1996. I would say that Tim took it bravely when he was refused a full licence. However, he asked the committee to consider him for a permit only. The Jockey Club gives permits out like confetti to any Tom, Dick or Harry. Well no, not quite! But permits are granted to Lady Connell, Countess Goes-Saurau, Lady Elizabeth Mays-Smith, the Honourable Mrs Arthur, Lady Susan Brook ...

Need I go further? I think my readers are getting the message.

Tim wrote an earlier letter to the Jockey Club in 1996 as follows:

23rd September, 1996
The Jockey Club
Licensing Department
Dear Sirs,

I would thank you for your recent letter. I am obviously unhappy that you feel unable to grant me a training licence.

Unfortunately, in your letter you did not give any guidance as to why my application was refused and I would appreciate any comments you may feel appropriate to make on why my licence was refused and in what area the Licensing Committee was unhappy. I do feel that I can make a contribution to the racing industry and would like to pursue the granting of a training licence in the future. Therefore, any assistance would be gratefully appreciated.

Turning to this current jump season, I am considering schooling some of my horses for either hurdling or chasing. Would it be possible for me to obtain a permit holders licence for this current year? I would appreciate your comments and assistance in this area also.

I look forward to hearing from you.
Yours faithfully,

Mr. T. Dawson

This next letter was the response in 1996 from the Jockey Club to Tim's letter. And, at the time we both believed the Jockey Club's integrity. Today, we know it's full of deceit.

31st October 1996
Tim Dawson
Dear Mr. Dawson,

I refer to your letter, dated 23rd September, 1996 and apologies for the delay in replying.

I have consulted with the Licensing Committee again and have been asked to inform you that the Committee would not look favourably upon an application for a Permit to Train.

*I believe it is unlikely that the Committee would look favourably upon an application for a **Trainer's Licence or Permit to Train in the foreseeable future.** As you are obviously keen to hold a Licence to Train, I should point out that successful appli-*

cants have normally been employed in racing establishments for several years with a minimum of two years employment in the role of Assistant Trainer. Those applicants have usually been employed 'independently' and can supply supporting references from employers other than those who are currently training horses for them.

Successful applicants are also able to produce evidence of a demand for their services from members of the public.

I hope this is of some assistance to you.

Yours sincerely,

Richard L. Smith
Secretary to the Licensing Committee

This is important. I want to draw the reader's attention here and ask you to consider the following: when Classic Thoroughbreds went belly up in 1990 (this dream child of Jockey Club member and millionaire owner, Robert Sangster and his crew, namely: Chairman Vincent O'Brian and Michael Smurfit), they were never penalised by the Jockey Club, yet small investors had lost millions. Robert Sangster has been a Jockey Club member since 1972 and remains one to this day. He is one of the clique, while I'm just a whipping-boy.

I would like to refresh the Jockey Club's memory here because they have evidently blanked it out. It commenced in 1984 when Sangster's team decided to launch Classic Thoroughbred plc with D. Desmond who was the Dublin stockbroker handling the deal. The plan was that they would float it on the Dublin Stock Exchange. They would buy yearlings at the sales and, in order to demonstrate their success, pointed out how they had bought yearlings in the past and marketed them as stallions for millions of pounds.

Sangster and his chums then recruited the Chairman of the Irish Racing Board, Michael Smurfit, one of Ireland's richest men, to join their scheme. Vincent O'Brian would be Chairman, but Sangster would take a backseat and just be a major shareholder, not making any waves.

He admitted that his name was used to win the trust of the public. The shares were priced at 30 pence each and private shareholders invested £12,000,000, mostly paid by small investors.

Personally, I couldn't care less about Robert Sangster and Michael Smurfit losing their money. But what about the little guy? 'Via the press, I knew about them all too well'. In 1989, Classic Thoroughbred plc reported a half year loss of $8.3 million and the horses they had bought for millions of pounds were not up to the mark - apart from one horse purchased called Royal Academy.

By 1990, Classic Thoroughbred shares were down to about three pence each and at an Extraordinary General Meeting the company was dissolved. One thing that will have to be explained to me some day is how Robert Sangster personally owned a quarter share in the one and only good horse that Classic Thoroughbred owned?

Of course, I am sure it would be all above board. I would just like to know, that's all. But doesn't the sheer hypocrisy of the Jockey Club shine through? One rule for members like Sangster, another rule for Ronnie Dawson.

Now, why would the Jockey Club do this to me? Well, I think the following is part it. They believed the rumours and the media reports of missing millions. I also removed one of Classic Bloodstock plc's horses from trainer, Stuart Williams (the horse lover): He proudly told me how he had used an electric cattle prod to get it running faster on the training gallops. I mentioned this electric prod business on the Classic plc private phone line. The newspapers were eavesdropping and the next day blew it up into something big. And Williams did a silly thing. In effect, he called me a liar in the press. Now he could call me a wally, a freak or a bastard - but not a liar. And so I brand him as a fool. He had only to state the truth. Instead, he tried to cover it up.

Next, we have the Jockey Club (Mr Plod) John Elsey knocking at my door for an explanation. I told the truth and produced a reliable witness who said he had, indeed, seen Williams using an electric prod on the horse. It was no big deal. I shouldn't have mentioned it in the first place, but I was naive and did so. Elsey, the Jockey Club investigator, went to interview Williams. Then he came back to me and said, Williams had said I was lying. I told Elsey straight. "Look, I will take a lie detector test on this one." I just can't believe Williams would lie over the matter. In my opinion, Elsey is not daft, he's an ex-copper. He knows full well, I believe, who was telling the truth. Quite honestly, I had never even heard of an electric prod in my life until William had mentioned it. But, anyway, Elsey said, "Look Ron, all this is not doing racing any good. Animal rights could get wind of it and cause trouble. Bad for the sport."

"You're right," I replied. "It's best for racing that it's forgotten." But Stuart Williams shouldn't have lied and he will always have to live with that lie."

Just as bad, I think, was the fact that Stuart Williams told me that he wasn't satisfied with Alan Mackay, our jockey. I pointed out to Williams about a vote of confidence the majority of shareholders had given Alan. They own the horses, not Williams. Also, Alan gave much of his free time to the benefit of shareholders visiting the yard. In addition, he rode out two or three lots of Classic Bloodstock's two-year olds every morning, free-of-charge.

He had just rode a nice Stuart trained Classic Horse to win called Classic Find. What was the problem? The problem was he wanted Kevin Darley to ride. Stuart gave the shareholders an ultimatum, either Alan goes or he didn't want the horses to train (what an ego!). Now Stuart knew that the company and myself were under a lot of pressure from the press. And the last thing I wanted was more trouble which the press boys would blow up and cause as much discontentment as possible. Stuart's timing was perfect. He gave me until 10.00 a.m. the following morning to come to a decision. It was easy for me really. No trainer is bigger than his owners. I sacked Stuart the following day. And I will tell you this. Williams could not stand Classic shareholders around his yard. But at Charnwood the welcome was warm and genuine.

Stuart repaid me for sacking him by going to Companies House and getting the names and addresses of all our shareholders and writing to them to offer a scheme to join his new racing venture called the Cherry Pickers. It failed. Stuart should realise in life that, when you have a few cronies telling you how good you are, it's never the majority speaking.

I had other trainers who similarly hit the headlines.

For example, there was Brian McMath, whom I sacked for incompetence and deceit. One of the tricks he tried to pull really backfired. He caused a lot of trouble in the press about how the horse passports for Classic Bloodstock had gone missing. The Sporting Life and the Racing Post gave it plenty of coverage. The problem with the passports was that Brian had hidden them and reported the apparent theft from Brian's office to the police and the Jockey Club in Portman's Square. What value could they possibly have to anyone? It was all so foolish for Brian to try and brew up trouble and mischief because he had been fired. I solved it very easily. As I wrote earlier, Brian went past my house on his horse. I leaned out of the bedroom window and called out:

"When the passports are found Brian, come over to my house and only then will I pay your wages." I love this story. Brian had caused so much trouble for Maureen and myself. Nobody believed us at first when we had sussed the real Brian. But like all little con men, I see right through them.

The passports mysteriously returned that same morning discovered back in Brian's office, he said they had got accidentally concealed under a copy of The Sporting Life. In my opinion, if Brian wants to get on in life, he really must stop telling lies. One evening I found Brian drunk and fighting with a jockey on the floor in my kitchen. "If you want to fight, do it outside!" I told them.

I once had two little kids, aged about twelve, knocking on my door for money Brian had apparently promised them some amount for working in the stables for him on the cheap (and to avoid paying proper staff). I chased the kids outside and told them that they should see Brian for their money. "Brian won't pay us!" they said. The next thing I know, they returned with their mothers. So, I paid the kids and told them not to come to the yard again. When I complained to Brian, he said he hadn't paid them because they hadn't worked hard enough.

I replied. "They are only little kids, Brian. They shouldn't even be in the stables." But that was Brian, tight as they come. Brian was sacked from his good job as a trainer for Classic Bloodstock after several warnings. He had valuable racehorses standing in their boxes on concrete without sufficient bedding. He was paid good money and promptly to ensure the well-being of the horses under his care. He did not do so and was not up to the job. It was my fault. I never should have given him the position in the first place.

It had really only taken a few weeks for me to realise what a dreadful mistake I had made in giving Brian the job as trainer for half the Classic Bloodstock plc horses. Brian was married to my favourite niece, and Tim's cousin, Marietta. But then I wanted both Brian and Marietta to get on in life. I really thought Brian had deserved his chance. He had told me that the excellent trainer, Mark Johnson had (he said) offered him the good job as his assistant, but Brian wanted to make his own mark. I could understand that. And, while Brian McMath couldn't provide me with any proof of his claims at that time, he said he would do so shortly, with other references. I never did see any!

It wasn't very long after that he came to Charnwood that we had a problem. My rose gardens were my pride and joy and, while I knew Charnwood horses would never probably hold a candle to that great 'Warren Place', trainer, Henry Cecil's horses, I thought I had a very good chance in the 'rose garden stakes', of which Henry's roses are claimed to be a priority in his life. Anyway, Brian's dogs were messing up my hallowed ground. The lawns and my rose beds. It upset me daily. Brian knew that I didn't want his dogs messing on my garden. The last incident was when I had some Classic shareholders around and a lady put her foot in it!

I told Brian firmly but fairly: "For the last time and tenth, keep your dogs off the rose garden lawns." That night, Brian called at the house with a bottle of whisky for me and a huge box of chocolates for Maureen. We both felt a bit uncomfortable, with Brian crying and wringing his cap in anguish. We thanked him, but I said that I would rather have a clean lawn. And it was true. For two days he succeeded. Then it was back to business (excuse the pun).

Everything was becoming very difficult. Maureen was upset because the horses had very little bedding and, sometimes, if Tim wasn't at the stables in the evening, the horses wouldn't have enough water to drink. But that wasn't such a problem as Maureen would do the buckets before nightfall. But the bedding was.

Once again, Brian came over to the house with chocolates for Maureen, wringing his cap with crocodile tears. A truly worthy Oscar winning performance. He told us he wanted some money for a private matter. He called it a loan. I called it money down the drain. But I warned Brian again. "Brian, you get top money at Charnwood for the horses. Where is it going to? You have no proper staff. No head lad and the horses are neglected."

He promised me faithfully "on his grave," (I'd heard that so many times before!) that everything would be in order within three weeks. It wasn't. It got worse - so bad at one time that Tim, his assistant trainer, bought straw for bedding out of his own pocket.

My nerves were shattered. I couldn't sack him. He knew that, because he had a year contract. I offered to pay him compensation to go. He refused. So I did the only thing I could do - try and make it work until his year was up.

Anyway, Tim did all he could to help me, even kow-towing to Brian's big ego. Then came an episode that finished the last of any hope. I had to make it work. "It was the straw that broke the camel's back" - probably, the only bit of straw in the stables.

Tim came in for breakfast and said: "*Charlie Big Time* is spot on Dad. I've never seen him better. Get your betting boots on, Dad. He is ready to win again."

Now, the previous year Tim had been working as close as he could with Gay Kelleway, learning all he could from her, and Gay won three times for me with Charlie and each time she had told me that Charlie was ready to win - and he did! Tim knew the secret. Despite what a lot of people have been led to believe, "Tim knows his horses." And that attention to detail puts a few trainers above others. Tim was happy that week. He had just won a good first in a big dog show with one of his Staffordshire Bull Terriers and also won best in show overall. It was a wonderful effort by him for mastering the perfection required to produce your dog spot-on for that day. (He did the same again in another show later that year).

As dog lovers, Maureen and I gave Tim our congratulations and cracked a bottle of champagne. Not that I needed any excuse for that. But there was little happiness in Charnwood, so we had something to celebrate. Tim then said: "Dad, I had Rob (our vet) do Charlie's Blood yesterday. It's as I suspected - perfect."

"Okay Tim, what did Brian say?" I asked.

"He just said that the blood tells you nothing."

"Right Tim. This is what we will do. I will go over to the stables and speak to Brian - not to undermine his opinion," I added.

So I spoke to Brian: "How has Charlie been doing?" I asked nonchalantly.

"He needs another three weeks to be ready," he replied.

"Tim thinks he's spot on," I replied very politely.

Brian replied with a nastiness that even I had never witnessed before. "Tim doesn't know what he's talking about!"

I kept cool and returned to the house.

The next morning, after going around the stables, Tim came in for breakfast. He was also responsible for feeding Charlie a special diet, so had obviously seen him again that morning.

"Dad, I'm telling you. Get your betting boots on, good and proper!" Now I know Tim had always placed a major emphasis on the blood tests, he could even read them himself, although they baffled me. But Charlie was telling Tim something else also.

"Okay Tim. I have Charlie entered in a race at the weekend." I told him. "I was just going to give him a run just to keep him loose."

"No Dad, you can't do that, given his present handicap mark and the way he is, he will win!"

"Okay son, what I have to do then is persuade Brian. It's his decision."

So I went over to the stables and spoke to Brian again.

"My word Brian, Charlie is a credit to you. I have never seen him better. You've done a fantastic job. Well done! I want him to run at the weekend." Then I turned and walked back into the house, without giving him the time to reply.

The day of the race Brian had two runners; one in the afternoon, owned by an owner and friend of his who had some kind of taxi business in London. (And likes a bet, I had heard) and Charlie who would run at the evening meeting. Brian called at the house at 7.30 a.m. and said I will saddle the horse at the afternoon meeting while Tim would saddle Charlie in the evening.

"Okay Brian," I said, "but try and make the evening meeting to watch him run." "You may have your first winner since coming to Charnwood," he replied. "The horse that is running this afternoon will win for sure."

"Okay Brian. But will you please tell your other owners for me that I will be backing Charlie."

"Aye," he replied.

Tim came in at breakfast happy that he was going to saddle Charlie for the race.

"Brian told me his horse will win this afternoon," I told him.

"Dad, its back is not right, it shouldn't run," I tried to explain to Brian, but he just walked away.

"Okay son, don't worry, I know how it is. Good luck tonight."

"Well, I want my money on Charlie," said Tim and gave me his wedge of £1,000 in £50 notes.

"Okay son, I will start putting it on with mine here and there during the course of the day." Tim's grand made me realise just how serious he was. I also knew that Tim would also back Charlie at the course and I suspected he would have his private punters on too. My first job was to put the horse out on my hotline for my clients.

In the afternoon, Brian's horse got well beat. But I thought that, if Brian had given his other owners my message regarding Charlie then, at least they would recover their losses. In fact, Brian told them not to back Charlie and stayed in London that evening, instead of coming to see Charlie race.

Tim knew Charlie so, for one and a half hours before the race, he had the lad out walking him. Charlie has rheumatism and the walking gets his joints working smoothly. In the saddling enclosure, Tim had no specific instructions for our jockey, Alan Mackay, "Alan knows Charlie's idiosyncrasies probably better than he knows his wifes," he joked.

Both Tim and Alan knew old Charlie was all fired-up and well-focused on the business in hand. Alan would coax Charlie to believe that he could, indeed, win this one. Once Charlie came out the stalls, he immediately got a couple of backhanders to show him he wasn't out for a picnic. Charlie was as fit as a flea and didn't want any more reminders. He was all set to "go like a bat out of hell." Well, not quite, but at least he would get a move on.

Alan Mackay, the pilot, was confident. Tim was confident. And me? I just prayed Charlie would draw from that confidence placed in him and deliver pennies from heaven. And yes! Backed from 10/1 down to 9/2, Charlie won easily.

After that, Brian and Tim's working relationship went further downhill in so much as Brian tried every trick in the book to discredit Tim to others who would listen. Thankfully, I suspect only idiots did. We shall see.

Today, I wonder whether Brian could have put the boot in with his "lies and wringing cap with crocodile tears' to the Jockey Club to prevent Tim from getting a permit to train. Nah! Could the steward be that bloody daft! Although I do wonder if it was McMath that put the boot in for Tim. If so, then he is a thoroughly unworthy person, but then I suspect that obviously doesn't count, particularly if you have friends who have the ear of the stewards at Portman Square.

Eventually, I got rid of "Life with Brian", although I had to cop him a few thousand quid. The best money I ever spent!

Tim would always try and get me winners to put on our race line, especially those on which I could tell my clients this is a strong bet. And, while I could give you so many instances of getting these big betting opportunities, I just want to give you here just one example of Tim's professionalism.

Tim knew about a horse in a claiming race at Southwell from a racing contact of his. He told me about it and so I put it on my tipping line. It was a filly called *Legally Delicious*. Tim said to me: "Dad, you know I would like to go to the Southwell racecourse and bid for this horse in the claimer. It will win today but will be favourite. And if we put four grand on her between us, the winnings will pay for the horse. I agreed and gave Tim half the bet - £2,000. The horse won very easily and Tim put his claim in. His was the only one. Jack Banks, the trainer who lost the horse came up to Tim and said: "I wish you all the bad luck in the world with that filly." Jack Banks shows his true colours with that remark; a nasty piece of goods. Banks is one of those jumped-up trainers who are bad for the sport.

Anyway, Tim gets the horse back to Charnwood and we found out that she was a cripple. In other words Tim had bought "a pig in a poke".

"Look Dad, don't worry, we'll sell the filly on," he told me.

"No-one will buy her, she can't walk, Tim," I replied.

"You're right, Dad, she can't walk - but she can run!" he answered. "And I'll do exactly as Banksy did with the filly, train her and feed her the same and find out everything I can about the filly."

Now, as I have said elsewhere, Tim has a lot of friends in racing. He got *Legally Delicious*' menu from a friend in Bank's yard. She was on a special diet. He got the vet to inject her knees with cortisone and, for three weeks, trained that filly as if she was walking on glass. He did everything that Banks had done. One of Tim's favourite sayings to me about horses is: "If it's not broken, don't try and fix it." And that's what his aim was with this filly.

Two weeks later, Tim said: "Right Dad, she is ready to win. Put her in the same claimer at the same race track in Southwell and at the same weight as when she won."

"Right Tim. Anything else?"

"Yes Dad. Get your betting boots polished. She'll be a certainty, I promise you." I looked at Maureen and jokingly said. "Well you heard him, lass. Get into the kitchen and polish my betting boots!"

The next day I went over to the office in the yard and our jockey, Alan Mackay was with Tim being shown the video of *Legally Delicious'* last race which was on the day Tim had bought her. "That's how you have to ride her," he told Alan. They went through the video together about four or five times. Then, Tim put Alan on the spot.

"Look Alan, when you come out of the saddling enclosure, don't go down to the start with the others. Go the long way round to the start and bring her round. If the stewards fine you, I will pay it." Tim looked at me quizzically. "Dad," he said. "When Banksy laid this filly out for a gamble, Jimmy Quinn rode her that day and it's exactly what he did. We mustn't change the winning formula."

I smiled to myself and told Tim I was going back to the house. "I want to make sure Maureen's polished those boots!" He knew the terminology as well as I. In the old days, your spare cash would be kept under the stairs in your riding boots (hence they became known as your betting boots).

The day of the race I put on my hotline that this filly was a very good bet. Tim and I also put our private punters on and decided we would also put on eight grand between us. One hour before the race, Tim gave Old Delicious an approved Jockey Club pain killer called 'None Bute', so the match is lit. Nothing left to chance, and Maureen's done a nice job on the boots!

Tim gave Alan his final instructions in the saddling ring. "Don't worry, Dad. If Alan does what I have told him, there's no danger. But as in all well-laid plans of mice and men, Alan blew it. Well not quite - the horse won, but only by a head. Upon dismounting, Alan's expression was grave.

"I came too soon," he said. "I should have waited."

"That's okay," replied Tim. "I know how it can be sometimes. At least she's won. (The third horse was ten lengths back). Now, unlike the time Tim claimed her with the only claim, there were eight claims that night. The gentleman who got the horse had Tim shaking him by the hand and explaining all the secrets of the filly. (That's the difference between Jeff Banks and Tim - Tim's a gentleman).

Anyway, the successful claimant said to Tim: "I thank you for all your kindness and, if you get your licence, you can count on two horses from me. As we all know, Tim never got that licence, although I know. with much sorrow, what a good trainer he would have made.

After Stuart Williams, my next trainer was Roger Harris who is currently in prison on a million pound drug rap for smuggling dope worth millions in a horse-box from Spain. Am I unlucky with trainers or what! The Jockey Club refused my son a licence to train, despite all the qualifications needed and the financial backing. His face didn't fit that's all. Perhaps he's too honest!

"I wouldn't want Tim to be associated with some of the racehorse trainers I know," I told him. "This business is full of sharks from top to bottom. The only saving grace is their disguise - a whistle and flute (suit)."

Now I want to give you a little story here showing how top trainers can make fools of themselves. And the unfortunate trainer I have picked on as an example falls on Ben Hanbury's shoulders this time. But, believe me, there are a lot more making fools of themselves than him. This is one of those little stories you cannot finger everyone, so to speak. So I will be gentle - well sort of!

Now our Ben trains a horse and the horse is useless, could not win a race even if it started ten minutes before the others. So Ben sends it to the sales because as a two year old colt, this horse could not run for toffee. I suspect that Ben thought this two year old was a sprinter and if it did not sprint (short trips, 5 or 6 furlongs), then Ben would give it the boot from his yard, as obviously the poor young nag had not lived up to Ben's expectations.

And our Ben has more expectations than Pip in Dicken's book, Great Expectations. Now, our Ben dresses like Arnold Palmer would at St Andrews. In fact, I have always suspected Ben's car boot was filled with iron. Well, a three, four, five and six iron and, possibly, a putter. But I can't confirm it as I have never had the pleasure of looking in Ben's car boot. But every time, I have seen Ben on the race course, or the gallops, or even at the sales, I have thought: "I bet he's got a nine iron somewhere on his person, or left it in his boot". Yes, just like a hole in one, you've got it in one. Ben dresses like a golfer!

Back to the horses. This horse *Indian Jockey* is a waste of space to Ben in his luxury Newmarket yard. Three times he has put him on the racecourse. Three times the horse shows nothing. Well, our Ben, being a pretty good trainer who looks like a golfer, makes a mistake.

Ben sends the horse to the Newmarket sales, obviously to also please the owner who must be feeling that feeding this two year old is like giving food to a muppet. I mean, our Ben knows his horses and this nag, *Indian Jockey* is useless. It clearly does not obviously strike our Ben that he should maybe give the horse a chance over a longer distance.

So the horse fetches buttons at the sales and the owner must now suffer more nightmares than I do. Because the lads who have now got this horse gave it a few trial spins over a mile and it proved it had ability.

Now, the next thing the new lads think is: "We need a bit of help. Who is the best man for the job?" Well, that was pretty obvious: Tim Dawson who, for his age, knows more about putting the bookies away than anyone. So the horse is brought to the trial gallops. Tim provides the ingredients to try and prove or disprove that the lads have indeed got one for a tilt at the ring. He puts our top work jockey, Paul Burke on my horse, *Environmentalist* who was in good form and is a fair four year old handicapper, while Alan Mackay is set to ride the three year old *Indian Jockey* over one mile, one furlong on the trial gallop.

On a Sunday morning, so early the birds are not even out of bed and the gallops are deserted. Not a tout (work watcher) in sight of the trial gallop. At full racing pace, Indian Jockey left Tim gob-smacked as *Environmentalist* was passed on a tight rein with Alan looking like he was riding a pretty decent horse. Anyway, the lads plan to run the horse in a selling race. But Alan and Tim said to them. "IF you do that, you could lose the horse. This horse is too good for a seller." But as I say, these lads were bent on landing a gamble. So the decision is made and the plan is that they will put Alan down to ride it at Nottingham the following Friday. But the lads are not from the local nut house, so when Alan asks them what the horse is called, they say: "Its name is *Fill yer Boots*. Well, thought Alan. Fair enough. At least , it's not one of those Arab named horses you can't pronounce."

So, when Alan looks in the paper at the selling race on Friday morning, he sees he is down for *Indian Jockey*. So the lads (rightly so), had tried a fast one to keep it quiet.

In any case, it was a good plan. But obviously Tim and I wanted a bit of the action because we had provided the tools as required. So a compromise was reached. I would not put the horse on my hotline until 11.45 a.m., thus allowing the lads to get a bit of their readies (money) on with early morning price bookmakers. I put the message that night before on my hotline: "Ring back tomorrow at, or after 11.45 a.m. for a hot one."

Clearly, later when I saw from my computer printout chart that, not only had my regular clients rung back, but half the bloody nation, I realised that obviously they, my clients, had passed my number on, en-route to work. From the engine driver, to Maggie in the coffee-shop to the girl at W.H. Smiths. In fact, I would damn well say to just about every Tom, Dick and Harry they talked to that morning.

But there were twenty-three runners in this race. "A bookmakers benefit race on paper."

Hell, the favourite is 5/1. But this little beauty is 7/1 and half the world is on it. But most, I suspect, like 'Coffee Shop Maggie' just put on a quid. Anyway, the horse wins on a tight rein by six wickets (six lengths) with the jockey pulling its back teeth out (stopping it winning by half the track). Now the lads with their pockets full of the bookies money had not listened to Tim and Alan's advice and so lost the horse at the ensuing selling auction to trainer, Martin Pipe for 7,500 guineas. I suspect he would have gone to 20,000 guineas.

Now, Martin Pipe is no fool. He knows a horse's potential when he sees one. And this horse, Indian Jockey goes on and wins more races for Pipey than I have had Ruby Murray's (curries) at my local Bombay Curry House.

If the previous Ben Hanbury's owner had stabbed himself for every race the horse went and won, he would have more holes than a pin cushion. So the moral of this story might be: "Do not give a horse to Ben Hanbury to train." Actually, it is not, because our Ben is a pretty good trainer, whatever you may think..

The true moral to this story is: If your horse is useless at sprint distance, give your trainer a gentle nudge and say: "Give it a go over a longer distance. There's a good chap. I paid for it so far, so one more try won't matter. And then we may not make such bloody fools of ourselves."

Here's another little story you might find interesting. Colin Williams trained three two year old horses for me in his stables. They weren't much good as they were bred to be three years olds. I knew Colin would always do his best for me if he had the right horses, but he very much appreciated the support I gave him.

Anyway, one evening there was a knock on my door. It was Colin and he had called around to tell me he would have a winner the following day and I could have a big bet. It had no form and would be at big odds.

I had a couple of Scotches with Colin and his parting words were: "No danger tomorrow, Ronnie, it's a cert." I slept well that night dreaming of pound notes. Next morning, to my surprise, Colin was on my doorstep again, very agitated.

"Bloody blacksmith has plated the horse with racing shoes and pricked his foot. The horse is lame!"

"That's bad luck, Colin," I said. "Never mind, there's always another day."

"No, there isn't," he replied. "The horse is going back to Ireland next week. I will just have to run him lame."

"Hell Colin, we can't bet on him now on three legs."

"For one year I have been patiently getting this horse ready," he replied. "He would have won half the track fully sound. Now he will still win, but not as easy." That remark stopped me in my tracks. Hell, before he went lame, this horse must have been the biggest certainty to look through a bridle.

"Best of luck today, Colin," I told him. "But I will halve my bet!"

The horse won at a canter at the good price of 20/1. "That's my boy!"

Trainer Stuart Williams
Told lies over a minor issue
to the Jockey Club investigator,
to blacken my name, I suspect.

Bob Champion
Classic Bloodstock PLC II Trainer,
despite The Sunday Peoples
attempt to lead it's readers to think
otherwise

My lovely wife and step daughter, Kate, on our wedding day in Mombassa, Africa January 20th 1995

Our Wedding Reception, with my Best Man Ray, my Mum, our bridesmade Renata and my stepdaughterKate.

Cutting the Wedding Cake full of happiness and joy

The yacht that took us for
a trip on the Indian Ocean

In the Hotel gardens with my wife,
and her daughter Kate,

Sailing down to Mombassa with the 'Cameroon Boys' to our 'plane for Nairobi

Tvasa National Park, where we met up with my Mum, World Wide Elsie, after our Safari Honeymoon

At Dinner with my Mum and our Bridesmaid Renata, at Their Safari Lodge, in Tvasa National Park, Kenya

On our honeymoon Safari
in Kenya, Africa, 1995

In my wheelchair in 1995,
after our return from Africa,
with Maureens Mother, Joan,
who died so unexpectedly
later that year,
and Maureens Dad,
Bob Hacking,
ex Blackburn Rovers footballer

CHAPTER TWENTY

I was happily married to Maureen in Kenya on her birthday, the 20th January, 1995, at the Serena Beach Hotel. Afterwards, we sailed down to Mombassa for a wedding breakfast with my sailing friends, the Cameroon boys. We left here via small plane to our honeymoon destination on the Maasai Mara Game Reserve; a luxury lodge deep into Kenya.

Finally, a week later, we travelled overland on safari to Tvasa East National Park, where we met up with 'worldwide Elsie', my mother (she is 82 now and has just returned from a holiday in Australia) - she gets around a bit, hence her nickname! She also came to Kenya for our wedding. Our bridesmaid, Kate, my step-daughter, and Renata our bridesmaid, met up with us also at Tvasa.

Naturally, we had a wonderful time and saw some fantastic sights. We were back in England in February ready for the launch of plc11 on the 26th of the month but few days later I was in hospital fighting a serious illness. When I went to Africa I took a chance with my Systemic Lupus. Because of this, there were certain injections I couldn't have and I caught some sort of tropical disease, maybe just caused by an mosquito bite. The doctors couldn't identify what I had contracted. They never could, all they did was give it a number.

I was drifting in and out of consciousness in dreadful pain. My kidneys had packed in, my arm was full of poison and I had a dangerous blood clot in a bad place. I was not well at all and, during this time, plc 11 was being launched. When I was finally semi-recovered, I discharged myself from hospital, although I was still ill. By late March, I had bad angina and constant kidney infections. Maureen got me out of Charnwood before the stress killed me and we flew to Spain for a bit of peace and quiet.

It was fine but I was still not feeling well, so we flew back to England to Papworth Heart Hospital, Huntingdon where I managed to get a angloplatsy. I was subsequently transferred to Addenbrooks Hospital in Cambridge for a kidney biopsy to see what damage had been caused by my Lupus and the effect of the tropical disease. I had also contracted salmonella so was placed in an isolation ward. Things were not going my way!

When I had my biopsy for some unknown reason, (such as the long needle scoop slipping when a kidney sample was taken ...), something caused me to slip three discs. I was in agony and when I discharged myself from hospital earlier than was sensible, I could hardly stand. But I had had enough of hospitals.

Unfortunately for me though, I got progressively worse. In the end, I was in a wheelchair and on a very high dose of morphine which was a relief for my pain. During this time, Tim was handling my betting business and our first big hit that season was a loser. I couldn't walk and the stress of Charnwood Stables and Classic Bloodstock and the constant harassment by the press saw me and Maureen, once again, off to Spain.

It was arranged that Tim would take care of the business and he was also made a director of Classic Bloodstock later that year so that he could do my job. This was essentially looking after the shareholders, showing them around the stables and meeting them at the racecourse when we had runners. It was a thankless, unpaid task. But my son did it well and the majority of shareholders appreciated this and he was warmly received at all times - except, of course, by those foolish newspaper hacks.

Whilst we were in Spain, we bought a modest, but lovely villa with sweeping panoramic views of the sea and mountains behind. We paid just £95,000 for it although, strangely enough, just three years later, The

News of the World reckoned it was worth closer to a £1 million.

Meanwhile, on the betting front and on our behalf, Tim had three mega hits, and overseas punters were on each time. Beautiful, just beautiful! With that sort of news (not to mention the morphine!), I was on cloud nine. But very bad news indeed was just around the corner. Maureen's much loved mother, Joan, went into hospital for a routine female operation, but there were serious complications. We both flew back to Maureen's home in Southport. I was in the wheelchair, Maureen had pushed me all over Spain - and she was still pushing. At the hospital we received the dreadful news, Maureen's Mum was dying of ovarian cancer and had as little as ten to twelve weeks left. I was shocked while Maureen was, naturally, devastated. It had come out of the blue.

Maureen's Mum wanted to go home to die, but obviously her daughter couldn't take care of both her mother and me, so I returned to Spain alone. I couldn't face my main home, Charnwood, without Maureen. While we had been waiting for our Spanish property purchase to go through, we had rented a penthouse flat overlooking the sea in Calpe. My mother flew out to help me cope and we both stayed there in the meantime.

After a few weeks, Maureen flew back to relieve my Mum for a spell as the doctors had told her that her mother still had some time left. The plan was to stay a week before returning to her mother. Maureen was with me just three days when she received a call from her brother, Graham. Her mother had died peacefully in her sleep.

To express how sad I was for my dear wife are words I can't find. I cried for Maureen for I knew, as an only daughter, just how close she had always been to her mother. So, back to England Maureen went, alone this time. I was of no use. The only bit of good news at that time was when I received a date for being admitted to hospital for my operation. But it didn't mean much to me right then.

My operation was partially successful. I was very, very sore and had to be given large doses of morphine by injection while in hospital. Once discharged, I was on crutches for months. But the main agony had gone, all that remained was to be weaned off the morphine which could take many months. Ultimately, it took one year to be off it completely. And a further operation to shrink a disc some time later, again in hospital.

Needless to say, we had an unhappy Christmas. Maureen was still in shock, losing her mother so suddenly. I was regaining my strength however, although I knew I would never be really well again. 1995 was not a vintage happy family year, but four winners from six big bets was satisfactory on that front, at least.

That following January I made plans for my last holiday; after which I intended to stay put forever in my new much loved home in Spain. But first the 'holiday'. 1996 was to prove to be full of surprises.

We had decided before we went away to have our villa modernised, including a couple of extensions built and the garden landscaped. And we had no intention of being there whilst this was being done. Now let Ronnie Dawson, explater and 'Jack the lad' take you on a little trip. I was owed a bit of money by a guy who had been on my books for years. The problem was he had legged it to Miami. He wasn't dodging me, but he was dodging someone. Anyway, he wanted to pay his dues, or so he said. But I would have to fly out there and collect. It's a long way to go to find someone not at home. Anyway, I wanted to give Maureen a break to help take her mind off past events (and current ones in England for that matter). So we flew from Alicante to Madrid to London and from there to Florida for a few weeks holiday. Miami's just down the road, so to speak - a few hundred miles, but the right country.

Well I had a punter, I had known this guy for thirty years and some of his family years before then. They were as poor as church mice. But somewhere in life, this guy got a leg up, ending up in the North Sea oil business. He likes a bet - don't they all? And puts his pad at our disposal at Kissemee in Florida. I always ring him when I have a good bet. He settled his dues promptly and has always told me his pad is available to me if I ever went to Florida.

When Maureen and I arrived at Orlando Airport, a limo was waiting for us. It had a TV and a bar. We soon saw that this lad had had more than a leg up in life - he'd struck oil because the 'pad' was a magnificent place, indoor and outside swimming pool, six bedrooms, six bathrooms - the business. We were met by the housekeeper and chose the bedroom with the water bed (I don't recommend them). Joking, I said to Maureen. "Cor, how the other half live! I must remember to put his odds up when I get home." ('odds up' i.e. pay more for racing information).

"Okay, well they only lived in a scruffy old council house when he was a kid, but the lad's hit the big time nowadays."

We went to Disneyland, Seaworld and the Kennedy Space Centre .... But I was itching to move on to Miami but just couldn't get this bloke to answer his phone. Every day I tried to get through. Finally, on the seventh day he answered. "Surprise, surprise," I say. "It's me, Ronnie Dawson and I'm only down the road."

He was ecstatic. "Get down here! I'll book you into The Shelbourne Hotel, it's in art-deco in downtown Miami. You'll love it."

"Great!" I replied. "But have you got my readies (money)?".

"Sure have, man,"

"Okay, I'll be there tomorrow, book me into The Shelbourne." I told Maureen the plan and to start packing. We're off!

I then had the idea to go down to Lake Tahoe and get this fellow with his seaplane to fly us down to Miami as I knew it was for hire and it was something neither of us had done before.

So, we go to the lake, no problem. This is a good trip for the pilot. We strike a deal. 10 a.m. tomorrow morning. He's got to charge a bit extra because he was coming back alone while we planned to get a scheduled flight back to Orlando, once my business with the dodger was completed.

"Look Maureen, leave the kitchen sink and pack light for this trip." I usually have a large hold-all for holidays, Maureen usually has three or four large suitcases. Anyway, to get on with the story, the Seaplane is a bit ropy, very noisy but gets off the lake okay. As we are flying over it, the pilot points to alligators basking on the banks in the morning sun. Definitely not a good place to run out of petrol. But it was a good trip, overall. We can only communicate with the pilot through our head phones. I thought of John Wayne in the film, Flying Seas Bees. Eat your heart out, there's a new kid on the block.

Eventually, we arrive in Miami and there's a place for docking sea planes. We say goodbye and thanks to our pilot. Fifteen minutes later, we've arrived at the Sherbourne via taxi. There's a bit of building work still going on inside the place. I'm suddenly concerned that we may not be expected. I go up to the desk. Yes, we are expected and, furthermore, can order anything we want. Apparently, the Dodger is picking up the full tab. We settle in and try and get hold of him on the phone to just say that we have arrived. No joy. After two days, I'm getting worried.

"We'll give it another day and if there is still no joy then we'll just fly back to Orlando." I told Maureen. At the same time, we were enjoying Miami, it was great, especially the art-deco quarter. Then my room phone rings. It's the man himself. Apparently, he's in the foyer and asks if he can come up. The door opens and there he is - a big guy (I don't know why I keep referring to him as the Dodger, naturally it's not his real name!).

Hugs all round. Maureen's impressed. After fifteen years of giving this guy racing tips, it's the first time we've actually met. I poured out two large Bourbons to make us feel at home. There follows the usual small talk about business, family, the weather back in England. What does he think of the ole U.S.A., etc. There is no mention of my readies. Then, with a big grin he hands me a fat envelope. "Dollars," he said. "No pounds."

Hell, I wasn't bothered if it was French francs. I wasn't sure I would ever get my dues. Then, when we were on our second Bourbon, he came out with a beauty.

"How would you and Maureen like a free mini-cruise to the Bahamas, Nassau in fact?"

"Well, I wouldn't mind." I replied honestly. "What's the score?" I wasn't really concentrating, my mind was on how much was in that envelope he had just given me.

"Look Ron, I need a favour. You get a cruise. It leaves the day after tomorrow. I will also give you $2,000 and all you have to do is deliver a shoe-box package to an address in Nassau. The ship docks there for a whole day while tourists sightsee."

It had to be drugs I reasoned, my mind racing and told him as much.

"Ron, " he replied. "I've always been straight with you. I promise you it's not drugs." He was telling the truth. It was my gut feeling. To myself, I muttered "$2,000..."

"Listen, okay I will pay you $3,000," he said. (Dodger seemed desperate) Hell, I had already made my mind up. I would have done it for a $2,000 pay day, and a free cruise; life is full of surprises.

Anyway, to get on with my story, my instructions are to collect the package off him at reception in the morning. He told me that it must never be out of my sight until it was delivered; that was his only condition.

"No problem," I replied sincerely.

The cruise left from Palm Beach the next day, up the coast and, furthermore, he wanted us out of the Sherbourne that day. Apparently, he would book us into a hotel on Singer Island near Palm Beach which was our supposed departure point. Maureen then threw a wobbly. She had just remembered that she has packed light. Like all women in life going on a cruise, she wants to look the part. Dodger can see there's a problem brewing.

"Look Maureen," he said. "There's a boutique on Collins Avenue called 'Shelly's'. Just go there, pick out a few things. It's down to me. I'll arrange it, no problem." I thought this guy must have robbed a bank or something. He was definitely into a bit of heavy money.

Anyway, Maureen's happy. I'm happy and Dodger, well he looks very pleased with himself. The next morning at noon I picked up the package from Dodger in reception. He had it in a hold-all. He opened it up and showed me the box inside. It was well taped up. It looked a pretty big shoe-box to me, must have belonged to someone with a size 12 foot. Next, he handed me our cruise ticket and the envelope with the $3,000. A firm handshake and the parting words: "Got yer an outside cabin. Enjoy the trip."

Maureen's got her new gear from Shelly's. I've got two envelopes full of dollars. The one containing my dues, by far the biggest. Then it's a taxi to Singer Island which is about an hour's drive. The only problem was that the cruise was leaving from Fort Lauderdale not Palm Beach which we found out just in time. I looked at the tickets Dodger has slipped us for the cruise.

"Maureen, look at this? The ships called 'The Fantasy'." Aptly named at the moment, I thought. As it turned out, it was a beautiful new cruise ship owned by the Carnival Lines. We had the most romantic cruise anyone could wish for and the food was superb. No doubt about it, this cruise was the business. We loved it.

When we got off at Nassau, I felt a bit conspicuous with the big hold-all. But there was no customs so I felt easier. We had gone through customs a little apprehensively when we boarded the boat and when we embarked back at Fort Lauderdale, we would again. But that wouldn't be a problem as I wouldn't have the hold-all then.

To spare you all the details. In Nassau, I found the address very easily. It was a boutique. A Shelly's again. I went inside while Maureen stayed outside. I was obviously expected. Three guys and two girls in the shop. I asked for Moses, the guy came forward, took the hold-all into a back room and told me to stay put, while the other two blokes stayed with me. A few minutes later, he came out, beaming like a Cheshire cat. Thanked me profusely. "Nice one, man, nice one." Whatever that means and, believe it or not, slips me an envelope from behind the counter. I just know it's money. I wasn't expecting anything more. Of course, I took it. If it's a mistake I will be back on the boat. "Forget the sightseeing, Maureen," I said. "We'll leg it back on board, quick like."

Back on the Fantasy, safe and sound, I count the money - $2,000, it's a bonus I hadn't expected. I never did learn what was in that box, none of my business, but I was curious. We had an appropriately eventful cruise home. I've always enjoyed playing a little roulette. True, it can be boring but I like it because if you can concentrate for a few hours you can really make a bit of money. I have this system and have found that it works best when you are playing three tables simultaneously with two other players in your team. On this particular ship there were only two tables in the casino, so Maureen played one while I played the other. After four hours, my table was level, but Maureen had won $600. We had

had enough, it's hard work, so turned in to our outside cabin and we had a few drinks watching the lights of Nassau fade as we steamed away back to Fort Lauderdale.

All that week, we had both eaten too much and by this time I was dying for something down to earth like beans on toast. Eventually we were back in our Florida base where we had two options. We had been away from home for nearly three weeks and it had been an unexpected adventure. I was still on my morphine but managing with a low dose.

"Let's blow the money!" I told Maureen. "After all, we got it for nothing and we deserve to, after everything we went through last year. Money is for enjoying, it's life. Let's fly!"

Needless to say, Maureen readily agreed. The next thing to decide was where we would go. I wanted to see Georgia as I love history, especially the American Civil War, while Maureen was keen to see Los Angeles. We compromised. I had always fancied a train journey on Amtrak, the American railway. So, from downtown Kissimee, we caught the train to Savanna in Georgia, changing at Jacksonville. The train connection was four hours late so, by the time we reached Savannah, it was nearly midnight. Luckily, our hotel had been booked in advance by Amtrak. I enjoyed Savannah very much and we did a lot of sightseeing. I particularly appreciated the American Civil War Museum and the beautiful old colonial style homes.

But it was time to move on and, before we knew it, we were back at our base in Kissemee and it was time for Maureen's choice - Los Angeles. It was a long flight and we had to go via Atlanta. Thankfully, we managed to sleep a bit. We finally landed safely and went straight to the hotel we had booked - The Beverly Hills Hilton. Why not? Film star, Eddie Murphy did! And I will tell you something else as well. I nicked a dressing gown with its gold motif: "Beverly Hills Hilton" just like Eddie Murphy did in Beverly Hills Cops. To my mind, they charge enough anyway to cover the cost of a dressing gown.

We went shopping on the famous Rodeo Drive. I only bought a $100 tie, Maureen a Gucci scarf for $200. The prices were frightening. We did the Hollywood Universal Studios tour which Maureen enjoyed. This was real Hollywood at last. However, to cut a long story short, overall we really didn't like Los Angeles too much and three days later left for San Francisco. We booked in at the Fairmont Hotel on Nobb Hill. It was the hotel used in the film and TV series, 'Hotel'. We liked San Francisco. We took the boat over to Alcatraz prison on the rock. I thought of past inmates like Al Capone. Sims of 'The Life' also crossed my mind. Sims probably had visions of me being locked up somewhere like this. I also enjoyed the boat trip back to the real world.

The next trip was over the spectacular Golden Gate Bridge. Apparently, nine men died building it. Maureen and I were truly enjoying ourselves. That awful year, 1995 seemed a long way behind us. I decided that, although I liked the parts of America I had seen, the good ole USA wasn't my cup of tea for a long stay and that, in another two weeks or so, I would be ready to go home. In the meantime, where to next?

I knew a guy living in Vancouver, Canada. We had always kept in touch, ever since I had first put him up in my flat some twenty years previously when he came over for a holiday and couldn't find accommodation because it was the week of the horse sales. All my family have a long tradition of helping out others. It's in our blood, I suppose. My Granddad once took in a young chap called Abe Acton who he found hungry and homeless in Barrow. That same young lad went off to the 1914-18 war and was killed in action winning the Victoria Cross. Private Abraham Acton VC. Although he was no relation, my father always spoke of him with pride. Abraham's letters of the war he sent home to his real parents but my family have some copies. They are so heartbreaking. He was a true hero of the country.

Yet another true hero was my wife Maureens great uncle The Reverend Arthur Proctor V.C. He won his illustrious medal for "Bravery beyond the call of duty" in the Great War 1914-18 whilst serving on the Western Front. But unlike Abe Acton, the Reverend survived the war. He now lies in Exeter Cathedral.

Back to the story.

So Thomas, my punter, had come to Newmarket every few years for the July meeting or the Houghton Sales. I didn't have his address but I did have a phone number in my dues book. Anyway, we got a flight and booked in at the Waterfront Hotel, but I couldn't get a reply from his number. That night, Maureen and I dined in Vancouver city's revolving restaurant. The view was stunning. The next day, I tried the number again. A woman answered and told me that my friend, Thomas, was up at the Whistler Ski Resort. She gave me the phone number.

"Listen Maureen," I told her. "I'll just ring him up and say we are in Canada and see what he says. I don't want to intrude." So I rang Thomas and got through the first time.

"Surprise, surprise, it's Ronnie Dawson," I told him. "I'm in Canada."

Well, of course, Canada is a pretty big place and I could have been 2,000 miles away.

"Exactly whereabouts are you, Ronnie?"

"I'm at the Waterfront Hotel in Vancouver."

"Great! Can you get up here to Whistler?"

"I've got my wife with me, Maureen."

"Well, that's even better," Thomas replied. "I always did want to meet her."

"Okay then, Thomas. How do I get to this place, Whistler?"

"At 6 0-clock every morning there's a train which comes from downtown Vancouver. It takes about two hours. It'll be packed with skiers, but you'll get on. I will be there at Whistler Station to meet you. Check out of the Waterfront Hotel and stay up here with us for as long as you like."

So we checked out of the Waterfront very early the next morning. That train journey up to Whistler was truly memorable. Dawn was just breaking as we left Vancouver Station. I had managed to persuade Maureen to take just one case. She couldn't turn up looking like she's packed for six months and the hotel was happy to look after her luggage.

The views were spectacular. The rivers were full of dead salmon after spawning with scores of bald eagles everywhere, feasting on the fish.

Thomas was there to meet us. We had a terrific visit getting happily merry on Jack Daniels and exchanging stories. We stayed in a guest room of Thomas' very pleasant ski lodge. In all, we were a group of ten. They were all friendly and warm people which was just as well as outside, it was freezing cold. But after a few days, my joint pains were flaring up. I needed sunshine. We decided that we would have one last visit somewhere, then return home. But where? Thomas and his party discussed it with us and the general consensus was Hawaii. Apparently you could get a direct flight from Vancouver.

We said goodbye to our host and realised that we would probably never meet again. Two days later we were ensconced in the Hyatt Twin Towers Hotel on Wakiki Beach, Hawaii. It was beautiful, warm, friendly - terrific in every way and we gave the place our best shot. Personally, I found the highlight was, of course, Pearl Harbour. As I mentioned earlier, I love war history. Maureen's best day was watching the World Surfing Championships which was on at the time. Then, in the evenings, the Kilavea volcano was spewing red hot lava. It was truly spectacular scenery.

But ultimately, I was ready for home - and Spain. I had no desire to return to England. There were no direct flights available at such short notice, so the journey took us two nights and a day. The long way home. Finally, we arrived in Spain, exhausted but happy.

Back to backing winners in 1997, with the flat season only weeks away and beckoning me. My adventure was over. That was my last one. Never again. These days, two hours on a plane back and forth to England is about my limit. You wouldn't get me further if you paid me. But I believe money is for enjoying life, if you are lucky enough to make it. And, more importantly, make it from something you enjoy doing. Mine is tipping winners. Good 'n it!

Spain 1996, ready to leave for America to collect my 'dues' from the 'Dodger'

Miami 1995

Ron at Kennedy Space
Centre, Florida

**Maureen in the
limo' sent to pick us up at
Orlando Airport
by my oil punter**

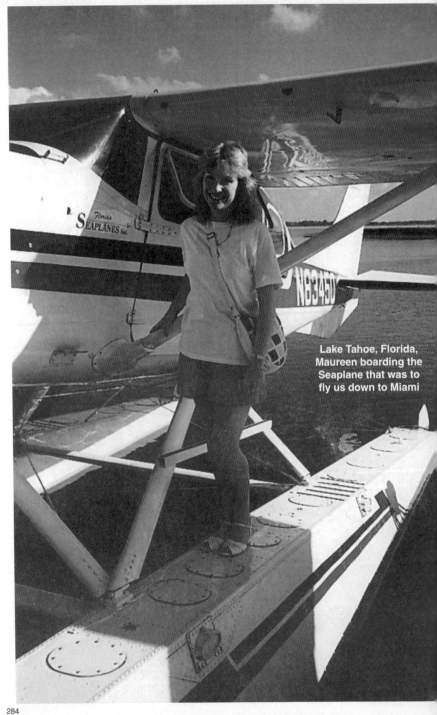

Lake Tahoe, Florida, Maureen boarding the Seaplane that was to fly us down to Miami

The Shelbourn Hotel, Miami, where we met the 'Dodger' who is now in prison for 18 years.

Ronnie Dawson leaving the 'Fantasy' in Nassau to deliver the package for Dodger

THE Shelborne BEACH HOTEL

OCEANFRONT ON MIAMI BEACH

Where the world ... Miami Beach...

FANTASY

Our Hotel on Nob Hill, San Francisco, used for the film and T.V. series 'Hotel'.
We could see Alcatraz from our bedroom window.

Alcatraz Prison, San Francisco, 1996.
I think Sporting Life reporter Sim's wishes I was a resident there

Ron nd Maureen under the
American Flag
at Pearl Harbour

Maureen up at Whistler Ski
Resort in Canada, as a guest
of my punter Thomas

CHAPTER TWENTY-ONE

The year, 1996, had truly been a happy one although, later that year, saw me back in hospital. But it was the following year - 1997, that was to bring myself and my family much heartache. The reason I am including this episode of my life is primarily as a warning to others. I now know that they could so very easily fall foul of the system and be thrown into a pit of vipers who are there to legally inject their poison (i.e. bankruptcy) at the behest of the Department of Trade and Industry (DTI)

I smugly never imagined that this could ever happen to me but, all too soon, I was brought down-to-earth with a shattering experience that will stay with me forever. More to the point, is that I saw first-hand the true light of our so-called establishment, namely that their reputed 'fine principles are, in fact, heartless and indifferent and the only thing they have in mind is an overriding lust for money; in this case - my money.

Let me backtrack a little and start at the beginning. In the summer of 1996, my brother Rick and I had a visit from the VAT inspector, Mr. Nash. We have never minded these visits because, at least when they were over, my books were tidied up somewhat. But this particular encounter was to prove a bombshell.

Apparently, the Customs and Excise Department had decided that all subscriptions to a so-called racing club would be liable for VAT I could go along with that, I decided, if that was the law. Far worse than this was the fact that this decision was to be backdated two years which meant that I was going to be forced to pay VAT on subscriptions for this entire additional period (1994-5). I protested to Mr Nash. "Why was I not informed?" If I had been, I would have made allowances and put a percentage of the membership subscriptions to one side. "Why had it taken two years, without one letter to inform me of this ruling. And why had I not had a VAT visit by Mr Nash for nearly two years in order to inform me of my position?

Mr Nash's response was to blame the government for cut-backs. "We have had to cut back our visits," he told me gravely. Obviously, I felt bitter. I had to find £67,000 out of the blue immediately. I didn't have it, although I did have my assets, of course, which were worth over £1 million. I really didn't think that it was any big deal. I was so naive! Me, the old shrewdie, the supposed smart arse who relied on the advice of his legal advisor, instead of his more reliable gut feeling.

Anyway, the gist of it was that the VAT wanted their money. I think I had a very strong case against the VAT and wanted to take this case to the tribunal court. To his credit, even Mr. Nash thought I had a valid argument due to the lack of information provided by the Customs and Excise Department and the gap of two years before that fateful VAT inspector's visit. But, to be fair, previously in 1995, Mr Nash had told me that a ruling would be forthcoming.

When it apparently was not, I wrongly assumed that the racing club was not subject to VAT and, furthermore, as I explained to Nash, all the major racing clubs who were advertising in the press for members were not advertising the fact that subscriptions were liable for VAT

As I have said, I thought the best move would be to fight the case at a VAT tribunal. I had already won one of those types of cases against Customs and Excise in 1992, so knew how fairly they were conducted. However, to my dismay, my accountant, Mr Irish of Stephenson and Davies told me he had taken advice on the matter and that we would not only lose the case, but that we would also incur additional costs.

To say I found this puzzling is an understatement. Up until this point, both my brother, Richard (who was my manager and bookkeeper) and myself felt we had a strong case. But, back then, I highly respected my financial advisor, Mr. Irish. My wife, Maureen, also had the utmost confidence in him. Indeed, on two previous occasions we had flown him out to Spain to discuss our finances. I truly believed that he was highly efficient at his job.

It seems like he suffered from short arms and deep pockets. But Maureen and I thought that, if he is tight with his own money, he will be the same with ours! At the same time, Maureen and myself were the opposite - over-generous. I was always the first to put my hand in my pocket, it's just way I am.

Andy amazed us on several occasions. One time, I remember that we flew him to Spain. As always, our hospitality was top-class and Andy never once had to open his wallet. I used to say to Maureen that it was stapled to his jacket! (She would reply that, as she had never seen it, she couldn't comment!).

Anyway, on with my story. The VAT wanted their money. I was in Spain and the bailiffs put a writ for bankruptcy through the letter-box of an empty house on my estate. Hence I was not aware of the summons until it was too late. The case came to court undefended and the irons were put on me.

Meanwhile, Mr. Irish had transferred my main property, Charnwood, into a trust for inheritance tax avoidance. In the meantime, I had paid the last £50,000 I had to the Nat West Bank in Newmarket to clear the remaining mortgage on the complex. I had bought the stables freehold in 1990 for £325,000 and spent £400,000 on improvements so, by this time, it was a valuable asset. But I didn't need it. It was a monument to my tenacity at a time. I wanted to prove I could do something. Now, it is surplus to my requirements in life.

What I should have done or, rather, what my legal advisor, Mr. Irish should have told me to do, was to pay that fifty grand to the VAT He didn't. He advised me to pay-off my stables so that the deeds could then be placed offshore. If Andy gave Maureen and I any advice, we took it as gospel. Neither of us really understood or appreciated the complexity of business finance. My only gift is that I can make money - not handle it carefully,

Meanwhile, costs were rising and, to make matters worse, they had frozen the money belonging to the 852 investors of Classic Gold. They said that they could do this as I had opened the account in the name of R. Dawson - Classic Gold, which was true. But, as I pointed out, not one penny of that money belonged to me and my only concern was the well-being of the Classic Gold horses. They had to be fed and looked after.

This plea fell on deaf ears. Compassion was not a part of the official receiver and his solicitors. All they seemed to care about was money! So I arranged a meeting with the O.R., Mr. Chris Nutting of K.P.M.G. and flew to England. I had previously made a full and clear disclosure of all my assets which totalled around £1.3 million at that time. I offered at once my deeds from Charnwood which more than covered my debts and arranged for them to be delivered to Mr. Paul Bromfield of the renowned solicitor's firm, Hammond Suddard who were the official receivers' solicitors. Mr. Bromfield assured me at that meeting that, once they were in possession of the deeds, they would have no further interests in the money (i.e. the £19,000 belonging to Classic Gold). This made good sense to me as it would to anyone.

I, therefore, arranged for Mr. Bromfield to be sent the deeds for Charnwood which, at the time of writing, he has in his possession.

"Paul, please keep to your promise and release the money for the welfare of the horses. You know full-well that it is not mine," I pleaded. He wouldn't. I call it deceit. He calls it, "In pursuant to Section 284 of the Insolvency Act, 1986."

Conveniently, he now categorically states that he never told me he would in the first place and has pointed out that he had a legal duty to the official receiver to retain these funds. For four long months, he tried every trick in the book to try and prove that some of the Classic Gold money belonged to me. I had apparently committed a breach of the bankruptcy rules and they were entitled to freeze all the money! It's so pathetic, it beggars belief.

"But Paul, "I told him. "You don't need to do that, you've got the deeds for Charnwood," I told him. "What about the welfare of the horses?" I thought he was going to reply: "Give them cake," like Marie-Antoinette!

So now I hope you understand the true situation, dear reader, for the same could befall you some day, as it could anyone. The official receiver and its appointed solicitors owe a duty to the creditors. The bigger the creditors, the more money they make. To my mind, their only interest in you is to try and find more debt so they can make more money from you and, furthermore, they apparently can do this with the full blessing of the DTI They have no concern for any personal feelings. They can latch on like leeches and bleed you of as much blood as they are legally allowed. Only now am I becoming aware of the misery of thousands of families in a similar position.

I know I am more fortunate than most as I have the assets to more than cover my liabilities which is just as well as the official receiver cannot sell your property for under its market value. But I think of all those poor families who are devastated for reasons they have no control over. Like those truck drivers who were forced into bankruptcy because of the French lorry driver strike and its ensuing blockage of British trucks. For me, in the case of anyone making money from this imposed misery, and to feed from it would make me vomit!

My family solicitor was surprised, to say the least, when he found out that Mr. Irish, my financial advisor, thought bankruptcy would be to my benefit. Believe me when I say that your family solicitor is the one person you should listen to. For thirty years, he has acted for me. Oh, why did I not ask and take his advice before it was too late. My solicitor, Melvin Skelton of Bendell and Sons is of the old school: solid, reliable, honest and a credit to his profession.

To my disadvantage I allowed myself to be manipulated by my accountant Andy Irish. Due to my illnesses, I spent much of 1995 and part of 1996 in great pain, which meant I was taking many drugs, including high doses of morphine, (which took a while to get free from) I state this not so much as a defence, but more as an explanation as to how Mr. Irish could be able to use my condition for his own advantage.

Andy Irish would visit me, either in my hospital bed, or later at Charnwood Stables or in Spain, to present papers for signing, even getting me to sign a complete chequebook of blank cheques, now I know that we are told never to give someone a blank cheque, but when your own accountant asks you to do so, to keep the businesses running, you have to be in far better health than I was to refuse. I accept that he had been my choice of accountant, and with my then business outlook, his high flyer manner was attractive, but when he got control of my affairs, his schemes brought me to near destitution.

In 1995, when Andy wanted to take his mistress to America on an all expenses paid jaunt, to buy "cheap" racehorses for Classic Bloodstock PLC II, I should have said no. But to my disgrace I allowed him to go, signing his pre-prepared letters of authority that he presented. When you dance with the devil, it's not surprising when he starts calling the tune. Looking back now I am ashamed that I did not stand up against his abuse of shareholders money on that and other occassions, but hindsight is always perfect, and again in retrospect I have paid for his devious ways and my compliance with them.

Take the instance when I 'sold' my racing addresses list to Classic Bloodstock PLC II in an endeavour to save it from collapse. In theory I got £100,000 (in shares) for the list, but in practice I paid the capital gains tax for shares which have no value. Sure if the company had gone as planned, they would have seen me a return, but the fact remains that I paid the government to give away my mailing list, on Mr. Irish's advice, and he even confiscated a cheque for £35,000 that I received for the sale of some of my racehorses, to pay the tax due to the government.

During those days I was too ill to make decisions, certainly the launch of PLC II should have been delayed until I was fit enough to resume control of the day to day affairs of the companies, but I trusted Mr. Irish to take control of my affairs. People like me tend to trust high paid, educated professionals, at least until you realise that some of them are just smooth financial predators, seeking to devour those they may. Why do the most dangerous and devious people always appear to be the most respectable and righteous, because they find it easier to prey on their victims I guess.

I most certainly will try and see if I can get re-compensation through the courts for the wrong advice my financial advisor gave me.

Mr. Irish is now saying in his latest fax that he wasn't qualified to give us advice on bankruptcy and, furthermore, the advice he took on our behalf from the sources has, on hindsight, proved to be bad. Bloody right it has! Since I made some money, the educated are all waiting for their grub. They let the entrepreneurs make a few quid and then get their knives and forks out.

In life many people are waiting like vultures in order to feed themselves off you and, if possible, those bones must be picked clean. They do it legally in most cases.

When I complained of what I thought was incompetence on behalf of Hammond Suddards over the Classic Gold account, I was put firmly in my place by the K.P.M.G. receiver, Mr. Steve Treherne who faxed me that the combined resources of K.P.M.G. and Hammond Suddards were more than capable of sorting out Classic Gold - bloody right! They should be and, at what cost in additional expenses to Ronnie Dawson? I remember distinctly how Chris Nutting, the (O.R.) at K.P.M.G. told me with enthusiasm how some chap - a millionaire, wouldn't pay a £600 bill on a principle and he ended up £100,000 out of pocket. Nutting's eyes glowed as he related that particular story. It's not nice the way I see it, but then I'm not a parasite living off the misery of others.

Here follows a copy of a fax and letter I sent to Paul Bromfield at Hammond Suddard .

Paul Bromfield

Thursday, April 24th

Dear Paul,

With reference to my phone call to you yesterday, and your concern that I have written about you and official receivers, Chris Nutting and Steve Treherne in my autobiography Conmen, Cheats and Liars. As I have subsequently explained, when faxing you the copy of the front cover of the book, my primary intention in deciding to publish this story was to tell the truth "warts and all" about my life. And, I believe that this should come as no surprise to you. Indeed, after receiving an extremely sarcastic letter from Mr Treherne, I clearly replied that I considered that Mr Hammond Suddard was inexplicably 'nit picking' and blowing the situation way out of proportion with regard to the Classic Gold account. I was, thereafter, rudely told to, in effect, 'shut up'.

Furthermore, if you remember at our first meeting which was held, at my request, at the K.P.M.G. offices that, when I mentioned 'Jersey', Chris Nutting leapt from his chair and screamed accusingly at me that I was "covering something up." He shocked me with his belligerence. The young secretary and yourself, Mr Bromfield, were present at the time and I said that I was not in the habit of covering anything up. In fact, I offered you the substantial property of Charnwood to hold as (more than) sufficient security against any so-called world-wide debts I was supposed to have incurred.

As I recall, your response to this was that in that case, once you were in possession of the property deeds for Charnwood, you would not be interested in any additional assets. This is obvious in my opinion and makes perfect common-sense.

What was to become apparent to me over the ensuing months was the case of the O.R. for K.P.M.G. who seemed only intent in trying to find out if I owed any other moneys for, if I did, and they could uncover it, they would get more money.

As I stated to you during our meeting, to the best of my knowledge, apart from the VAT, I would have income tax liabilities in the future of around £100,000.

After the bad advice I have received from my financial advisors (which no doubt led me into your clutches), I have been made to suffer untold stress over the miserable amount of money belonging to Classic Gold. Now, just three months later and, on merely a technicality, you have found a way to retain the same. This is despite all my pleas on behalf of the 842 Classic Gold investors, clarifying the situation regarding the welfare of the horses which has always been uppermost in my mind. My pleas apparently fell on deaf ears. This, despite the fact that you were holding assets far greater than you required. I also pointed out how unfair it was that the Classic Gold trust were having to pay solicitors to try and recover the remaining little money from their quarter of a million outlay.

However, Hammond Suddard were not for moving. Of course, I realise now that, in my opinion, the more work you do, regardless of ethics - other than hard nose business, your interests only lie in making money from the fallen. However, what I felt particularly bad about was the fact that although I delivered as promised you could not compromise in any way over the welfare of dumb animals. I was driven to such despair.

As I explained to you in numerous faxes (we both have copies), in my opinion it was some of the very people who are educated and thus privileged who were to prove to me the conmen, cheats and liars of the world. As you warned me yesterday, ("Be careful what you write in your book about Hammond Suddard"). My reply was that I will only tell the truth. And, if I didn't you could sue me. I promise you that I only want the people to know the true *and real situation. Deceit from others has played a major role in my life and I have no intention of emulating the same to others.*

In my book, Paul, I have documented all faxes from the Jockey Club, newspaper editors, solicitors and/or inserted in the order of the chapters of my life.

I might remind you also that, when I wrote to Chris Nutting asking for an explanation of my £12,000 solicitor fees, I received no reply. But you know well, Paul, that I now have nearly £100,000 worth of costs to date on a VAT bill that I feel my accountant gave me bad advice regarding the same. Also, I imagine the general public would perceive this as greed in the extreme (with costs and interest of over £100,000). Similarly, I can't believe that people in this country in a similar position, i.e. who are made bankrupt, realise to the extent the official receivers and their solicitors feed their families in style from those less fortunate than themselves.

If you find a part of this letter which is untruthful in any way, please fax by return and I will delete it from my story, Conmen, Cheats and Liars. I suspect, because of the chapter in my book which refers to the official receivers and their solicitors (I have taken no prisoners!), I can expect no favours in the future. So be it. Yours faithfully,

Ron Dawson

nb: At the time of publication, Paul Bromfield declined to answer my two questions.

The next fax I sent to Paul is included hereafter:

Paul Bromfield

Monday, 27th April, 1998

Dear Paul,

My solicitors have now responded to me regarding your latest fax dated 23rd April, 1998 in which you state that you are retaining the money that belongs to Classic Gold as you have apparently discovered a loophole to do so legally (pursuant to Section 284 of the insolvency act, 1986). May I just remind you that it has been exactly six months since I first tried to have the money released from O.R. Mr. Brown of Cambridge.

Please could you explain why you chose not to retain my money from my horses sold at the Newmarket October sales in 1997, which I believe were sold in excess of twenty-five thousand pounds? Surely, this was far less a priority than the Classic Gold money which was needed in order to pay for the Classic Gold horses' welfare. (And surely falls under your 'pursuant to Section 284 of the insolvency act, 1986)?

Finally, I am pleased you could not find anything unduly adverse in my fax to you on Friday, 24th April. You will see in my book Paul, that I have only told the truth to the best of my knowledge and also that I blame no-one for my problems - other than my financial advisors and, of course, myself.
My best wishes,

Ron Dawson

I did receive a previous fax from Hammond Suddard informing me that they will not hesitate to take action against me if I criticise them for any undue delay in sorting out the Classic Gold mess. I can put their mind at rest. I am sick of the pettiness of it all. So, the threats from Hammond Suddard regarding Paul Bromfield, Chris Nutting and Steve Treverne dealing with my problems is a mere side issue to me. Furthermore, if they think they can button me up with threats, they best think again.

I am talking here, in general, about the untold misery and humiliation that can befall those that don't necessarily even have a failed business, but have merely suffered a single unfortunate event in their lives. I hate greed of any kind and parasites of any form.

Now, I have been told by many that my book is going to stir up a hornet's nest. Well, so be it and, if it can only help one person to avoid the trap I have fallen into, it will be well worth it to me.

People who think they can steamroller over you must become accountable to someone. As I wrote to Steve Treherne, I must stick up for myself and ask questions over the spiralling costs to Maureen and myself. We can't just lie down cowering in a corner. It's obvious that I will be pleased once I have got certain people out of my life, but no one is to blame for this unhappy episode but myself. I should have never put my trust in others.

However, in defence of my selection of accountant, Mr. Andrew Irish, I truly believed him to be one of the finest in his profession - but it appears, only on tax advice. He should have said, "Look, pay-off most of your bankruptcy with the £50,000 you have and leave your £40,000 mortgage on Charnwood for now. Because, in any case, if you move Charnwood into an offshore trust, two years prior to your bankruptcy, it will not be out of the clutches of the official receiver.

In fact, despite all the solicitor's costs I incurred in this trust being set up, it was not put into trust until after the date of my bankruptcy, never mind, two years previously. So, here I find myself in a position that I should never have been in, because it turns into a horror film story and, as I tell it, I hope it will, in turn, be remembered by you, in case you were ever to fall foul of the system. Heaven forbid! As in horse racing, beware of sharks, in a whistle and flute.

So, in good faith, I arranged for the deeds of Charnwood to be put into the hands of the official receiver's solicitors. "Please sell the property as quickly as possible at its market price, pay off my VAT debt and any income tax I may owe," I told them. But, of course, I wasn't prepared for the legal daylight robbery that was to be revealed. From out of my sale proceeds, DTI fees would be payable at 15% on the first £50,000, 11.25% on the next £50,000 and 9.75% on the remainder of the sale proceeds.

It doesn't end there. Next in line for his cut is the trustee in bankruptcy. He is entitled to elect for payment of his remuneration on what is known as the official receiver's scale. On the sale of Charnwood, he cops 20% on the first £5,000. 10% on the next £5,000, 10% on the next £90,000 and 5% on the next £50,000. Between K.P.M.G. and the DTI, that's a total of £85,000 on top of an initial VAT bill of £60,000 which, with interest, equals £80,000 which in turn equals £165,000. Is that it then? You must be joking!

The official receiver is also entitled on the same scale paid out to creditors and I am not allowed to pay the increasing interest on my VAT or income tax debt to stop it spiralling out of control. For instance, let's assume my stables - Charnwood, takes twelve months to sell and only at what it cost me (which was three quarters of a million). Then, the interest on VAT and my income tax would be about £40,000. So now the official receiver is ready to eat his next piece of tasty legal cake. The money he pays out of my money to my creditors will be 10% on the first £5,000, 7.5% on the next £5,000, 5% on the next £90,000 and 2.5% on the remainder. So, the total is at least £15,000. Thus, in total, between the DTI and the O.R., they've copped about 100,000 grand of my family's money, all completely legal.

Now, I won't dwell on the £10,000-£20,000 solicitor's fees that will be on top of that, otherwise I may be accused of nit picking. In any case, this is peanuts compared to what the main K.P.M.G. men legally nick. If anyone wins the lottery, a fiver towards my fighting fund won't go amiss. Seriously now, I invested my greatest assets on my boys, long before the O.R. could get his snout in the trough.

It's true that, other than the Classic Gold fiasco, I have no complaints against Mr. Paul Bromfield of Hammond Suddards - despite my many abrasive letters to him. Hold on a minute, it's just struck me that the 19,000 quid that belongs to Classic Gold - they are trying to keep it! And the O.R. will get their cut out of that too. Well, it may be legal like, but it makes me cringe. Pigs at the trough is an image going through my mind right now. My Dad would turn in his grave. Those very people are making more money out of his son in one hit than he probably made in forty five years of sweat and toil in the shipyard.

Chris Nutting, the official receiver is doubtless a most pleasant chap, it's not his fault. God forgive him. And, despite Steve Treverne's high-handedness to me, I have put that down to him having a bad day in the office! They all have a job to do. They may have families to feed and, I believe that the legal system is obscene regarding the amount of money they allow to be nicked by those operating within the law. I most certainly wouldn't feel comfortable feeding my family on misery pie. I would just like to add here (to allay any fears) that, while bankruptcy is an unpleasant experience, providing you are honest over your assets and you try to work with the official receivers, it can be a little less painful. Robbery without violence springs to mind.

When other people in large businesses go bankrupt on purpose and leave small creditors and family businesses in the lurch (especially as they don't seem to have suffered much themselves) - this is criminal in my opinion. As for Ronnie Dawson, I will just get up, dust myself down and get on with my life - and make another million.

I'll tell you a joke first: "How do you tell when a lawyer is lying?" Answer: "His lips are moving!"

And in April 1998, all that you have read above was the situation. But things were to change for the worse. The manager at K.P.M.G. who was the official receiver in my case called Chris Nutting, now begins to show his true colours. He left no stone unturned in his quest to discover more debt. Gloatingly, he would fax, write and telephone me of any few quid he could discover. One occasion in particular, I remember I asked him if I could see my tax appeal assessment. He didn't like that so to put me in my place, he faxed me thirty-five sheets of my old tax papers. Yes, it would all be charged to me.

Now you may say that to do this witch hunt of trying to find debt is his job. And in that, I would admit is true. But in all my life, I had never had the misfortune to meet this kind of person before. For in Maureen's and my mind he became so odious to us and, in my honest opinion, someone who was glorifying himself in seeing Maureen and I lose our beautiful racing stables. For instance he said to me, "Oh these stables are so lovely with very nice houses. Pity you are going to lose them."

The pleasure he was getting from our misery was hard to believe. I said to Maureen, "You know, love, I suspect he's "getting off" on our predicament."

Do you have any idea how much power these people have? How about this - they had my yard valued. I paid for the valuation. Yet I'm not allowed to see that valuation. Now isn't that a disgrace. I enclose a letter here in answer to mine asking for that information.

24th September, 1998

Dear Mr Dawson

Thank you for your fax message regarding the document prepared by Estate Agents, Knight Frank.

I have spoken to both the solicitors acting for the Trustee in Bankruptcy and Knight Frank and I have been informed that the document is privileged to the Trustee and therefore I regret that I cannot forward a copy to you.

Yours sincerely,

C. Nutting
for the Trustee in Bankruptcy of Ronald Dawson

Now this sort of thing is one to cause nightmares. You do not know what valuation the O.R. has gotten. He has you blindfold and in irons. As a bankrupt it appears you have no rights. You are expected to suffer without a wimper.

As I said, I desperately wanted to pay my debts. I even found a buyer for my stables, an Arab, Kamil Mahdi at £495,000. No, not the £800,000 they had cost me after tax, but I had to pay my debts and in a buyers market could expect no more than half a million.

Chris Nutting was put out on that, but he recovered quickly. "Look, I will have it valued," he told me. "Yes, but I am paying," I said. "There's no need, I'll accept that figure. I need to get my life back."

"Okay," he told me. "I will get two valuers in now."

"That's a couple of thousand!" I replied. "Why do you want to bleed me so?"

"It's the law," he said. "I can do what I want." Maureen was in tears.

"Mr Nutting," I replied. "I have found a buyer. He will pay cash. Why do I have to pay all these extra DTI fees to the government?"

"It's the law," he repeated and I could imagine the smirk on his face. I even put horns on him in my imagination.

"Mr Nutting," I said. "Do you know why I was made bankrupt? I have always paid my debts."

He replied (and this is the truth). "Don't try and wind me up. I listened to you once, never again."

I was amazed at my calmness when replying and Maureen looked at me in amazement. As a family we had been through such pain and anguish. I had I felt been de-humanised by this bankruptcy receiver."

"Mr Nutting, until my dying day, I will try for vindication at the way I have been unethically treated by Customs and Excise." I replied. "It is they who made me bankrupt. You may eat your misery pie and fill your belly and mind with pleasure at the job you do.

"I just want to write to you with a letter laying out my grievances to the VAT which I have already sent to the Adjudicator. You can see that, while enjoying your obvious pleasure at Maureen's and my expense and agony, in years to come, if I ever get vindicated, you will know that the damages I will receive will far outweigh all the debts and DTI feels and your solicitor's cost and K.P.M.G. money in total. And that would, in itself, spoil your joy (because I would tell you). So much so that just the thought of it to me is like a taste of heaven."

"Look, everyone has to make a bit of money out of you," he replied. "Every penny we take off you, we do within the Law."

"God Bless You, Mr Nutting," I replied, still calm and put down the phone.

Anyway, dear reader, I pray that none of you ever meet this man. For, at first, you will feel secure (after his initial bullying) as he has charm and is smarmy. But don't be deceived. In my opinion, he has more heads than the Lernaean Hydra. And I believe his battle cry is "bleed the buggers dry!"

I turned to my Maureen to witness all the distress I have caused her. Losing half a million is a lot of pain but the degradation of bankruptcy is worse. You are treated worse than a second-class citizen. Your bank manager now forgets the good business you had with his bank. Ours, David William Gardner of the Nat West Bank no longer replies to our letters. Ever day is like a nail in your coffin. Such is the now apparent horror and feeling of despair at your impending doom. I can only say that I hope none of my readers fall into the trap. It's a daily agony as your life is put under a microscope and dismantled.

But I tried so hard to reverse the damage done. I really did. And tried so hard to win a reprieve, such as writing endlessly to the VAT). And I look now at what I still have, not what I have lost. A lovely wife and wonderful children. Many friends in every land, financially still secure. A joyful life in a lovely place but, for now, during this painful time, I have had my last throw of the dice.

This is my grouse against Custom and Excise (VAT).

In 1990, I started my first racing club. Club members were not charged by me as I understood Sport and Leisure were non-VATable. In 1991-1992-1993-1994-1995-1996, every single year, I paid Custom and Excise VAT earned on my phone lines every year. They, the VAT were happy. In April,1994, I had a VAT visit by Bob Nash, the VAT inspector. He was so happy. The club member subscriptions were the same as previous years (no VAT). I did the same in 1995.

So, I did not charge my members VAT. In 1996, I did the same as I had always done. So for 6 years, while I paid huge amounts to the VAT on my phone business, I did not charge my club members VAT. I mostly collect club subscriptions each year from 1st January to 31st March. So how can the VAT say, "we told you before 1st January, 1994 that your racing club is 'vatable':" I challenge the VAT to give me evidence of this. They cannot. Full stop. Nor for 1994 or 1995. Not until the summer of 1996.

Now, unknown to me, and I bet a thousand to one you probably did not know either, the VAT ruling changed from January 1st, 1994. This is because, they, the penny pinching Custom and Excise won a tribunal case against "the Royal Pigeon Racing Association". You can't get much more money grabbing than that!

The R.P.A. pigeon lads defending themselves at the tribunal on the E.U. Sixth Directive: Sports and Leisure. The R.P.A. lost its case because now, this is important (activities which are purely recreational in nature or entail no significant element of physical activity designed to improve physical fitness do not qualify for exemption). Case ref. LON/94/2910A. Yet, what does qualify is, say, crossbow (see full list at the end of story). So, if you are in a crossbow club that's a physical business? It's stupid.

So, Custom and Excise armed with that tribunal success against the RPA, wrote to me on 28th August, 1996, over two years later, together with a letter and schedule, saying that I should have been charging my members VAT on their subscriptions since January 1st, 1994 and they, the VAT on examination of my books, asked me for £56,146.94. Later, a default surcharge of £98.23. Plus, an interest of £9,481.55 which is a total of £66,106.72. I protested but they, the VAT wouldn't budge. I told them that I had been misled into believing that my racing clubs were not 'vatable'. "Why didn't they tell me in 1993 when they won their case against RPA?" I asked.

"We don't have to," they replied. "You should be aware of it."

"How?" I asked.

"Because it was probably in the VAT news."

"I have never seen or heard of that paper!" I told them. (Has anyone?)

So they, the VAT left me high and dry and then they made me bankrupt. Yet I have paid them hundreds of thousands in VAT which I knew was 'vatable' on my business.

Now on 12th June, 1988, Brian Bliss informs me that, because of Section 94 of the VAT act, subscription by racing club members are liable for VAT (that is true, it is the law). Then he goes on to explain that my brother, Richard was advised that he should see an accountant. That is a lie. On something so important as that, don't you think that someone like my brother wouldn't inform me? After all, if that is a new ruling, it is no skin off our nose.

We just add VAT to the members' subscription. "Easy as pie". So come on! Who does Mr Bliss think he is kidding? I suspect now that they did mean to inform us but, because of overwork, neglect, call it what you will, they overlooked it. Otherwise, where is a letter before December 31st, 1993 informing me of new VAT liabilities? There was none. The VAT are crooks.

No, not a whisper about the change in VAT law. And they know it. So, I was in a no-win situation. If I charge my club members VAT, I could be acting illegally. I even asked the VAT for a ruling (as had my brother/manager Rick). I had done this every year since 1990, just in case there was any change. They declined to give one, as usual, either verbally or by letter. Not until June, 1996 did they draw my attention to it after examining my club brochure.

Now, if that is how the government wants to treat small businessmen, then this country of ours, for sure, has problems. Just for the record: Ref 701/45/94 H.M. Custom and Excise gives a list of sporting activities which qualify for exemption. There are 114 on that list which include such obscure sports and leisure names as Biathlon, Boccia, Camogie, Kabaddi, Luge Pètanque, Shinty (I know that one is a form of hocky), Tackwondo and a lot more I have never heard of. But, no, pigeon racing is not on that list of 114 sports which are exempt, but horse racing is. And that is my business, horse racing. And, if the Custom and Excise want to be more exact, they should at least make a comment next to horse racing. A question mark would do. Then I could have twisted their arm more often to give me a ruling or, believed if horse racing is on the list, it should not be taken literally.

Anyone looking at that official Custom and Excise list would have done what I did and carried on as usual, thinking that, if they changed the 'goal posts', they would at least let me know. They didn't. And if that is not pulling the wool over the eyes of a small businessman, I am Little Miss Bo-Peep!

I will always carry with me, all my life, the misery imposed on me and my family by the Custom and Excise. Even the VAT inspector who came to do my books, while apologising for his lack of visits, which he blamed on government cut-backs (Chris Ashby at the VAT complaints team now says on Friday 21st August that was not the case). I have asked for a copy of any letter confirming my new VAT status after 31st December 1993. Also, the dates I was visited by the VAT inspector, Bob Nash who was clearly uncomfortable in what his superiors had ordered him to do, which was to backdate my VAT assessment for nearly two years.

Throughout that time, not only did they deprive me of a visit, they could not afford a 12 pence stamp to let me know my new VAT racing club status. So you could say, for the cost of a 12 pence stamp, I was made bankrupt! My accountant asked for the assessment to be reconsidered and this was taken by an independent member of staff who confirmed the original VAT decision.

Here is a full list issued by H.M. Custom and Excise 701/45/94

Annex D

SPORTS ACTIVITIES WHICH QUALIFY FOR EXCEPTION

Aikido, American Football, Angling, Archery, Arm Wrestling, Association Football, Athletics, Badminton, Ballooning, Baseball, Basketball, Baton Twirling, Biathlon, Bicycle Polo, Billiards, Bobsleigh, Boccia, Bowls, Boxing, Camogie, Canoeing, Caving, Chinese Martial Arts, Cricket, Croquet, Pentathlon, Crossbow, Curling, Cycling, Dragon Boat Racing, Movement and Dance, Equestrian, Exercise and Fitness, Fencing, Field Sports, Fives, Flying, Gaelic Football, Gliding, Golf, Gymnastics, Handball, Hand/Para Gliding, Highland Games, Hockey, Horse Racing, Hovering, Hurling, Ice Hockey, Ice Skating, Jet Skiing, Ju Jitsu, Judo, Kabaddi, Karate, Kendo, Konfball, Lacrosse, Lawn Tennis, Life Saving, Luge, Modern Pentathlon, Motor Cycling, Motor Sports, Netball, Orienteering, Parachuting, Pétanque, Polo, Pony Trekking Pool, Quoits, Racquetball, Rambling, Real Tennis, Roller Hockey, Roller Skating, Rounders, Rowing, Rugby League, Rugby Union, Sailing/Yachting, Sand and Land Yachting, Shinty, Shooting, Skateboarding, Skiing, Skipping, Snooker, Snowboarding, Softball, Sombo Wrestling, Squash, Street Hockey, Sub-Aqua, Surf Life Saving, Surfing, Swimming, Table Tennis, Taikwondo, Tang Soo Doo, Ten Pin Bowling, Trampolining, Triathlon, Volleyball, Water Skiing, Weightlifting, Wrestling, Yoga

Now I bet that, unless you work in the right Custom and Excise Department you did not know that. I am full of little gems of information. Yuk.

Now I would like my reader to go back a bit, to the time I was trying to register Classic Gold and I told the Jockey Club that I was trying to find a way round racing clubs paying 17.5% on their subscriptions. And the Jockey Club bigots, instead of working with me, turned their fangs of venom on me.

And, because I was trying to do something for racing on the VAT situation, I felt isolated and abandoned by the Jockey Club stance. This eventually led to Tim and I getting our (10) ten year sentence. But nonetheless because I support horse racing, I studied in depth the E.U.

Sixth Directive: Sport and Leisure. I also took much legal advice with a great deal of correspondence from me to the Custom and Excise.

So, it gives me great pleasure to give the Jockey Club a bloody nose because I have, at last, found a chink in the Custom and Excise ruling on members of a racing club paying VAT in the future. And it will save thousands of racing fans a lot of money in the future. I will wait for the horse racing board or Jockey Club to give me a ring and I will give them then some good news. I am waiting for the call! So, anyone reading my book and paying 17.5% VAT on club membership, ring Portman Square to ask if they have contacted me yet.

Friday, 25th September, 1998

Now came an event that greatly saddened me, but knowing horse racing trainers like Gay Kelleway, it does not entirely surprise me. For deceit again is in my life.

Despite my utter contempt for Gay Kelleway's ethics, I remained friends with her mother and father, Paul and Gillian who now live close by to me in Spain. Maureen and I enjoy their company so when I was approached to lease half my stables to their son, Anthony for one year, I agreed. I really wanted to let my complete yard, however, as one unit for £50,000 a year which would have given me £20,000 a year profit, after tax and running expenses. Indeed, this was part of the reason for putting my stables into a trust. As my health was very poor, it would give Maureen and daughter, Kate, an income for the future.

I have another feeling of unease. I only found out by accident when my manager, Richard rang the Jockey Club Estate Agent, Peter Amos on Friday that he understood Anthony Kelleway was to make a case of buying my property under, (I understand), Section 48 of the Landlord and Tenant Act 1987. And, when I immediately phoned to Mr. Chris Nutting, the trustee in my bankruptcy, he confirmed this was correct. I was stunned. Furthermore, I have been kept in the dark over this important development. Of course, it may be the case as Mr. Nutting confirmed to me on the 24th September in reply to my request to know the valuation of the property by Frank Knight Estate Agents (which I had paid for).

My trustee in bankruptcy wrote to me that Mr. Nutting's solicitors and Frank Knight had both confirmed that the information or document is the privilege of the trustee in bankruptcy. So, it seems that I am not allowed, by law, to know the valuation of my own property! And, despite paying for that valuation! I most certainly will challenge this issue in due course through the courts. The bankruptcy laws are draconian in my opinion and want changing!

So, it could be the case that my trustee in bankruptcy, Chris Nutting does not have to inform me of any developments. And, if this is the case, it makes me uneasy. Because, when I challenged Mr. Nutting on Friday 25th September, he told me that his solicitor, Paul Bromfield of Hammond Suddards had his firm's property advisors looking at the legality of Kelleway's intentions which, in my opinion, amounts to a conspiracy between Kelleway and the assistant trainer's father, Mr. Michael Carr who, I understand, is putting up most of the money.

I intend to write to Mr. Nutting on Monday morning, the 28th September to ask him this: "How long have they known of Kelleway's plot? Also, why were neither myself nor my manager not asked, first of all, whether Kelleway had kept to his lease? Perhaps Mr. Nutting will confirm to me again tomorrow that they do not have to tell me by law, as in the case of the valuation. Well, if that is correct, this is a very serious flaw in the legal system. Because, if the Official Receiver had asked me, or my manager, Richard, whether Kelleway had kept to his lease, the answer would have been - "No"!

For now, forget the allegations of theft. Kelleway deliberately damaged my rose-garden lawns with his horses, despite three warnings. He should not have his horses on the rose lawns. His reply was, "I can do what I like."

He has now paid for that wilful damage, but it caused me much stress. But 11 months and no water or horse-walker electricity payments, not to mention, other non payments to date. It's too much so I look at "Forfeiture" in the lease contract (7) which states that when there is a breach of any obligations on the part of the tenant, the tenancy will immediately be determined without prejudice to any other rights of the landlord. This is subject to any statuary restrictions on the landlord's power to do so. A court order will be required if anyone is residing at the premises. So I will ask the Official Receiver tomorrow, Monday 28th September to contact his solicitors immediately and apply for Mr. Kelleway's ejection and for Mr. Nutting's confirmation that no attempt was made to assist Mr. Kelleway unethically to purchase Charnwood.

The saddest part of this whole episode to me, is that it ended *Paul Kellerways and my relationship. I have always tried to chose my friends carefully, and in Paul I found a person I wanted as my friend. Both Maureen and I have always had much respect for Paul. He is a lovely person, once you get to know him. Of course he had to put his son first, any loving father would do the same thing, I understand that. But with my financial problems, I also have to put my own family first

Bankruptcy? My advice, told from experience, is to try very hard to ensure that it never befalls you.

Paul died in early 1999 from a sudden illness, I deeply regret that our friendship was damaged and not restored when he died.

CHAPTER TWENTY-TWO

There is a lot more I could write about horse racing. For example, on how I believe that the mega influx of Arab money is not necessary good for British racing. Sure, we can probably now boast of having, once again, based in the British Isles, the finest bloodstock in the world. But on the other side of the coin are the small owners whose horses can't compete in a minor or average race because they are up against several Arab owned horses in the same event which have cost a fortune or been bred from the finest bloodstock. I've known a seven horse maiden race where six of the runners are Arab owned.

And then there is the problem of stable staff; good lads are hard to find these days in racing. All trainers need them, but if you want to find these good lads en masse, look in the Arab owned yards. The Arabs can afford to pay the best wages. Of course, I think these lads should have good money, but what it leaves is a two-tier system that will see a worsening situation in the stable labour market with small and middle of the road trainers unable to keep the few good lads they do have because they just can't pay them top money. And, if the trainers do pay that much more, they have to pass that cost on to the racehorse owner who then finds it too expensive and exits from the game. These days, the average cost to keep a racehorse in training in Newmarket is about £13,000 per year (my calculations).

I would think that the average cost to the Arabs is about double that amount, say £25,000. They have higher labour costs and a structure of managers to oversee trainers and top jockey retainers. The best quality of hay and straw. The list is endless. No wonder the Arabs are now moaning about the low prize money. I have a solution: Why don't they half the number of racehorses they own? Then racing might just be able to slowly get back on the right track.

Now I do want to say a few words about the use of the whip in racing. On Tuesday, August 18th 1998 things got pretty brutal in a race at York: the £350,000 Juddmonte stakes. It was here that three champion jockeys, past and present, got suspensions for over-use of the whip. Pat Eddery (eight days), Frankie Dettori (four days) and Kieron Fallon (three days). All felt the wrath of the stewards after a dramatic race in which all three horses finished in a line at the winning post with only inches between them. Now, Eddery gave the winning filly, the Luca Cumani trained, *One So Wonderful* twenty-three lashes, about par for convicts in penal servitude at Botany Bay, Australia, in around 1788, just for asking for a glass of water!

I have never before seriously advocated the use of the whip although I know, only too well, that some horses need a few reminders to keep them focused. Now we are nearly down the road from where the RSPCA are - on the verge of charging jockeys with cruelty. And it can be done. If the 1911 Protection of Animals Act was implemented, I am sure certain jockeys would be in the dock. And, if a persistent offender under the Law could do a stretch or two, perhaps only 3-6 months but he would have a criminal record and, in some instances, be deemed by the stewards, :not a fit and proper person" and lose his licence. Now that would be bad for racing.

The Jockey Club mouthpiece, Johnnie (Hang 'em High) Maxse puts plenty of his oar in on this one and I believe rightly so. But they, at the Jockey Club, are really at a loss about what to do. So this is my suggestion.

Let's look at the race: The Juddmonte prize money, £350,000 say, for convenience of rounded figures, the jock gets his 10%, that's £35,000 for winning. Well, how about this. Any jockey found guilty of a serious whip offence will forgo his 10% prize money. Okay, let's take it a step further, a big step, and say that, if any horse wins a race whose jockey is found guilty of excessive use of the whip, then the total prize money is forfeited. I look at it like this. Why should the jockey be blamed and condemned as much as he is when it is the owner who wants his jockey to pull out every stop to win? That pressure is on jockeys to win at all costs, if the owner is penalised also, it's gone in a flash, isn't it? No not quite, because some-one who has got a bit of very heavy money, like say the Aga Khan or Robert Sangster or one of the mega rich Arabs is not exactly racing for prize money. Three hun-dred grand I should imagine would equate to about three quid to Sheikh Mohammed. - or perhaps just threepence.

So, let's go the whole hog. "One small step for a rich man, but a giant step for horse kind." If any jockey is found guilty of excessive use of the whip, the horse will be disqualified. And the instructions from an owner and his trainer to their jockey in the saddling ring would then be, "I don't want this horse winning at all costs. Win if you can, but go very easy on the whip." And I bet you 5/4 that the excessive whipping is out of racing in a flash. No owner is going to lose an important race with his horse that could put a million pounds on his stud value, only to lose it for a few extra cracks of the whip. And I don't think they will give their jockey the "tin tack" (sack) for not using enough force with the whip.

The only thing is: Has the Jockey Club got the bottle to go down that road?

I doubt it and I will tell you why.

As many of our biggest, richest or titled owners are members of the Jockey Club, they would be reluctant to impose my ideas of punishment on their own. On other ordinary people's horses, yes. Knowing the two sides of the Jockey Club, I think you would have the "Ronnie Dawson" rule applied, a two-tier system. One rule for the Ronnies and one rule for Honourable Members (list provided).

Could you picture His Royal Highness (multi-billionnaire, Sheikh Mohammed) standing "on the mat" with his jockey in front of the stewards? No, neither can I. So keep your whips in good order, jockey lads. The owner keeps you primed to do his dirty work for him and, unless the Jockey Club implements my ideas, there is not damn much you jockeys can do about it!

How can a man who has just been given a racing ban of ten years write something impartial on the Jockey Club? You may ask. Well, I will try to answer.

These events took place during the first week of August, 1998. I want to try and show readers here just how much the Jockey Club have to contend with. And I also want to take the liberty here of saying that, despite my anger and vendetta against the Jockey club over Tim, I have a grudging admiration for the way they try so hard to keep the interests of the racing public to the fore.

Back to that first week in August .... There were three big issues that week, all reported to Portman Square, and one small issue the following week which I will outline later.

The first issue concerns trainer, Geoff Lewis, who was up in arms over his horse who finished fourth in a controversial race won by that glamorous Italian jockey and housewives' favourite, Frankie Dettori.

The story goes like this: Lewis threatens to report Dettori to the Disciplinary Committee for conning the starter. Frankie's mount called *Threat* won this particular race after Frankie had screamed at the starter that there had been a false start. Then, as the race was restarted, Frankie got a flyer and won the race. Then, his trainer Gosden got his pennyworth in with his opinion. (A pennyworth is a bit much, I reckon, for Gosden's opinion). But anyway, to give you his bit of wisdom, Gosden said: "I feel strongly that Frankie did the right thing," and then added one of his rare pearls of wisdom: "for the horse". Well, he had to add that on.

Did he say it because Frankie was fined 400 quid by the stewards for misleading the starter? Lewis called the £400 fine a sick joke. I am not sure here what Lewis was referring to - 400 nicker is like a bit of loose change to Frankie and a ten year ban from racing would be more appropriate. But then John Maxse said Lewis is entitled to put his case to the Disciplinary Department. I suspect it is a welcome relief to Frankie that "hang 'em high" Maxse is not one of the disciplinary crew at Portman Square.

The next fiasco was like something out of a Carry-On film. At Hamilton Park on 2nd August in the E.B.F. Malt Fillies handicap, a horse which should never have run in the race took part. The horse which should have run in the race - *Royal Dream* was, in fact, fast asleep in its racing stable box and, in its place, was the little two year old called *Periguex* which the unsuspecting public backed to 7/2, second favourite. But the poor young two year old had obviously no chance against the winner, a big five year old called *Naisant*. *Periguex*, bless his little cotton socks, finished last, beaten so far it was embarrassing. I would suspect that the poor Periguex will now suffer from an inferiority complex for the rest of his life.

The connections claim a clear case of mistaken identity. In other words, the owners would not know their own horse if they saw it and the person responsible for saddling him would not know it either, even if it kicked him. To be fair, serious as the implications are, I believe this is a straightforward case of mistaken identity. This case has also been referred to the stewards at the Jockey Club headquarters on Portman Square.

Let us hope old "Hang 'em High" Jockey Club sheriff and mouth piece, Johnnie Maxse doesn't put his oar in on this one to the press. It is confusing enough as it is.

Another controversy occurred the same week, 5th August, for the Jockey Club boys and concerned my old mate from the good old/bad old days, Barry Hills. The old maestro was fined £1,500 under Rule 151 (non-triers). The fine is peanuts for Barrington who has come a long way since his early days as a mere stable lad. J.D. Smith, his jockey, gets a ten day enforced holiday which, I suspect, he will spend in Barbados or the Seychelles. The horse does very well out of this also. In fact, you could say that the stewards have been particularly kind on this occasion, giving the poor, unsuspecting animal forty days box rest. Lucky nag. If word gets out to other horses by word of neigh, I have a gut feeling you will have a lot more horses that are non-triers. After all, the last thing these nags want is to be woken up every morning at 5.30 am and led out in inclement weather and made to gallop their brains out just to satisfy some rich owner. I am sure they would rather laze about around the stables and not have to race for forty days. It would go like this:

The Three Nags

Cast:

Neigh	Dobbin, the chestnut
Neigh, Neigh	Lady, the dappled grey
Neigh, Neigh, Neigh	Millie, the black horse

Dobbin: the chestnut: *"I hope my jockey is not trying today."*

Lady: the dappled grey: *"Neigh, neigh. I hope my jockey is not going to try either."*

Dobbin: *"Neigh. If he gets caught stopping me from winning, I will get a holiday."*

Lady: *"Neigh, neigh. Perhaps we might spend it together in a field."*

Millie *"Neigh, neigh, neigh. It's all very well for you two thoroughbreds getting forty days vacation from the race track. But what about little me? My jockey was so desperate to win the race as the owner had bet £10,000 on us to do just that. I got*

*my bottom smacked twenty times. I'm as sore as
can be. Despite me being half-beaten to death, I
get no holiday from racing yet. My jockey gets a
ten day holiday for whipping me too much, it's
just not fair. I only hope the next jockey who rides
me is found to be a non trier, then I will get a
long holiday like you two lucky nags.*

Dobbin:*"Neigh. Now Millie, jealously will get you nowhere!"*

*So the Jockey Club boys have another problem.
I suggest they find a way to interrogate these
horses and find out if they were indeed hooked
(stopped from winning) or did it just look that
way to the stewards in the stands.*

Now for a little story. This is a beaut!

On August 1st at Market Rasen, Classic Gold's horse,
Charlie's Gold wins a hurdle race over two miles at the
rewarding odds of 16/1. I told everybody on my racing
tips line to back it e/w. (This was a horse my son Tim
bought on behalf of Classic Gold investors. The fourth to
win from the five purchased): Anyway, trainer Anthony
Kelleway who trains this horse at my stables at
Charnwood in Newmarket, decides to run the horse
again, this time on the flat at Wolverhampton on August 7th. I find out all about the horse again and, because of the information which I am given, put it on my
stable news hotline again with the message: "You must
back this horse again today". And, despite the fact that
in its last three races on the flat, had seen it out with the
washing (beaten out of sight), this horse worked on the
trial ground with Anthony Kelleway's Royal Ascot winner, *Dovedon Star* and, surprise, surprise old *Dovedon*
could not get past *Charlie's Gold*.

Anyway, to cut the story short, *Charlie's Gold*, God
Bless him, won at the big odds of 25/1. Everyone was
happy.

Well, not quite. The stewards of the Jockey Club referred the victory of *Charlie's Gold* (yes, you've got it in one) to Portman Square where, no doubt, Anthony - poor lad, will have his collar felt. Even Anthony's dad, Paul Kelleway, who is also ensconced here in Spain and lives just over the mountain, won a four figure pick-up on old Charlie Boy. I did very well and of course, the wife got her new outfit. All the boys in the Classic Gold club had a tickle (won money). The boys who ring my hotline won a few pounds. My brother, Rick, won a nice few quid and for this, poor Anthony has a day out at Portman Square in London to look forward to. Let's hope that the stewards are sensible on this occasion. I must say old 'Hang 'em High' Johnnie Maxse has made no comment in the press. So far ....

Let me tell you now of one small jiggery pokery the stewards didn't get hold of concerning a horse Tim bought on behalf of Classic Gold Syndicates called *Pursuit of Gold*.

This fellow cost £70,000, bought by Tim. The day he arrived at my stables in a horse-box straight from the horse sales at Newmarket, a freak disaster happened. He kicked out in his box and hit the wall, breaking his pedal bone in his foot, £70,000 down the drain, or so it seemed.

Tim was devastated. One minute he is proudly getting a very athletic looking horse out of the horse-box then, within a flash, the horse is lame. The situation then was in September, 1995. For a whole year, the horse was in his box ensconced in plaster, then rubber pads and, finally he was able to walk normal.

Tim nursed that horse like a mother would a baby. Then, in July 1997, he was nearly fully fit and ran his first race at Newmarket over one mile. He finished last, beaten so far it was nearly night fall when he reached the finishing line.

A few weeks later *Pursuit of Gold* runs at Bath. This time over 6 furlongs (3/4 of a mile). He should have been in the betting as a 100/1 no hoper. Instead, he was a 33/

1 chance in the early betting, finishing up at 8/1 third favourite. And, if he hadn't been draw number 16 of the sixteen runners, I was going to have £10,000 on him. For know to me and Tim and to trainer, Kelleway and jockey, Alan Mackey. *Pursuit of Gold* was a lot better than anyone could suspect. But his dreadful poor draw that day sapped my confidence to a bet of only £2000 on 'the nose'.

Alan knew the task in hand full well. Not only did he have to get the horse out of the stalls fast, he had to use up valuable early speed to force him up with the pack into a better position far too soon than he would have liked.

At half-way the horse has ten in front of him with a furlong to go, he still has five in front of him, but he is into top gear. Alan waves the whip to threaten and in true grit style, the horse from a hopeless draw is with the leaders in a dash to the winning post. Then, with only yards to go, he passes them all except the favourite who is giving his all for his powerful jockey. The noise in the betting shop reaches a crescendo as every friend of mine has backed him on my advice.

For a split second, the horse is beat, but he won't go down without a fight and, with a final supreme effort of horse and jockey, he flashes past the post locked in racing combat with the gallant favourite. A photograph is announced. My heart is like a hammer pounding. So much I imagine that everyone in the now hushed betting shop can hear it. Then, it comes over the Tanoy. "First - number 16!"

Pandemonium breaks out. Local personality, Blackpool Frank is waving a copy of my book in the air in a sign of triumph. All my friends are hugging each other or shaking hands, as one does with a feeling of euphoria, having won money from the bookmakers who look on from behind their betting shop counter wearing a look of despondency and ruin (that's put on). But they couldn't lay the flood of money off with other bookmak-ers. "Why not?" you say. Well this betting shop is in Benidorm on the Costa Blanca.

So, my lads, if you are off to Spain for your holiday and like a bet. You can leave your missus on the beach with the squawking kids and enjoy the quiet sanctuary of this betting shop called 'Maggie Mays' with full TV coverage of racing from England. Well, quiet that is, if Ronnie has not engineered a coup.

Now I will turn to a more in-depth look at the Jockey Club and refer to their publication: The Review, 1997-1998. The first thing I want to draw your attention to is on page 14 which is under the heading, '**Fit and Proper Person**'. (Now this 'fit and proper' bit does not concern a person's health or whether he has a glass eye or a wooden leg. No, it means he aint fit and proper like - he's an evil bastard, criminal crook, murderer, conman, cheat and liar. Yes, that about covers it!)

"The Licensing Committee has explicit power under the rules to refuse to issue permits to whom, in its opinion are not fit and proper persons to hold permits or licences. One application was refused last year."

It doesn't take the brains of Einstein to work out that the person they could be referring to in 1996 as this "un-fit and not a proper person" is my son, Tim. He applied for a licence in 1996 and was refused. Now please note the words in the review: "its opinion". Okay, fair enough. So my son and the world knows that in the Licensing Committee's opinion, my son Tim could be the one named as not a fit and proper person. If so he is branded with this slur on his character. Everyone I know in racing believes they are referring to Tim.

Exactly seven times between Tim and I, we have asked the Jockey Club for an explanation. They refused, tak-ing the coward's way out: "We do not have to give a rea-son:" Is it really any wonder why Tim and I hold the whole damn lot of them in such contempt. I most certainly wouldn't want them on my side in a war.

The following is a copy of the last letter I have sent to the leader of the disciplinary tribe, Malcolm Wallace. And I promise this - Malcolm Wallace appears to me as if he's from the soft toy department. And, if he won't be honest over my son then, by the time I have finished with him, he won't know if he's Arthur or Martha.

Tim wrote this letter to the Jockey Club.

12th August, 1998
Malcolm Wallace
The Jockey Club
Dear Sir,

In its 1997-1998 "Review", the Licensing Department is stating in its records that only one licence was refused in 1996 on the grounds that the person who applied was "not a fit and proper person to hold a licence.

I believe that, because of the wording of your letter to me on the 31st October, 1996, I must be the one you refer to "as not a fit and proper person.

And, to top that, you have banned me from racing for (10) ten years for running two horses in my name. The two horses I bought for the syndicate of which I am a member!

You know full well, that racing those two horses was only a temporary measure until you registered Classic Gold. What harm was done, what great crime do you want the unsuspecting racing public to believe I have been guilty of.

Your actions towards me and my father are a disgrace. Ordinary people should be made aware of the way I believe you have conspired to justify your pitiful attempts to blacken our names.
I am very disappointed in your worthless stance.
Yours faithfully,

Tim Dawson

Tim and my bitterness is towards the obvious lack of fair play by the Jockey Club crew. Let's look into them a bit more. In the 1997/8 Review, in the largest of bold type letters, we have this statement:

"The Jockey Club will continue to warn of the detrimental effects that a ban on hunting would have on racing and fight to oppose any legislation."

Well, in my opinion, if you believe that claptrap, you are ready for the nut house. These many country squires, Jockey Club types are the very people, I believe, that glory in blood sports. These are the very upmarket twits that pass their judgement on a person and call him, not a fit and proper person. I will leave you, the reader, to judge who are the fit and proper persons.

Even at this late hour, I will say to these stewards of the Jockey Club whose Patrons are Her Majesty the Queen and its illustrious members who include:

H.H. Prince Khalid bin Abdullah
The Marquees of Abergavenny
The Viscount Allendale
The Hon. Sir John Astor
Sir John K. Barlow, Bt.
Capt. The Hon. Sir Nicholas Beaumont
Col. Sir Piers Bengough
Gen. Sir Cecil Blacker
The Earl Cadogan
The Earl of Carnarvon
Sir Michael Connell
Sir John Cotterell, Bt
The Lord Daresbury
The Duke of Devonshire
Sir William S. Dugdale, Bt
The Lord Fairhaven
Brigadier the Lord Grimthorpe
The Earl of Halifax
The Countess of Halifax
Sir Ernest Harrison
Marquess of Hartington
Major W.R. Hern

The Lord Howard de Walden
Capt. Marcos Lemos
The Viscount Leverhulme
R.J. McAlpine, Esq.
The Lord McGowan
H.H. Sheikh Maktoub bin Rashid al Maktoum
H.H. Sheikh Hamdan bin Rasid al Maktoum
H.H. Sheikh Mohammed bin Rashid al Maktoum
H.H. Sheikh Ahmed bin Rashid al Maktoum
Brig. A.H. Parker Bowles
Sir Thomas Pilkington Bt
Sir Evelyn de Rothchild
The Duke of Roxburghe
H.H. Prince Fahd Salman
R.E. Sangster, Esq.
The Earl of Scarborough
The Duke of Sutherland
The Viscount Ullswater
The Lord Vestey
The Lord Weinstock
Lady Richard Wellesley
The Lord Westbury
The Lord Wolverton
The Marquees of Zetland

And others of distinction.

No wonder it's called the world's most exclusive club. Yes, I checked the list myself. No Sir Ronnie Dawson. So, to the stewards of the Jockey Club I say, how about giving Tim a fair crack of the whip and try and recover yourselves as stewards worthy of the above illustrious ladies and gentlemen of fair mind and without prejudice. And give a loyal subject of Her Majesty. Tim Dawson, fair justice.

I would just like to clear up one mystery to those readers who are confused as to why it's called 'The Jockey

Club'. After all no jockeys are allowed to be members. It's got me baffled also. I can only think that possibly all its members are jockeying for a more prestigious position in life or, in the case of its stewards or secretaries, they are all jockeying with each other for promotion.

Now, because I delved deeply into Tim's case in 1990 and wanted the truth out, the whole truth and nothing but the truth, I have let the stewards of the hook. Because, without saying that Tim's enforced, non-coerced statement in 1990 was untrue, he did mislead the stewards. So it will be very interesting for me to see what they will do about it. Will they try and justify a "fit and proper" person bit over the young man's actions in 1990 - nine years ago? I don't think so. Because, to do so would put the stewards in contempt by Her Majesty's subjects. Who can say? You have done enough damage to the lad. At least he had the guts to stand up and be counted.

The Horse Racing Board in itself comes out of all this sorry episode with no credit. In fact, as I say in another part of this book, the supposedly illustrious multi-millionaire, Peter Saville, who is now a prominent member of that board is, in my opinion, a two-faced twit. And that is the trouble with racing. These people who get on their high horse and dispel their wisdom on to the unsuspecting public should look into their own cupboard for skeletons.

I am being really kind when I call them hypocrites. In 1994 and 1995, Wetherby's racing untouchables sold me their mailing list to post out the Classic Bloodstock plc prospectus to their clients. In 1996, when I objected strongly to the editor of the "Owners Magazine": the horse racing board rag which had allowed that tarnished writer, Dominic Prince, to write his spiteful, nasty piece of journalistic claptrap about Classic Bloodstock, the editor wrote back to me in an offhand way saying, in effect - "tough!" I suspect, because this unworthy editor is another who believed all the Classic Bloodstock rumours and innuendoes of Ronnie Dawson and his son, Tim nicking a sackful of shareholder's money. No proof, mind you. But who needs any when a load of wankers are dispelling their tittle-tattle over their gin and tonics. So, I surmise that this particular, should I say - gentleman, (not what I am inclined to call him at all) has also put the boot into me and Tim and joined the bandwagon of the old school tie brigade. Guilty as hell, the pair of them, is how they think.

He was either heaven bent on damaging Tim's and my reputation in a magazine that went out to around 20,000 other owners, persuaded by his cronies or the derogatory press reports that we were thieves. No doubt, he will give us his explanation on subpoena in my son's pending libel action.

Let Wetherbies sell the owners list to Ronnie Dawson. And let him send out his prospectus. That mailing list sale makes the racing bodies a few quid. Then the next thing they are slamming us in a racing publication. Talk about double standards in the racing hierarchy.

On the very day I am writing this, I see yet another Classic Bloodstock plc horse has just won *Classic Find*. Four years since I started Classic plc and they are still winning and this one is backed from 20/1 down to 12/1. Sims and his Racing Post fellow journalist, Green take note.

Incidentally, I wrote a letter to Alan Byrne, the Racing Post editor, saying that if his paper wanted to do something positive for racing, they should look into the reasons of the Jockey Club actions against Tim. I gave him my number to give me a call saying perhaps we could work together.

I have never even had an acknowledgement. That is what I am up against - editors who do not want to get onto any good stories. Why should they? When they can dispel to their readers a load of rubbish. These sort of people are so weak they would fall over in a breeze.

Far left at the back, Classic Eagle rounds Tattenham Corner in the English Derby to finish 10th.

CHAPTER TWENTY-THREE

The Jockey Club.

How can a man who has just been given a racing ban of ten years write something impartial, you may ask. Well, I will try to answer. In 1967, a new candidate was put forward for election as a member of the Jockey Club. He was black-balled. His name was Christopher Soames

The story goes that Lord Willoughey de Broke was the blackballer (the villain of the piece). Apparently, it had something to do with Christopher Soames who served in the Cold Stream Guards at Tubruk in the North African campaign in World War 2. From all accounts, we have a very decent man blackballed for some obscure event over twenty years previously. Lord Soames, as he later became known following a distinguished political career, was elected at a later date. The upper-class thought racing was run solely for their benefit and they still do today, I think.

Now, if we look back to the 1960's, the Jockey Club's rules of membership were something like this.

The Club does not want as members:

1. film stars or entertainers.

2. professional sportsmen

3. jockeys or trainers

4. foreign born people.

5. working class tradesmen

6. persons of low rank

Now that does not leave an opening for Ronnie Dawson to get into that exclusive club for the knighthood I expected for launching a Classic Bloodstock scheme. This is now no longer on the agenda. The words: "Arise Sir Ronnie, Jockey Club member and tipster..." is now but just a dream.

Seriously though, in all fairness to the Jockey Club, they have improved over the years - but slowly. Yes, they still have their little idiosyncrasies, but at least they have eased the rules for new members to be elected. But many drink like fishes, suffer from gout and bet like mad. So, if you follow these principles, you could have a chance of being elected to the club providing, of course, you don't have the principles of Ronnie Dawson. Straight dealing is obviously not a prerequisite..

Of course, the membership is made up with its usual sprinkling of Dukes, Earls, Lords, Sirs and Generals. And, in the past, even a King. The most famous Jockey Club member was probably Admiral Henry Rous who died in 1877. He is best-known for his stance against any big hitters in the Jockey Club membership whose horse betting winnings were in excess of £100,000. Well, hang on a minute Admiral. Just what was a hundred grand worth in those days? Especially for the ordinary man.

The fact remains that, even today, Jockey Club members are a breed apart. I've had runners at Royal Ascot to provide the entertainment for others - so to speak.

And from the owner's basic stand, you can gaze in wonderment at the array of Jockey Club members with the best seats in the house. I often wonder if they had to pay to get in, would the upper circle still be full of the well-heeled country types or would they be elsewhere? I am sure of one thing - they wouldn't be in the stalls with Ronnie Dawson.

Some day you, dear reader, may wish to call and see me, perhaps have a glass of wine with me (I drink any kind!) while I sign your book.

In case that is on your mind, I've included a copy of my personal/business card opposite, (front & back!)with some of the services I can offer.

I have sent my card to the Jockey Club so they know the quality of the guy they are up against in my quest for justice.

In the year 2000, I am going to write another book. By then, my final VAT battle will be won or lost. But in the meantime, before the exciting new millennium, my life will be one of battles. The libel actions against the many newspapers who have branded myself and my son Tim, "the family from Hell" in The Sporting Life to "Race Kings £8 million horse-racing scam" in my birthplace, Barrow-in Furness' town rag and, in between, all the others that have put in their threepenny worth of slur without a speck of proof. I real-ise these libel cases will take much of my now precious time over the ensuing months.

OTHER CLAIMS TO FAME

Aeroplanes Piloted
Jockey Clubs Sorted
Tax Offices Torched
Savings Minded
Ships Sunk
Traitors Beheaded
Churchmen Defrocked
Ships Built
Governments Advised
Border Disputes Settled
Wives Sampled
Newspapers Shreaded

For further undertakings I can offer, read my book "HELP" Vols. I, II, & III.

Card Sharps Hung
Brothels Inspected
Drugs Confiscated
Castles Stormed
Ghosts Dispirited
Allotments Dug
Currys Tasted
Bigots Educated
Trees Uprooted
Stories Told
Bulls Fought

Tigers Tamed
Bars Emptied
Virgins Converted
Swiss Accounts Verified
Orgies Organised

Wars Fought
Revolutions Started
Alligators Castrated
Official Receivers Fed
Uprisings Quelled

Ronnie Dawson
(ENTREPRENEUR)

Tel/Fax: 00 34 96 574 8518

Casual Hero
International Lover
Philosopher/Author
VAT Problems Prolonged

Tipster
Bon Vivant
World Traveller
Soldier of Fortune

I want you, my reader, to try and under-stand what it is like for Tim to be cast out like a piece of dirt from all his friends in racing: trainers and jockeys, some of whom Tim went to school with and, by order of the Jockey Club, never to be able to take your place in the sport you love. (Well not for 10 years...).

I am going to put the Jockey Club boys in such a spin, they will be spinning like a kiddie's top. Oh, I relish the coming action. But that is enough Ronnie my lad. You're boiling over. Okay. We will leave it for now.

Yet imagine, if that stalwart, the First Duke of Wellington was admitted as a member of the Jockey Club for beating the hell out of Napoleon's team at Waterloo when, in so doing, he killed the Emperor's finest soldiers, many of whom would not surrender because of their French pride. Well, for that alone, if he wanted to be a club member, how could they refuse him? Mind you, he was a bit lucky at Waterloo, with the tough as boots Prussian General, Blucher (who, as a foreigner would not have got Jockey Club membership) turning up on time to save our Wellie from a military disaster.

And, as history tells us, none fought braver than the French Guard that day. Although, as in every war, none ever fought braver than the common British soldier.

But even if he had won a sackful of Victoria crosses, that would not have got him into the Jockey Club but if your ancestor had been swinging his battle axe with good effect at the Battle of Bosworth Field in 1485, King Henry V11 would have given him a right few acres. Perhaps nearly a whole county. And 500 years later, you could be a Jockey Club member, it is that simple!

Well, sort of, but you see as many of the illustrious Jockey Club members are very big landowners. Yes, it does help to have a few thousand acres to your name. Throw in a title, a good school, a member of Lloyds perhaps, speak with an educated voice (nothing wrong with that). Snobbery will be a help rather than a hindrance, a pedigree, family one (not a horse one!) and you are into the world's most exclusive club. That's all it takes.

Ronnie lad, sorry. You fail on all seven. Oh well, there you go!

Seriously again, what was the sense of the Jockey Club boys putting the irons on me for ten years. One year would have done the job better, kept me in line. But ten years? I have got nothing to lose, I can run wild and there is not a damn thing the boys in the club can do about it. If they had been chess players, they would have seen the folly of their move. The truth is, brains have never been a pre-requisite for members to join the Jockey Club.

I remember when I was at Goodwood Races. It was 31 July, 1998 and, for a laugh, Tim and I decided to put to the test the disqualification ban imposed by the Jockey Club - in disguise, of course. Tim sported a handlebar moustache with John Lennon glasses. I went for a goatee beard with the addition of darkened eye-brows. Okay, we had it all done professionally and it cost a few quid but it was worth every penny!

The reason we chose Friday the 31st July and Good-wood Races was mainly because a horse was running that day in the first race at 2.15 p.m. which belonged to Classic Gold investors called *Gift of Gold*. And we wanted a couple of owner's badges (it's easy when you know how).

To test his nerve, Tim went into the weighing room and wasn't recognised. But you know I am sure that, even if he was, the jockeys wouldn't have said anything. Tim had their respect since standing firm with me over the trainer Stuart William's episode when he wanted to give jockey, Alan Mackay the boot. Jockey's have to live with trainers' whims. Let's face it. When a horse gets beat that's fancied, blame the jockey. That's the most common practice.

Anyway, to get on with my story. My heart was pounding and I sidled up to a racecourse official and noncha-lantly said: "Pity about the poor summer," then got chat-ting and led the conversation around to undesirables. How would you ever know if a disqualified person was on the racecourse with all these people thronging about?" I asked innocently.

"Smell them out a mile off, sir," he replied. "There's something about that kind, shifty like."

"But what if he was in disguise?"

"Wouldn't fool me, sir. I served with the Met.(obviously an ex-copper). We are trained to spot a wrong one. You see, sir it's all down to experience."

"Well, that's wonderful," I replied, doffing my Goodwood straw trilby with its standard brown ribbon at a pretty young lady going past. "Could have been the Duchess of the Paradise Massage Parlour for all I know," I told him, subtly changing the subject. "But one thing racing does attract is plenty of pretty fillies to relieve the punter of a few quid."

As pre-arranged, I met Tim in the Sea Food Bar; two plates of prawns with a bottle of Moet-Chandon to wash them down with was the order. I could see by the twinkle in Tim's eye that he was enjoying the challenge. People were certainly staring at us. I suddenly felt a little uncomfortable. Then I twigged why! Well, there we were, with faces brown and tanned, amongst a sea of whities. But real recognition? No way! As long as we kept our voices down amongst the "la-de-da's", we were safe. A shout from me: "Right lad, let's have another bottle then!" could have given the game away.

There is something strange, yet exciting about leading a double life. Your heart pounds every time someone looks quizzically at you. I am sure I saw Lord Lucan in a blue dress with matching hat. No, I am mistaken, probably part of the pickpocket look-out squad. I never did think moustaches went with blue hats.

Anyway, we left before the last race to beat the four hour traffic jam leaving the course. We both skimmed our Goodwood trilbies like frisbees across the car park then got into our taxi and headed back to our London hotel in high spirits. Our flight next morning to Valencia was still twelve hours away, so we had time for a bit of fun in the city. We had had a good day out, backed a winner, strutted our stuff and harmed no one. I don't take life too seriously, apart from my betting activities; that's serious business. But the rest of it is just a bit of fun.

England is a smashing place, a lovely country, full of lovely people and just a few prats. Tim and I will continue to go racing. If we are caught we will be escorted from the course (that's all). Perhaps then I will get some more publicity for my book.

I believe racing needs a few colourful characters, not robots in straw hats or Ascot topper and tails and with bookmakers that are now nothing but glorified accountants. I much preferred the days of "Prince Honolulu," the tipster who used to do his song and dance before flogging you a tip (it usually lost). The bookie who would lay you a bet of £10,000 to £800 without giving you a ticket. The toff buying everyone champagne who has just done a seven year stretch for embezzlement in the city with a cracking young golden girl on his arm. None of this kowtowing you have today with phoney posh accents trying to impress everyone, including the stable cat. Okay, they, the stewards are trying to clean up racing. But don't scrub too clean or we will end up like France where going racing is like watching paint dry. Let the colour and intrigue stay and you will have a lot more fun and games. Hide and seek is not a bad game. I played it as a kid. I never thought I would still be playing it in my retirement. Oh well, bring on the dancing girls.

Writing about doffing my hat at Goodwood to the 'Duchess of the Paradise Massage Club' leads me on to another story.

In racing, many characters have nicknames. For instance, my ex-partner, Kevin and his astute friend, Roger Marshall are known on the racecourse as Bodie and Doyle. I am known as Clogger. Not a glamorous nickname. I think I got mine for booting the bookies, or giving lots of my many trainers the boot!

Years ago, when I first arrived in Newmarket penniless, I got a room on tick at Waterwich House. A semiderelict slum that one day had been the living quarters for stable staff, probably around 1850. On my left were the notorious double act of racecourse conmen, Kinlan and Bloater ('Bloater' from Yarmouth) and on my right, Snuffi, who acquired his nickname when, as a stable lad for Noel Murless, played his part in snuffing out the favourite for the Derby with a needle full of dope. Snuffi turned Queen's evidence which sent two of his doping accomplices to prison, which left Snuffi for the rest of his life wishing he had eyes in the back of his head.

Well, I could tell you some stories about racing characters I have known, but I will give you one.

One of many loveable rogues and iffy characters that go to make up the racing scene.

I knew this face called John and as he progressed through life, he picked up the nickname, "Honest John". I remember one occasion so well.

I was at the races when I spied Honest John. You couldn't miss him, loud checked jacket, bow-tie, wispy silver hair. He could have passed as 'Lord Lotsofdough'. that was Honest John and on his arm this day, he had a sweetie, dressed all in white with a white parasol. She looked like she had just dropped down from Heaven.

Anyway, Honest John spots me, six strides in a flash, he is with me and pulls me to one side as one does. And he asked me to lend him a quick hundred. I frowned. As Honest John had never paid me back a quick anything.

"Okay Clogger," he said. "I can just manage on a fast fifty," glancing his eyes across to his racy filly all in white. For a second, a thought flashed through my head. It was a wedding job!

I gave him a slow tenner with the words. "It's a gift, Honest John, not a loan," I said. What was the point.

Then he called me the 'Great Esteemed One', bowed, thanked me generously and gave me the winner for the 3.30 race which meant to me it was one I could now definitely eliminate from the field of six runners.

Anyway, Honest John moves over to the bar with his new-found wealth, my ten pound note, when this gent from out of the blue, introduces himself to me. And the gist of his approach is the gent in the bow tie with the stunning lady in white. Who was she? Blah, blah, blah.

Apparently, she had been giving my new-found friend the eye. Hell! I would bet she would have given Nelson the eye which I am sure he would have appreciated. Anyway, the gent wants an introduction. I warn him: "Keep away from Honest John or you will be leaving this race-course without your shirt." But the gent is adamant. So, I take his arm and steer him over to introduce him to Honest John. Then, I leg it quick like to enjoy my racing. After the next race, I pass the expensive Barry Copes' champagne and seafood bar and there is seated the happy looking trio with a lobster a piece and a bottle of Moet-Chandon with Honest John quaffing it down like a "good 'un".

I return to my same spot after the next race and they have another bottle in an ice-bucket. This time, accompanied with the dead one upside down as the champagne quaffers like to do. I had to smile because the gent is having his leg rubbed in a "close encounter of the stocking kind."

Anyway, I returned later to Barry Copes' bar for a Pimm's. The gent is sat all alone with yet another bottle of bubbly. He beckons me over and says he has got a right story for me.

Apparently, the young lady is Honest John's young sister called Annabelle who has just been let down by some cad who has done a runner with all Annabelle's money. And, to make matters worse, the beautiful Annabelle owed a bookie a monkey (£500) which she had bet on a horse on credit for her cad lover who has done the runner when it lost. And, the arrangement is that sweet Annabelle has agreed to satisfy the lusty bookie's needs this very night in a hotel in Newmarket to service the debt. A task she is going to find very hard. (I bet she will). And she has told her brother, Honest John she was wishing it was my friend from out of the blue she was going to do it with. Well, the gent being the gent he is, gives Honest John five hundred in readies to square up the bookie and a further bung of two hundred when Annabelle went to the powder room. So he had Honest John's blessing for a night of lust with his beautiful sister.

So he, from out of the blue, can step into the bookie's shoes, or out of them as the case would be at bedtime. So, Honest John and his sweet sister, Annabelle have gone to give the bookmaker the Spanish Archer (El Bow) with his whack of five hundred in cash and a mouthful of abuse for even thinking the delightful Annabelle was his for the night, and the gent from out of the blue, was to take care of the now relieved tearful Annabelle.

Oh dear! I emptied my glass, got up, shook my head in sorrow and slipped away. On leaving the course later, after the last race, there was my friend from out of the blue, a forlorn solitary figure now with four empty champagne bottles dead in his bucket. Honest John and sweet Annabelle long gone with an easy seven hundred in his sky rocket (pocket). Well, I did warn him to stay away from Honest John. He's lost his shirt on the 'Red Hot Fillies Stakes' to a plausible rogue.

If you go racing, put your money on a four legged filly, not a two legged one and, if you are going to make the racetrack your hunting ground, get a good nickname. And, if your Christian name is John, you have got a starter for ten.

Incidentally, my son Tim is known as 'The Captain'. Now there is a story I could tell ....

Of course, I've had some memorable times in the racing game and met many characters of all kinds. And, yes, I also had my sad times. No one can expect the good times without some bad times. I've made a lot of money from racing, that's all I know. I can't remember ever losing a punter. Well, that's not true, when he died I lost him. I have always tried to be honest with my clients. They are all important to me.

Here's one for you:

A well-known tipster was killed in a multi-car pile up on the MI. Anyway, they got his punter to identify the body in the morgue and, after opening the first three drawers, he said on each occasion:

"No, that's not him!"

Anyway, when they opened the fourth drawer, he said, "That's him! Not in the first three - as usual!"

I remember a few years ago talking to tipster John Blake and saying: "Why do you go on with it all, John? You certainly don't need the money!"

"I wouldn't know what to do with myself if I packed it in," he replied.

And he's right, of course, I feel exactly the same way, it's not the money, it's the buzz I get for putting my punters on the winners. The big difference between John and me is that my burial plot will be small, his will be large. It has to be. There will be Mr Blake, Mr Harrington, Mr Wells, Mr Francis and others of Blakes' aliases all in the box as well. May they rest in peace. As I come close to closing this chapter of my life, I would like to thank my brother Richard who has stood by me like a rock or a trojan whilst the press tried to destroy me and picked me up when I was low. "Don't let the buggers get you down," he would tell me.

Now for another little story. And this is of another bookmaking sting. But I will have to word it carefully, sort of "army style", no names, no pack drill. Well, yes, I will put most names in the frame, but to avoid any trou-

ble or kickback I will say some of this story could be rumour. But I know a very great part of it is true. Perhaps
all of it is. I suspect a little gloss has been added over the
years, as that News of the World ace snoop, Colin Cooper,
said "a bit of gloss is good for selling newspapers." However, despite the thoughts of me some day ending up ce-
mented into a motorway bridge, here it goes.

May 11th, 1995 was a delicious day, the day *Legally
Delicious*, trained by Tim, ran at Southwell. That morning Tim and our jockey, Alan met at Newmarket racecourse to fly up to Southwell racecourse in our hired six
seater plane landing in a farmer's field near the racecourse. As pre-arranged, the farmer who likes a bet (a
heavy punter) is waiting in his field in his Landrover to
whisk Tim and Alan to the racecourse.

Well, we all know that Delicious won her race that
day. But this very day was to be a day of drama. That
very afternoon, Alan had had the choice of two other rides.
He could have gone to Brighton to ride *Persian Affair*. It
won at 15/2 or he could have gone to Chester to ride
bookie, Jack Brown's horse, *Dawalab*. It won at 3/1, but
he wanted to ride Tim's horse because, firstly, Tim had
laid it out for the race and had booked Alan a week or so
earlier when Tim and Alan studied the video.

In any case, Alan was a mate of Tim's and thought of
Tim as the genuine article. (Still does, I suspect, since Tim
possibly saved Alan's riding career at a later date following
an accident and Tim's dash to the hospital). And, of course,
to keep you, the reader, aware of certain facts, as Tim had
trained the horse and, if everything turned out as we expected, Tim would be the new trainer at Charnwood the
following year with about forty horses in his care.

So, as I have said previously, Roger Harris held the
licence for Tim who trained them but only in the nom de
plume of assistant trainer. But, in his first year in training without name, Tim had seven winners and thirty

placed horses plus a tenth in the Derby. After Gay Kelleway, Tim proved my second best trainer, but I am drifting, so back to the story.

Unknown to many, but known to me and Tim, race-horse owner, Hugh "Shuggie" O'Donnel who had planned a major sting for that day with four horses, all of which he was connected to in one way or another. And Shuggie had laid out a good bit of money (a few thousand) for his E/W yankee bet. (Each/way doubles, trebles and the accumulator).

Now, if Shuggie will forgive me, he has a reputation as a shady guy while, to me, he is upright and straight dealing. The word "Glasgow" (gangster) is often mentioned. (You know how these rumours get about). Shuggie, they say, has some lucrative massage parlours in Scotland. The girls are hand-picked and as my many friends say to me, who have visited the joints: "You have got to 'hand' it to the girls, they are never 'off-hand' to their customers."

Shuggie who had visited me on occasion at Charnwood Stables was a lovely character. One time I was at Stansted Airport in my wheelchair with Maureen after a UK hospital visit waiting for my flight to Spain when Shuggie flew down to Stansted from Glasgow with his minder for a sort of surprise business meeting with me at the airport. That's Shuggie - considerate. His cement mixers were in Glasgow and I was not part of any Redimix concreting jobs for the time being. (I'm kidding!).

So Shuggie's was to operate a major sting to give the bookmaker a bit of pain on May 11th. Shuggie's first two horses of his four horses bet won with the odds at 15/2 and 3/1. However, he had not included Legally Delicious in his multi-bet thinking that, once Tim and I had got our money on, you are talking the favourite which she was - no good each way. But now, of course, Shuggie's sting is well on track. However, the next two horses were not running until the evening meeting being held at Hamilton racecourse up in Scotland. This time the jockey was my mate, Alan Mackay.

Tim did his rounds, collecting off the bookies at Southwell over *Legally Delicious*, (one could not pay but had to send a cheque later). Despite what people think, bookies are usually dead straight. Afterwards the lads, Tim and Alan legged it quick like from Southwell race-course to the waiting Landrover. The happy farmer, who likes a bet was obviously now of the firm opinion that picking up Tim to and from his field and taking him to and from the waiting plane was a damn sight more prof-itable than farming.

So, he drives the lads to the little plane which is ready to whisk the adventurous lads up and away to Hamil-ton's small airport and destiny of kinds. There, a Shuggie minder is waiting on the tarmac to drive the lads to the racecourse. Tim told me later that the hardest part that day was stopping the happy farmer from getting on the plane as well. He obviously wanted a bit more of the ac-tion. Milking bookmakers was clearly more lucrative than milking his cows!

Although the night in Scotland was cold, the warming thought was that, if Alan wins on Shuggie's two horses, Shuggie could cop the best part of a million pounds. And so Alan would get a kickback (a nice present).

Sadly, it didn't quite go to plan and Alan's first ride called *Mentalasanything* finished second, beaten only by three-quarters of a length by Kevin Darley on Noyan.. But at least it was placed and if Alan could win on his last ride, King Curran in the last race, the race track rumour was that Shuggie would be happy with three quarters of a million pick up and a new Merc for Alan. I expect his minders also had visions of holidays on yachts in the Caribbean.

They were under starters' orders and I knew exactly what was going through Alan's mind as the stalls opened. He was going to give old King Curran the ride of his life. (Both those horses at Hamilton ran in Shuggie's wife's name - Mrs M. O'Donnel). The reason for this I won't give right here - I'm well out-of-order as it is.

Everyone knew just how determined Alan was to win this race, including the Almighty, following Alan's prayers. After all, there was a lot at stake financially and otherwise for my Scottish jockey, Alan Mackay and his main Scottish owner, Shuggie. Alan disappointed no one in the race to get Shuggie his money.

All the hopes of the Scottish punters who were well-aware of Shuggie's sting are focused on Alan and *King Curran*. Slow away, the gallant horse had hit the front with a furlong to go, clearly inspired by a few cracks of the persuader (whip). Both the jockey and horse gave their all. Jockey Alan allowed no slackening in his drive to the finishing line and victory. Then, out of the ensuing pack, came Kevin Darley on *Aljawab*. King Curran had little left in the tank, but the brave horse and his determined jock with his persuader flashing, flew past the post first with Darley's horse being seemingly squeezed for room.

Sincere congratulations are in order. Back-slapping instead of horse-slapping are the order of the day. The bookies were stung by Shuggie's sting. But no! Just as a smiling and relieved Alan was taking off the saddle for the weighing in, over the loudspeaker came the dreaded message: "Stewards' enquiry", followed by the more severe message: "May be an objection".

The champagne stayed on ice then there was an uproar. Shuggie's minders were no longer looking like retired, benevolent ex-heavyweight fighters, but more like heavy weight fighters without the ex. Now, into the story comes rumour, or is it? I know what I believe and what I don't. Do not judge yet - just read.

There was trouble brewing. Shuggie was a legend in his own manor - generous and kind. (Did you know, dear reader, that Al Capone used to dish out free food to the poor in the days of the American depression?). Sorry I wrote that bit. I must be feeling hungry!

Back to the story. Supposedly there was a bit of 'argy bargy', a couple of doors ripped off their hinges, that sort of thing. But with the stewards locked in, the untouchables were safe. And, as the rumour goes, (you know how these silly stories go around), Alan allegedly said to Kevin Darley, the rider of the second horse which had suffered the interference. "If I lose this race Kevin, you won't be riding *Celtic Swing* in the 2,000 guineas at Newmarket." (Have you ever heard such a tale).

Now, as *Celtic Swing* was the best horse that multi-millionnaire Peter (Sack-em) Saville had ever owned and was favourite for that big race in two weeks' time, if that remark to Kevin Darley was true, poor Kevin must have had visions waking up in bed one morning with the horse's head as company.

But anyway, the story goes that Kevin Darley said to the stewards on "the mat" in the enquiry room. "It was as much my fault as Alan's" In other words, there was no one to blame. I suspect on this occasion with a baying hostile crowd outside which looked very much like a Wild West lynching mob, those words of wisdom of Darley's were like music to the ears of the stewards who, without further ado, announced: "Result stands".

The rumour goes that if Alan's horse had been dis-qualified, someone in his grief - a punter I suspect, could have had a few drinks too many because his betting ticket was useless and dropped his fag in sorrow, burning down the racecourse and perhaps the stewards along with it. Now, if you believe that story, "Well, there you go." I will say here that I like Shuggie and, if I have offended him, please let me know the size of the cheque you want from me for the church roof donation. I'm allergic to cement mixers.

The story is nearly finished, but not quite. Tim and Alan and enough jocks for a party, ensconced themselves with Tim's pilot into a hotel for a night of gentle relief. No, not one of Shuggie's parlours, I am unreliably told.

The next morning saw Tim and Alan and the pilot, Neil climbing over the airport fence at Hamilton Airport at 6.00 a.m. (It does not open until 8 a.m.). The plane was covered with six inches of snow (that's Scotland for you in May!). Somehow, it managed to get off the ground at the third attempt and flew back to Newmarket Race Course which is not a bad landing in daylight.

I say, daylight because old shiny shoes, Peter Amos, does not like the planes landing in the dark. In the past, when that's happened, our pilot has been guided by the white running rail of the racecourse next to the national stud side, then switched off his lights at the last moment. It is a bit scary, but okay if you have had a few beers. Peter Amos usually hears the plane as he lives in a house nearby, but it takes four miles by road to reach the national stud. Typically, he will jump in his Jeep and go like the clappers to catch the culprits who, by this time, have jumped into a car already parked nearby and waiting to receive the night time human cargo of various jockeys. Finally, you can bet that you will pass Peter Amos going like the clappers in the opposite direction as you speed into Newmarket and the pub.

Now, dear reader, you may think it is irresponsible actions, but it is living. Excitement, adventure and part of the wonderful sport of horse racing.

So, who are the real villains of the piece? The conmen, cheats and liars.. and who are those who are the 'Jack the lads'? I have my own thoughts and newspaper editors are definitely guilty of major charges. Those people who sit in their ivory towers, passing down their ideas of what they have decided the public should read. Why can't we have a press that reports facts honestly like the Daily Mail and let the people make up their own mind.

I often laugh, say when the British Government has made a so-called collective decision. Then, the next day, for instance in The Sun newspaper, The Sun reporters write an article and there you have in big, bold letters. 'What The Sun says - turn to page 6' And they offer their opinion. Who the hell wants to know what The Sun says? Some prick in an office dispatching his wisdom to the world. It's a comic newspaper for a bit of light reading. No more, no less.

Here's a true story about the Sun newspaper. I used to give their tipster, "Templegate" Derek Mitchell a few good tips. He always paid me well. Derek knew very little about horse-racing and was always bemoaning to me that he would rather cover tennis (In newspapers they stay loyal to their own staff and promote within to good jobs).

It was a Newmarket meeting and Derek was badly in need of a winning nap. Lucky for him, I had one, Alan Mackay rode it. His father-in-law, Eric Eldin trained it and this horse won at 10/1, Derek was chuffed, obviously he could savour the Sun racing headlines the next morning, telling readers how brilliant Templegate was.

Derek was insistent that I dine with him that night at The Rutland Hotel, Newmarket. I took a friend with me called Lyn to give a touch of glamour. We all met in the bar and Derek bungs me a couple of hundred in readies to show his appreciation for the winner.

Then into the dinner. Top-of-the-range with a couple of bottles of Bollinger Champagne to complement the meal. Obviously all courtesy of Sun newspapers. Though just of late, Derek's gaffers at the Sun headquarters had been showing concern over Derek's expense accounts. The problem was that Derek liked to stay in the bar all day entertaining a load of plonkers drinking their heads of courtesy of the Sun. Poor Derek would end up with a notebook full of tips which invariably lost. I tried to warn Derek he was a fool but being the guy he was, he couldn't turn the plonkers away. In any case, the Sun newspaper was picking up the tab. That was true, but for their money they were getting a bucketful of junk tips. But that's the Sun's problem not mine.

Later that evening after dinner in The Rutland over brandies, Derek put his cards on the table.

"Ronnie, I know you are well in with lots of trainers and jockeys. I bet you could know a few stories, bits of scandal and hanky panky. If you know any dirt, the Sun will pay you well," he added. "Of course, no one would need to know you were the source of the story!"

The day before, I had taken Derek as a guest to the member's only Marlborough Club in Newmarket and introduced him to some trainers and jockeys who were good friends of mine and now he wanted me to betray them for Sun money. And that was the last time I ever spoke to the Sun's "Templegate" Derek Mitchell.

He lost his job not much later. No doubt due to so many losing tips in the Sun via the bar plonkers.

As I write this, Sky TV is reporting about the exposure of the Newcastle directors, John Hall and Freddie Shepherd. No doubt they have been foolish. Foolish to get drunk and allow themselves to be set up by The News of the World. I don't know which bits are true and which are not. I do know this, The News of the World prints lies for its readers. I feel sorry for these guy's families and the Newcastle fans. The dirty ones here are not Hall and Shepherd in my opinion, but the low-down sneaky reporter, Mazher Mahmood who stoops so low he must wear permanent knee pads. What I would like to know is who was buying the drinks? The News of the World reporter, Mazher Mahmood, I suspect. Now the world over men spout a lot of untruths and brag their balls off when they've had a few drinks. When I was with The Sunday Mirror and drinking with the press boys in a Fleet Street pub, they were no different than the Halls and the Shepherds of the world. The only difference is that the press boys are hypocrites and if I was a Newcastle supporter (I am on TV) I'd tell The News of the World and The Sun to stick the papers up their ....

As Liverpool did, over the Hillsborough disaster. It's about time the tabloid press stopped conning the ordinary men and women in the street. The last Sun's football exposure with photographs of goalkeeper Grobbellar taking money, saw him walk free from the courts, after being judged by the people, a proper jury, not the Phil Hall editors of The News of the World. (My advice is buy The Daily Mail and enjoy a real newspaper).

The Newcastle public, I suspect, are being conned good and proper over Hall and Shepherd. 'It's how you write it,' as Sims would say.

And, to top it all, The News of the World is putting the set-up tape on a premium rate hotline for the callers to hear how a couple of drunks have made fools of themselves. Calls cost fifty pence a minute. Talk about milking a story.

On the 3rd August, it was announced that The News of the World's editor, Phil Hall, would join the press complaint council. I fail to see that, with seven editorial people on the panel, how they can administer fair play. I believe that this newspaper industry is a joke. It is so laughable - newspaper editors judging press complaints on what newspapers have written. Talk about jobs for the boys. I would not trust one of them to deliver papers as a paper boy.

This is how I suspect a complaint to a "press complaint council crew" from me could go.

The Cast
(newspaper editors sitting in judgement on Ronnie's complaint)

Tommy: Sporting Lie

Alan: News of the Screws

Joey: Sunday Pimple

Graham: Racing Boast

Alan: "That bloody Dawson has complained about our untrue story. Can't understand the bloody man. Told him we would pay him for the story, changed our minds. Bloody sour grapes if you ask me."

Tommy: "Don't worry, old chap. We called him and his mother's brood, 'the family from Hell'. And we didn't promise him any money for the privilege. Ha, ha!"

Joey: "Now you two. Don't worry about any complaints. Let's just ignore them. What do people expect us to write about - a church service?"

Graham: "Yes, that's the best way lads. Otherwise we'll keep talking and miss our lunch. But I think a church service story is a good idea. Anyone know any randy vicars? Oh, you all do."

Tommy: "Stone the crows. Is that the time already? 12 o'clock? We have been sat here for nearly ten minutes. Let's just say the complaint is without foundation. No truth in the matter. That covers it."

Graham: "You're right, Tommy. I agree with anything you say. I am hungry. I don't like these long ten minute sessions either. These people like the Dawsons have some nerve. Our paper gives the 'true date and true day every time on the front page'. So no one can say we don't always tell the truth."

Joey: "Anyone for golf this afternoon? I fancy a few rounds."

Alan: "The only rounds I fancy are at the bar. Ah, so we are unanimous on that also. Okay, your round, Joey.

End of the Press Complaints Meeting.

Verdict: Guilty of complaining. Bloody cheek!

When I left shipbuilding thirty-five years ago, I never knew where I would end up in life. But I was sure that I would be happy, carefree and do something I wanted to do. Tipping horses to punters just came naturally to me. And, I will always do it. As I will always put good genuine racing tips on my phone-lines. I reason it this way. What I do must be satisfactory to punters. The same people are with me for years. I do my best for them and always will.

In Spain, I now find it better than ever for finding the winners. I have nothing to distract me. I have my Sky racing channel, six hours a day. More, when we have evening racing. I have my Timeform library, The Sporting Life and The Racing Post on Internet. My form books are sent to me by express delivery. I have many loyal trainers and jockeys as friends and other excellent contacts built up over thirty years on my pay roll, every morning, seven days a week I'm on the phone 9 a.m.-10 a.m. and every evening 7 p.m.-8 p.m. to phone my racing contacts in England. There is very little going on in racing that I don't know about. I'm at the top of my profession and I want to stay there. Number one.

In April, 1998 my wife Maureen, the Company Secretary of Classic Bloodstock plc flew to England for an interview by the Department of Trade and Industry investigators. This meeting was held at Lytham St Annes, Lancashire under caution. According to Maureen, everything seemed very straightforward, except for one thing. The DTI investigators explained to Maureen that they thought there may have been an attempt at money laundering within the plc 11 company. Maureen was astounded to hear of this possibility, but was unable to help, other than be truthful under caution with all the questions asked of her.

Upon her return to Spain and myself, she told me of this new development. I was drinking a bottle of Don Perignon at the time. As I had made an appointment with the DTI investigator in Cambridge for May 6th, I felt that more information would be forthcoming at that time. One thing I was sure of was that, as Maureen had never handled any plc 11 money or written out any cheques, I was confident of her innocence in any such matters. You can tell if your wife has got a million stashed under the bed. When did you last look under your bed?

At my interview, certain things came to light. However, for me to add further to this at this stage could lead me into trouble with the DTI investigators. Having been informed at that meeting of certain irregularities, I was as helpful as I could be, but somewhat in the dark. I felt at that time what a relief it was that Maureen had no dealings with any moneys. No doubt, if the DTI are correct in their concerns, somebody must be worrying. I will add here that, for the sake of the destructive press and the biased Jockey Club, the DTI have not the slightest interest in my son, Tim. His financial involvement in Classic Bloodstock is zero.

I will just have a sip of champagne and a bit of caviar (I love the stuff) and carry on. Where was I? Oh yes, the missing millions? I am sure I didn't get that money, although my memory is bad at times.

The press have decided otherwise and followed, in turn, I suspect, by the Jockey Club. Is it any wonder that Tim feels so aggrieved. Okay, he did wrong in allowing his name to be used for entering and running the two Classic Gold horses, but that's all. The Jockey Club boys want you all to believe they've landed the biggest crook since Al Capone. Of course old Al served his ten years in Alcatraz, Tim is serving his ten lounging around his swimming pool or sailing my yacht.

But then everyone is in a prison of a kind. The Jockey Club stewards, I believe, operate a sort of Mafia Society, I mean. Most are all encased in Portman Square handing out sentences to anyone who has crossed them while jockeys and trainers are locked for hours in their cars as they shoot all over the country from one race track to another. Spending hours in traffic jams.

As for me and my ten years? Well, let's see, no more traffic jams, no more kow-towing to men in bowler hats at entrance gates. No more racing at Goodwood (unless in disguise) with ten thousand guys in lookalike straw trilbies with brown coloured bands. No more Royal Ascot's eyeing up the tasty birds (girls in all their gear), no more topper and tails sweating my socks off on a hot day, too sticky to sit down but smiling through all the discomforts. No more going up to a bookie and saying "Gimmee an even five grand, the favourite." No, it's all gone. Hey Maureen, how about a night at the Casino, a bit of action. You see if you're a sportsman like me, you will have your fun. Life is just one ball of fun. "Get me five grand from under the bed, love. I feel lucky tonight."

I have given my instructions for a new team of horses to be bought and put into training. Okay, they can't run in my name, but that's never impressed me. I will control them, their careers and their programme for my betting activities. (Graham Green of The Racing Post, I suspect, didn't like that comment of mine).

This was my final letter to the Jockey Club boys. "My last throw of the dice," to get justice for a truly nice lad, a true gentleman and a pleasure to call your friend - my dear son, Tim. For he is really the one who has lost his direction in life by a Jockey Club decision. It does not affect me the same. I have had my life in my beloved chosen sport.

Perhaps in the near future, we will see these faceless judges, of who Tim could be in their opinion, "Not a fit and proper person," It makes me feel sick somewhere deep down in my stomach. If it was your son branded like this, how would you react - hence this final letter.

This was my final letter to the Jockey Club before the publication of my book and they will have a copy before Tim and my appeal against our draconian sentence of ten years in the wilderness.

The Secretary and Managers
All Departments of the Jockey Club
September 1998

Dear Sir,

I am writing this letter in its entirety in my book, Conmen, Cheats and Liars and my readers are in no doubt to the depths of despair the Jockey Club stewards have put my family in, with their shady double standards.

This is my story.

In 1989, I started my racing clubs. They were very successful. I kept on average 15 horses a year in training and this, of course, fed back into the racing industry. In 1991, I fought a case at tribunal against the VAT on VAT added on my racehorse training fees. I won. And I believe this was a forerunner in much of the racing industry becoming less vatable.

Since 1989, apart from a twelve month business (1990-1991) spell in the Isle of Man, my son, Tim was at my side or with my trainers. In 1993, I brought into my stables a new trainer, Gay Kelleway from whom my son learned a lot. You could say he was Gay's shadow. In October 1994, I sacked Gay. I brought in a new trainer, Brian McMath, Tim as his official assistant. Brian's idea! And I gave Tim four of my own horses to train. (Unofficially), he trained four winners.

Also in spring 1994, I started up Classic Bloodstock. This plc, I understand is still in business today with several thousands of happy satisfied shareholders. And I say it with a smirk, since I resigned, the mistakes are obvious. Not least, selling for small money a full sister to this year's Oaks winner. A good example of the very reasons I bought the fillies. In 1995, I started plc 11. It failed. The reasons I give are well-documented in this book. Everyone played their part in its failure. The press, a few silly shareholders, the Jockey Club to some extent. And mainly - myself. Note here, I repeat, my son Tim had nothing to do with the Classic plc formation. He was only interested in training racehorses.

When I became ill in 1995 and it was certain I was not going to recover easily, Tim was the only obvious person to stand-in for me at short notice. He did so for me as a favour, until I could find another director.

I subsequently wrote to all shareholders on February 1st, 1996 asking if any shareholder would put his name forward for a position of director with Classic Bloodstock. I received thirteen replies. When I informed all these people (incidentally, one of them was Frazer Earle, leader of 'Classic Watch Boy Scouts') that the position carried no salary, they all decided they had other things to do.

In 1996, I employed trainer, Roger Harris. He was ideal. He had another business to run, his transport business. So, although he held the licence, Tim trained the horses. I agreed to this as Tim had proven to me in 1995 that he was capable. Peter Amos was aware Tim was training the horses. He had often called at Charnwood, but no Roger. Now, you know it is not the only case in racing when someone holds the licence for someone else to train. In 1996, Tim gave Charnwood its best year since 1990, apart from Gay Kelleway in 1994. He also trained Classic Eagle to run so well in the Derby, to the obvious dismay, I suspect, of my ex-trainer Williams.

So, you are now getting the picture of why it has hurt so much when you snubbed my lad's training application. I suspect you think "talent" is something in stockings and suspenders.

Now, despite all the bitter innuendoes in the press over Classic Bloodstock and the missing millions and the snide comments about Tim, we just got on with the job. However, we did take some comfort in Jockey Club spokesman, David Pipe's comments to the press - "Until any proof of any financial irregularities or DTI intervention, we plan no action". Well, that is fair enough and how it should be.

But it was not the true case because as we all know now, the Jockey Club have two faces. So they took on board the moaning

minnies - instead of the bedrock of the satisfied shareholders -
and threw their weight about.

I pause here to print a letter from Mr. and Mrs. Swansdale
which is typical of the anti-Dawson brigade:

Mr. R. Dawson
Charwood Stables
Hamilton Road
Newmarket
OB8 OTE
Friday, 28th August, 1998
Dear Mr. Dawson,
With your wealth you couldn't possibly understand how devas-
tated we were to lose £1,000 of our savings. Whether it was as a
result of a deliberate con, sheer incompetence or a conspiracy
makes no difference to the anger and despair we felt at the time.
I do not feel inclined to be taken in a second time and therefore if
you are so concerned in clearing your name, I challenge you to
send me a copy of your book free-of-charge so that I can decide
for myself. I promise you that if as a result of reading the book, I
concur with your grievance, I will write and say so.
Also, if you are really the victim of a conspiracy and wish to fight
back, I would have thought you would have sent this book free to all
those poor unfortunates who lost money in the Bloodstock venture.
Surely the cost of doing this would be peanuts compared with your
fortune or do you no longer own your villa in Spain and your Rolls
Royce? You obviously still own the stables and horses at Charnwood.
As far as I am concerned, if you do not accept the challenge, then
the mud will have to stick!
Yours sincerely,

Mr and Mrs Swansdale

Now we must ask ourselves, why did Mr and Mrs Swansdale
not just put in as most people did - £250? As Michael Walters said
in the City and Finance section of the Daily Mail on April 3rd,
1995: "As a modest investment for a bit of fun with all on offer, it's
good. But as a solid investment, it's all wrong." So this couple put
in a £1000 because they took a chance. And, if we had got a good
horse and won the Derby, they would have been moaning still,
wishing they had put in £10,000.

Of course, I replied personally to Mr and Mrs Swansdale's letter. It hurts me to see people lose money they can ill-afford to lose. And, of course, much as I would have liked to send ten thousand free books and bear the cost of the printing, post and package to all 10,000 shareholders, I cannot spare the £50,000 to do so at present. And, you at the Jockey Club know why. Yes, it is well-documented.

I wrote to you on the 4th November 1996 and explained to you that, although I would like to register Classic Gold, I was unhappy about the VAT situation of paying 17.5% out of the investors £250. And such was my adamant stance based on the E.U. 5th Directive: Sports and Leisure. I thought I had a good case. And, as I have always considered myself and Tim persons of principles, we had another crack at Customs and Excise. It was on unsafe ground as they ruled that, as members of a racing club play no physical part in their sport, they have to pay VAT But say if you joined a 'Crossbow Club' you would not. Now, isn't that stupid!

So, instead of the Jockey Club being interested in my theories, they showed their ignorance and made it clear it would be made difficult for me or Tim to register Classic Gold. Now, why should that be! Well, I suspect it was all part of a conspiracy within the Jockey Club for the past few years. I have already explained Classic Gold in an earlier chapter. I know I am an obstinate bastard at times. So obstinate that, if I believe in a cause or a friend say, I do not waver until the argument is won or lost. I like to think in a war, I would be a good soldier. You, at the Jockey Club, will get the message eventually. Now for those who have read my story will see, I am not without sin. "Let he who is without sin cast the first stone." I have never had a good opinion about myself. I have no ego and that is my strength and with a feeling deeply bred into me that right should overpower wrong. I want, no I demand, justice as is due to a common man.

Now we will turn yet again to Tim's training application. I believe you had no valid reason to refuse it! He came within all accepted criteria at the time. His references were good. Three years on a stud farm. Five years in racing. Of the two trainers who offered to supply references, one was a M.B.E. and does sterling charitable work on behalf of racing and other good causes. Tim also had a lot of horses to train, his, mine and others. Of course, we all know now that this was immaterial to the Licensing Committee, don't we?

What we had was a Jockey Club that operated double standards. For instance, if Tim had been an Arab, he could have found a more favourable response. For them, the rumours that abound in racing about certain irregularities would be swept under the carpet. But the lad, Tim, is not a bitter person, so he asks you only for a permit to train a few of his own horses under National Hunt Rules.

Your comments in a letter to him dated 31st October 1996 says: **"I believe it is unlikely that the Committee would look favourably upon an application for a trainer's licence or permit to train in the foreseeable future."** *The Oxford Dictionary explanation for foreseeable future is: 'The period during which the course of events can be predicted.' In other words, 'over our dead body'.*

And your comments, I believe, scream out as witness to your shame. You, I suspect, engineered a conspiracy. For, as on so many occasions when you have been asked to give a reason for your actions, you hide under something similar to the Official Secret Act, with those pitiful childish words: "We do not have to give a reason!"

Now, I want everyone who reads my book to be aware of our supposedly wonderful racing establishment at 42 Portman Square with its members of Lords and Ladies and Gentlemen of high standing (the full list is printed in an earlier chapter) that Ronnie Dawson brands its stewards as liars, in my horse racing world. Now, that is one hell of a stigma I brand you with for thousands of people who will read my book. So, I want to say to those I claim responsible for their double dealing. If what I say is not true, "sue me!" in a Court of Law. I also believe my readers will challenge you to do just that! But you won't, will you? And now let me go on.

I am not sure if all the racing public are aware of the Jockey Club licensing criteria. Until the 1997/1998 review which brought in some sort of fairness to give a level playing field to future trainers' application. No doubt the Jockey Club would agree that under these new mandatory training requirements, a great many of today's trainers would not have secured a licence. So let us explore the situation a little further. Up to about 1992, practically anyone could have a training licence. You just filled in a form.

Now, by putting these new criteria in place, it means less new trainers coming into racing. So, to keep the balance for now and to stop trainers cheating regularly on saying they have the minimum of twelve horses to train, they now only have to have six.

And now I am going to pull a rabbit out of the hat. Before this review came out, I was a thorn in the side of the Jockey Club over Tim's application refusal. And they tried every trick in the book to find a reason to give Tim which they could put in their own minds as a justification. For example, they wrote to Tim that "successful applicants are expected to produce evidence of demand for their services from members of the public."

My answer to that is to say that's a lie and for Tim to get through their newly laid minefield of their excuses, how about this for utter drivel, which should be an embarrassment to you. In your letter to Tim on the 31st October 1996, yes that "foreseeable future" one, you say "I should point out that those successful applicants have been employed 'independently' and can supply supporting references from employers other than those for whom they are currently training horses." That's another lie.

That is a classic example of Jockey Club gobbledegook. It is like reading from a Boy's Own comic. You really must stop conning Tim. It's not fitting of the Jockey Club.

In my opinion, the Licensing stewards are trying to fool some of the people some of the time, but they cannot fool all of the people all of the time. Are you saying no trainer from 1992 to 1997 was ever given a licence or permit on similar or less qualifying criteria that you refused Tim's application on? You cannot be serious.

Let me pull another rabbit out of the hat. Yes, I have a few in my hat. On Tim's licence application, he names 14 horses he owns himself. I have also promised him six new two-year olds. He has also informed the stewards he may train two or three Classic Bloodstock horses (That is up to the shareholders). But, as I suspect that the majority of shareholders liked hanging around Charnwood, they may have wanted Tim to train all the lot. But the Jockey Club were aware that Tim also had four or five other owners who wanted to give him horses. And, that is why we kept stable staff of eleven on full time at Charnwood, enough for at least thirty horses. And these stable staff were good, we also paid the best money in Newmarket outside the Arabs.

Tim had to prove to me he could do the job. He did with flying colours in 1996, so obviously he would be my choice of trainer at Charwood for 1997 and hopefully for the foreseeable future. My dream as a young man of some day owning my own racehorses and my own racing stables was now to reach the zenith of my life with my son as a racehorse trainer. My life's struggle with its highs and lows was in my mind now to pay me back in interest what every good man should aspire to do "putting down roots".

I will now look at permit holders, but only briefly.

Now, what is pretty obvious if we study the records on permit holders is that the biggest majority live on farms and they have one, two or three horses and rarely have a winner under the rules of racing. But what puts them above all others, say like Tim Dawson? Well, let's guess. How about blood sports, the hunting set, this green wellie brigade. But above all else, the majority are land owners. Their record under the Rules of Racing is dismal, but that matters not a jot to the Jockey Club. It keeps its supporters happy.

Note this licensing business prior to the 1998 review will not go away. I suspect the continuous cover up by the Jockey Club stewards only serves to taint those members of the Jockey Club. I see it like this. Surely honourable men only expect that the stewards who after all only act on behalf of these illustrious people to dispel the rules of racing with fairness to all. Let us face it when one of their own got blackballed by one of their own, there was uproar. But being gentlemen of quality, they only wanted to put things right. And this they did eventually to their credit.

But it is obvious to all who can grasp what I am trying to say. It was not the quality of Tim's licence application that the Jockey Club Licensing Committee found wanting. They showed that with their comments over Tim's permit to train. It was Tim Dawson that was the problem, not the criteria. Now I have tried so hard to squeeze the Jockey Club to spit out the truth. I have blamed Amos and McMath. The Jockey Club deny that was the case. Now the comments of Secretary, Lynn Williams to me: "it was the press". The Jockey Club deny this also. I say, I believe, that it was Tim you refer to in your review as not being a fit and proper person.

You deny you are referring to Tim, but say it is some other poor chap. I suspect you are lying! If it is none of the above, and we have established it cannot be the criteria prior to 1998 review. If it was, a hell of a lot of trainers would not have the licence they have. But like Starr with Clinton, I will chip away until the whole rotten facade crumbles. For you now know Ronnie only too well. I have researched the 1995-1996-1997 trainers and permit holders. And surprise, surprise, we have a few stories to tell don't we! My, my, ooh, certain criterion you wanted from Tim does not apply in all cases. Not by a long shot. And, if it did on a level playing field Tim would have had a full licence, never mind a piddling permit!

However, lucky for you for the time being. I am also at war with Customs and Excise led by the famous "general bankruptcy". And I do not have the energy to fight a war on two fronts. So I turn all my forces to do battle with general bankruptcy. Win or lose, he will know he has been in a war. If I dispose of him, in our final battle, which will be decided in the ensuing weeks, I will then turn my full force on you. Now that will be a hell of a scrap. In my mind it will be the foundation of my new racing story for the year 2000. Yours Faithfully

Ronnie Dawson

Three miles from our villa, I keep a speedboat at our local harbour.

My Villa in Spain, where Maureen and I have found much happiness
since we left the UK in late 1995

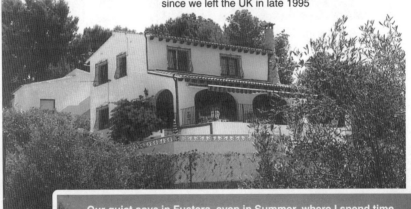

Our quiet cove in Fustera, even in Summer, where I spend time
reading and fishing at weekends.

Some of my family and three of my dogs, Christmas in Spain 1997

My 60th Birthday Party in Spain with my new wife Maureen and Tim
on my right hand side 'as usual'

CHAPTER TWENTY-FOUR

As you have read earlier in my story, I was made bankrupt by Custom and Excise on June 16th, 1997 (bloody awful thing, this bankruptcy business ...). I had tried so hard to escape from the irons put on me. I even read the biography of Houdini - twice! My accountants had tried to get Custom and Excise to reconsider the VAT assessment but they refused. So, I engaged a good solicitor and, after a three month fight on my behalf, he informed me that the position was hopeless. So, I brought up the big guns. A barrister which cost me 200 quid an hour. This guy was the real McCoy. He knew his onions and went for the soft underbelly of the VAT He fought the case on a misdirection and VAT negligence, but was utterly defeated. "Send more money!" he told me on the phone. "I'm going for the jugular this time!" "Go get 'em Butch," I replied. And sent a cheque. This man showed me exactly why barristers charge so much. He was good! For over a month, he hammered the VAT people with facts and figures. Personally, I think he should have just used the hammer! He threw everything at them. "He's in an asylum now." I went to visit him and took him a basket of fruit. I tried to console him with kind words like: "You can't win them all," (and "you still got well-paid.") I left him a humiliated figure, huddled in a corner of his padded cell eating orange-peel after he had discarded the inside.

The War 1998

On September 1st, 1998, I declared total war on the establishment. Having lost the three skirmishes with the VAT the previous months only hardened my resolve. My problem was raising a fresh army to fight with. The opposing forces were very strong and well dug-in. And, with their three victories behind them, when they repulsed my finest troops, they were in no mood to show me any respect or consideration. The official brigands had me by the short and curlies.

The opposing army, led by "General Bankruptcy", was most powerful. His allies consisted of Custom and Excise - Brian (Captain) Bliss. The trustee in my bankruptcy was Chris (Sergeant) Nutting. His solicitors, Hammond Suddards were led by Paul (Brigadier) Bromfield.

Other powerful allies of this lot were the 'law courts', the DTI (Department of Trade and Industry), bonded together via their lust for money (in this case, my money). This powerful coalition force was led by the world-famous 'General Bankruptcy' Victor of Thousands of Battles. To complicate my war position, I was trying to fight on three fronts. Not only was I opposing the famous General and his troops, I was fighting the newspaper industry for libel, particularly Alister (Major) Simms who, I suspect, had the title 'Major' bestowed on him by the press editors for writing major lies.

The other enemy was the supposedly distinguished Jockey Club who had a leader of sorts in Malcolm (Lance-Corporal) Wallace. No relation, I understand, to William Wallace, the Scottish warrior hero executed in 1305 by order of King Edward the First. I doubt whether Lance-Corporal Wallace has the steel to fight with me. No, I will not be drawn into comparisons with that other Lance-Corporal who got promoted to become leader of the Third Reich.

In any case, this lot will have to wait their turn to fight me. Right now, I turn my force onto General Bankruptcy and his troops. My accountant, my solicitors and a barrister, having tested the water against the VAT (without success) have proved to me that I had to find a chink in my enemy's armour. With my back to the wall, I had to also devise a limited damage plan to counter the expected wipe-out of my assets. I re-read my books - "Help" volumes 1, 11 and 111, picking out my best services like a Snake Charmer `War Strategist`. Solicitors Bullied, VAT Inspectors battered, etc.

But I also needed a master plan. When you are going to war, you have to have a contingency plan to fight a rearguard action to save something from the destruction your enemies were reaping on you. Old 'General Bankruptcy's' mission was nearly complete.

He had my homes and racing stables valued for a quick sale for half a million to the Arab, Kamil Mahdi. I wanted a full million for my stables to recover the cost of the £800,000 they had cost me to build with an extra 100 grand over to donate to the dogs' home. But, in a forced bankruptcy sale, I knew the £500,000 was all I could hope for. At this time, I knew that I was not going to get 'top dollar' for the stables. And, if the truth was known, I never expected to ever have to sell now or in the future. That's why the deeds had been placed offshore in my company in the Virgin Isles, to pass it on to my children. But that's life - "Some you win, some you lose."

Of course, if I won my war against Custom and Excise on, say, a technicality, I would be free of my bankruptcy. But, if I won my war against Custom and Excise due to maladministration by Custom and Excise, they could be sued for the shortfall on the 'top dollar' price of my stables. Plus, a lot more, such as: loss of my business, loss of my racehorses, undue stress .... Now, I have an ulcer - oh dozens of things! Even my wife, Maureen, is in a clinic. But that's all "pie in the sky" thinking! For now, just in case a miracle happens to me, I have put a plan together to get a million quid off the government in compensation. All I have to do is prove maladministration by Custom and Excise which is very, very unlikely to ever happen. A million quid? You can do a lot with a spare million. That's a fair whack of money, especially as it would be tax-free as compensation settlements are. "Dream on, Ronnie boy...". Being serious again; a million in compensation would not really be enough to compensate for the humiliation and agony of bankruptcy.

Now, I can identify with those people who have suffered this most ignominious event. I have always believed it is good for you to suffer the pain as others have. And it's those bad experiences through life that give you the opportunity to be a better person. But I still have a long road to travel. The final battle against General Bankruptcy and his troops was now to be fought. I declared total war and would take no prisoners out. For, if I could get others to learn and understand from my battles, I would still have achieved something positive.

My survival mode was now in overdrive, although my defeat was so likely I could taste it. Still, I wanted to give my enemy a bit of "bovver like". Acting on my reliable gut feeling - probably a tummy bug this time, I bombarded solicitor 'Brigadier' Bromfield with a constant barrage of abusive letters and faxes. I sent him my business card. I know that definitely shook him and I think he now suspects I'm nuts. But my bombardment had the desired effect. He never wrote to me again after telling me that all future contact must be through my solicitors. That gave me a bit of breathing space. Brigadier Bromfield was well "dug in" and obviously felt smug in the comfort that he would shortly have a nice piece of 'misery pie' baked with my money. I now turned my force onto the trustee in bankruptcy, Sergeant Nutting who was well entrenched in his bunker at K.P.M.G. headquarters. I slammed him with abusive letters and faxes and threw in a few bitter telephone calls for good measure. I informed him of one of my many talents was that of a 'certified Snake Charmer'. I suspect he thought that at least the certified part was correct. When I phoned him, I was convinced that I could hear music in the background. The record playing was "Money, Money, Money. Yes, I know what he wanted.".

Somehow in a decisive battle I had to beat General Bankruptcy and his troops. I needed to get the whole lot of them in a "pincher movement" Yes, I know it's called a "Pinser Movement", but "Pincher" I feel is right. They are trying to pinch my money. Next, I turned with my force in a feint attack against Captain Bliss and his division of Custom and Excise. I sent them enough paper to bog down their system for two years. Again, I added my business card as an afterthought, pointing out that one of my specialities was "VAT problems prolonged." That, I believe, worried them.

In reality, I was getting nowhere, just being a bloody nuisance. And like all armies, I now needed fresh supplies. I was completely exhausted of fax and writing paper. In one last desperate throw of the dice, I got out my famous books "Help" volume 1, 11 and 111. First page, volume 1, under 'A' was adjudicator specialist. Right, that's what I need, I decided - an independent adjudicator expert, like myself. I eventually found one: Elizabeth Filkin, Adjudicator. I read her official booklet on how to complain about Custom and Excise, the best bit in it was on page nine under the heading, "Compensation" (my favourite word) which read as follows: "Custom and Excise may provide you with financial redress if you suffer financial loss as a result of their maladministration." Right, Ronnie Boy, out comes my battle flags, sound the trumpet, bang the drums. I'm off to do battle now with my new found adjudicator, Elizabeth Filkin.

One last fight, one last chance. If I lose this battle, I have lost the war. When I go to war, it takes over my whole life. In wars you have to be focused on your enemy to know his strengths and weaknesses. People fight wars for all kinds of reasons: religion, greed, domination, bloody-mindedness, etc. "The killing fields are in every country." But I only fight wars when I feel I have suffered an injustice. Then with a feeling of right on my side, I go to war with a vengeance.

To a person who is a declared bankrupt then old 'General Bankruptcy' has no compassion to your plight. His aim rightly so is to get your money for every Tom, Dick and Harry who is on your creditor's list. It matters nothing to him that he can render you destitute.

The fact that he and his solicitors humiliate you is part of his battle strategy, I suspect. To bring you to your knees, make you feel wretched, to put you and your family through the hell of bankruptcy is part of the game - his game.

He has no compassion. His first duty is to your creditors. He couldn't care a cat's whisker that you feel you have suffered an injustice by Custom and Excise. He and his team of high rankers only want a share of the spoils. The more of your assets they can uncover, the bigger their cut. The percentages they are allowed by law to take from your money is, in my opinion, wicked. I believe they enjoy eating their share of misery pie more greedily if they have broken you and your family.

They go through the past years of your life with a nit comb. If I told you what they had pried into all legal like, you may feel the abhorration I have towards General Bankruptcy and his soldiers. In my mind, a more abominable gang you couldn't find. But with the full force of the law on his side he and his cronies offer you nothing but contempt.

So, if you can ever beat him off, I believe, it's your duty to humiliate him like he has thousands of others. It may not happen in his whole lifetime of nicking families' assets, but if you are ever fortunate enough to turn the tables on him, you are entitled to put "the boot in good and proper like," in memory of all the thousands who have been made destitute legally due to the bankruptcy system.

This brings me to the following: I truly feel deep inside that I am a victim of a cheating custom and excise decision. Yet no one will take heed. So now I can, to some measure, sympathise with those who are not guilty, but are rotting in prison or have rotted parts of their lives in the clink because they couldn't prove beyond all doubt of their innocence of the crimes for which they were prosecuted. And, that's the problem I have with Custom and Excise. They put the irons on me, and couldn't grasp the case I was trying to present.

Because I believe they know I realise someone nameless in their department has blundered. But they will not or cannot admit it.

My argument on a moral issue was not of any consequence to them. They could only reply, "You are responsible yourself for knowing the VAT law." In other words, if you get it wrong, it's your fault. In my defence, I can only repeat that the law is an ass. So you can see the futility of my case and why the Custom and Excise issue defeated my finest troops: my accountant, my solicitor and my barrister.

These troops were really just 'cannon fodder' because they all themselves live under the law, they also use the law to win their cases. So, when they come up against the law, up goes the white flag. But, as I said, the law is an ass and that was my defence to beat old "Grab 'Em" by the balls, yer old "General Bankruptcy" I would fight my considered injustice like a soldier defending his country from invasion by a cruel invader.

Stubbornly I have defended my precarious position for over a year now on nothing but scores of letters and faxes - to no avail. It seems to every one that I am doomed! But with the cunning of a street fighter and the dogged bravery of a fool (and not one rabbit left in my hat), I was facing a bitter defeat. And, while I would have to accept it, it would only serve to make me more bitter towards the establishment. I never could lose sight of a glimmer of hope with the adjudicator, but then I was asked by those very people, I was looking to for an eleventh hour reprieve: "Please don't send us any more details, you're swamping us."

But that was exactly the reasoning behind my actions. I would not just lay down and die, so I continued without abatement to try and get my argument across.

It is now November 11th, Armistice Day and I have just received a letter from the adjudicator's office; eleven pages of further questions to be answered. As I go through these I realise that, because of the slow deliberating and thoroughness of the adjudicators, I can see that I am probably not going to get a decision until next year. Tomorrow I will go to Malaga in the south of Spain to speak to my publisher and Josephine Quintero to discuss finalising my book. Malaga is a difficult place to get to from Alicante. Only night flights are available via Madrid. And arriving at 3 a.m. in the morning does not appeal to me. I could take the train like Cooper of The News of the Screws did. I suspect he is a trailblazer in media travel. Two days on a train? On seconds thought I will go by bus.... So I found myself early in the morning at Benidorm bus station ready for the twelve-hour trip.

The lovely thing about a bus trip is you see the countryside. The bad thing is you feel like 'Shaking Stevens' and with forty-five Spaniards for company there is no conversation. I am amusing myself happily with my own thoughts and, as the bus rattles on, I think to myself, 'I bet Jeffrey Archer didn't travel by bus to see his publisher!' Life is full of surprises.

Last week I heard a funny rumour. It was that 'he who is without sin,' Sims of The Sporting Lie. Yes, he who has dispelled much antagonism towards Tim and I. It's rumoured he has set himself up as a bloodstock agent. Well, it's well known that any Tom, Dick and Harry can call himself a bloodstock agent. It's the same as if you wanted to call yourself an estate agent. There are no compulsory qualifications.

But, come now, who could be so stupid as to buy a horse at the horse sales on the recommendation of Sims? Hands up any fools! Oh dear, so many! Well, as I said in an earlier chapter, a mug is born every minute. Thank God most of them live.

I just hope he never starts up a racing club. He's too devious in my opinion. It was good for me to see Classic Bloodstock horses are still winning. Two more this week. And yet another winner for my other venture, Classic

Gold. They are the five horses Tim bought for them. All have won now, some, more than once.

My health has been playing me up again of late. It's been because of all the stress. I went to the doctor who gave me some tablets. He told me to take one every day for the rest of my life ... there were only ten in the box. Tim's life is in ruins but, like Kevin Moorcroft before, Tim will get himself up and dust himself down and get on with things.

We have been working on a new project for the year 2000, 'Global International Thoroughbreds plc.' We have a huge new mailing list, China, Hong-Kong and Japan of 1.8 billion addresses and we are looking at India and North and South America, (not Australia, those boys are too smart for us!). I am sure it will be a big success. In fact, I know it will be - as long as the mailing lists are genuine.

At a board meeting in the Cayman Islands, the new Chairman of Global International Thoroughbreds plc, Tim proposed that all directors have yachts. This was seconded by his father, Ronnie.

Meanwhile, Maureen proposed that Tim and Ronnie have expensive plastic surgery to ensure racecourse admittance. This was similarly agreed. Tim then proposed that four mansions be purchased in various parts of the world to be used for parties. This was seconded by Maureen. Ronnie proposed that all directors are paid £1 million per year, carried unanimously - otherwise it is just not worth the hassle.

Now, to be serious, if you like a bet and would like to join my odds service, I now have a vacancy. Dodger is in prison for 18 years. My address is Charnwood Stables, Hamilton Road Newmarket CB8OTE.

Above:
Maureen and I celebrate our
third wedding anniversary.

Left:
My Jockey, Alan Mackay
returning from a racetrack.

Maureen at Charnwood
with her 'Cooney Crocket'
hat from Canada

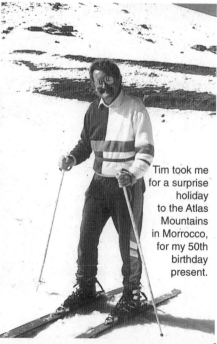

Tim took me
for a surprise
holiday
to the Atlas
Mountains
in Morrocco,
for my 50th
birthday
present.

Touring through Spain with my Jack Russell terrier called 'Jack' in his neckerchief

My youngest son David (left) with my stable manager Mark on holiday,
in Davids Beach Buggy, at my villa in Spain.

CHAPTER TWENTY-FIVE

On the bus journey back from Malaga, Costa del Sol to my home on the Costa Blanca, I could not shake off the apprehension of dark thoughts if I was to finally lose my adjudication. It was during that bus trip that I vowed I would fly to England and confront the adjudication managers at their offices at Haymarket House, London, taking further records of my business with me. The meeting was amicable but businesslike. At least they had a face to face confrontation with the guy they were dealing with, and were sympathetic to my problems. But that was all! They made it clear that Elizabeth Filkin would adjudicate my case on facts and true records. Nothing else. So I immediately got off my bended knees and asked for my bung of ten thousand in pound notes back. No, seriously. They just listened to my interpretation of why the VAT claims for money was, in my opinion, wrong.

Two days later, I was back in Spain with a feeling of doom. I made the decision though that I would finish my story properly. With the adjudicators win or lose verdict I would write down my feelings as events unfold. I have been a bankrupt now for 545 days, during which time I have suffered hundreds of sleepless nights and drunk hundreds of bottles of booze. Christmas was miserable as I was just counting the days to a decision. Win or lose.

It's now February 14th, St. Valentine's Day and still no verdict. What does it all mean? Because it's being drawn out, am I winning? Or does it mean I am losing! Though I have been assured again that my case is on the "Fast Track" and is a priority. This "Fast Track" for me is like the tortoise express. Daily, I am suffering emotional stress and physical abuse with drink.

As my bankruptcy drags on, the interest on monies I owe is spiralling out of control. But it's not just the thought of my England based assets being wiped out, it's the injustice of it all. For in my heart I know I do not deserve the stigma of bankruptcy. I am still adamant that I am a victim of a VAT double cross. I have a will of iron that keeps me fighting my corner when it would be so easy to roll over and die. I pray daily for the liberation of my shackles.

All the experts and barrack room lawyers give me no hope of winning my case. More disturbing thoughts are now being put onto me by KPMG Manager, Chris Nutting. I had informed him that my case was being looked at by the adjudicators and to wind him up. I foolishly put on an act of bravado in saying I thought I had a good chance of being reprieved from bankruptcy. I suspected from the tone of his voice that Nutting did not like to hear that I might yet get a last minute reprieve. He then replied to me in a letter that caused me a lot of distress. And these are his words which particularly troubled me. *'I would be grateful if you would let me know the name and address of the adjudication tribunal to enable your trustee in bankruptcy to deal with them direct. '*

I felt a lot of unease about this KPMG possible intention of interference with the adjudicator's good office. It is well documented in my first book that I had always treated KPMG and Manager, Chris Nutting along with solicitor, Bromfield with about as much respect I would give Saddam Hussain. So, if KPMG had any power to interfere with the adjudication managers, I could expect no KPMG favours.

A few days earlier I had once again tasted the full strength of bankruptcy laws when I asked if I could see the opinion of a barrister which I had paid for to assess the validity of Kelleway's lease. This was also, like the Estate Agent's valuation of Charnwood, refused me. Bankruptcy laws are pathetic. I have a suspicious mind which in my opinion is not without foundation. I have now been informed by a solicitor that KPMG have no authority to deal direct with the adjudication officers under bankruptcy laws. But I, like thousands of others, am in the official receivers' clutches. And I have to dance to their tune.

The draconian bankruptcy laws with its henchmen to operate them have you by the balls at all times. At the time of writing, I am having serious problems with Kelleway. He is behaving very badly towards my manager at Charnwood.

Kelleway is also turning a once beautiful property into a wreck. I phoned him to ask if he could please keep the stables in good order. Even I was taken aback by his venomous reply: "The more I wreck it, the cheaper I will buy it. You're f.......g bankrupt and can do f... all about it." And those words of Kelleway's are true. I am powerless to stop his despicable actions. This is a man I gave help to previously when he asked me for it.

Now I was very concerned over the intention of solicitor Bromfield and the KPMG Manager, Nutting. Could there be a plot to sell my property cheap? A "nod and a wink", a kickback, then a resale with somebody making a financial killing?

Let's look at it more closely. Kelleway pays rent £5,500 each quarter. This goes to solicitors Bromfield of Hammond Suddards or KPMG. This money was supposedly to be used solely for the upkeep of Charnwood but they decided to retain it. After all, they do get a percentage of all the money they can get their hands on. And Charnwood has fallen into disrepair, the electric gates are broken, many windows are smashed and all the houses and stables are desperate for a coat of paint. It will be hard to find a buyer. Kamil Mahdis' £1/2 million offer has gone because Kelleway wouldn't leave at the end of his one year lease as he promised me he would when I rented him the stables. Kelleway has now run amok and KPMG and its solicitors have not presented

Kelleway a bill for one bit of damage. Not one penny of rent money, £15,000 a year, have they used for the up-keep of the stables instead they have allowed Kelleway to turn the yard into one more fit for pigs than race-horses.

I realise it's not a KPMG problem if the yard goes to the dogs. As long as there is enough money from a sale to cover my creditors and for their cut of commission.

That's their main concern. KPMG and Hammond Suddard's I don't believe care a cat's whisker about the obvious depreciation of Charnwood. So have they found something out with their obvious intentions to deal di-rect with my adjudicators? Namely that my case is lost. So to hell with me! I am in the dark. I have had no hint of winning my case by the adjudication management. But I feel very concerned by KPMG power and secret intentions to try and deal directly with the adjudicator. What's their game! There is corruption in the Govern-ment. Corruption in the judiciary. Corruption is big busi-ness. Take corrupt Maxwell as a host for a gang of para-sites. There is corruption in the police - corruption eve-rywhere you look.

So why is it not possible to have corruption under the laws of bankruptcy? Kickbacks, manipulation, crooked estate agents, shady sales of property. It's all rife here in Spain. Is England really any different? I hope so. But I'm scared! One thing I will say is that the letter from KPMG about my adjudication, besides causing me much distress should be investigated by someone.

When you're bankrupt, your bank accounts are nicked. You can't remain in business, or start one up. And, if you earn any money above the cost of food and other basics for your family, you are liable to have it snatched by the official receivers. Believe me, you are helpless. You have no way of knowing or being entitled to know anything to do with your assets. I know I have done a lot of carping, but much of the reason is to try and warn others who may fall into the same trap.

My other problem is that I need money to pay solicitors and barristers in order to get my claims for compensation against my ex-accountants on the move. And, the same with the actions against the Jockey Club, as well as libel actions against the press.

Mentioning the press again, I would like to make a few more comments: The last few days it's been the Glen Hoddle business. Poor Glen! But at least he will get his life back now. Matt Dickenson of The Times, the reporter who has probably got his one and only moment of fame in his life on being granted an interview on football by Hoddle, betrayed the man by making a song and dance over Hoddle's personal beliefs. Matt 'Judas' Dickenson betrayed a decent Christian for his supposed reincarnation beliefs. Now, I'm not an expert, but I do know that Christians - who are promised eternal life - do not believe in reincarnation, so maybe our star reporter just heard what he wanted, or cannot tell the difference between a statement relating to problems we inherit 'generationally' (don't ask!) and instant karma.

Either way, had he checked his information, he would have known that reincarnation and religion have nothing to do with football - except that football is today's mass religion. Did Hoddle offend their High Priests? Then, after the media dogs uproar reached a crescendo for Hod's head, Matt 'Judas' Dickenson goes on Sky TV Sports a few days later and says: "Technically, Hoddle was a brilliant coach." This, from the Judas reporter who instigated Hod's downfall. His story in The Times lost us a good coach. We also had The Times editor, Peter Stothard on TV waving Dickenson's reporter's notebook (which reminded me of Chamberlain on his return visit from Hitler). Stothard smugly said: "My reporter is an honest guy." Well, now that is a miracle, because a few days earlier, TV Teletext reported a survey, which claimed that 80% of people thought reporters were liars. I bet you 20/1 you didn't read that survey in the paper did you? But you did read the headlines a few days later, following a couple of bogus TV documentaries. 'Can we believe anything we see on TV?' Bloody media hypocrites.

Poor Hod was crucified for speaking openly to a sneaky reporter. Hod obviously didn't think it was important to football. But when The Times are trying to sell papers to the public for only 30 pence and when you have a desperate circulation problem, you'll sell your soul for a controversial story.

In my opinion, The Times are unjust hypocrites, take Glen Hoddles views and apply Article 18. of the Universal Declaration of Human Rights 1948.:

> *"Everyone has the right to freedom of thought, conscience and religion. This right includes freedom to change his religion or belief, and freedom, either alone or in community with others and in public or private, to manifest his religion or beliefs in teaching, practice, worship and observance."*

Article 12 was 50 years old in December 1998. I suspect ex-Cambridge graduate, Dickenson has never even heard of it. The vindictiveness of the press that needed no helping hand to destroy our country's football manager, soon had the gullible public eating out of its hand.

Even our government joined in the butchery of the Christian. Tony Banks, our Minister of Sport drives his knife home. Then, Prime Minister Blair does not want to be seen - a Pontius Pilot with no actual blood on his hands - so he drives his knife in deepest of all and twists it home. Now, the flow of blood loss could not be stemmed and Glen Hoddle bled to death at Lancaster Gate, deserted by the very same F.A. officials who hired him, and because of their own skeletons in the cupboard, now cast him asunder to appease the demands of the press. It seems that everyone wanted a share of the Christian's destruction. The Chairman of the football task force, David Mellor said: "English football was being dragged down by Hoddle's bizarre beliefs." This quote is from an ex-government minister who could only score in bed with his mistress, the press said, when dressed in his Chelsea football kit. Now that David is bizarre!

The F.A. with its own previous tacky resignations over a bit of dodgy movement, left right and centre. Not a keeper amongst the lot of them, fawning now to the Nationwide Building Society sponsors. I can see in the future Nationwide MD. Mike Lazenby leading out our national football team at Wembley, now called the 'Nationwide Side'.

But not all people are fools. A few men of compassion and intelligence are supportive of Hoddle. Veteran campaigner for the disabled, Labour peer, Lord Ashley said about Hod's dismissal. "It's a sad day for British tolerance of free speech." Then Woolridge, the respected sport's journalist of The Daily Mail, said: "The job of an England football manager is untenable by an unrelenting vicious press." And, for that remark, Woolridge is obviously one of the 20% of honest journalists - not one of the 80% dishonest ones who are mostly employed by the downmarket tabloids.

Many years ago, I used to think there was a contract between the reader and his newspaper which should be one of explicit trust. The real scandal is we Brits have for reading tabloid trivia and believing its importance. If Times editor, Stothard and his supposedly honest reporter M.J.D ridiculed the now ex English coach, Hoddle for his metaphysical beliefs (which, incidentally, are the same as a few hundred million Hindus and Buddhists), what God given right have this pair to be so high and mighty? For they probably offended a greater world-wide majority with their criticism of Hoddle's beliefs with their newspaper's attempt to improve a disinterested readership. Was this more to do with The Times miserable circulation of with about 400,000 copies a day? Including the freebies?

Just for the record, Hoddle never got my vote in the beginning. I was a Jack Charlton man. Like in chess, a good defence is difficult to overcome and, just like Ramsey's 1966 World Cup winners, that would have been Jack's policy. I have often written, I think, that reporters are prats. But to show that I am no egoist, I will tell you this: I gave my next door neighbour a copy of my book to read, asking him to give me an honest frank opinion. He said: "It's a load of crap and makes you look a prat!" Well, there you go! But, surely I am not a prat in the same league as the media? A few days after the Hoddle sensation, we have a much bigger clanger dropped by the Chief Inspector of Schools, Chris Woodhouse, who said: "Sexual affairs between teachers and pupils can sometimes be educative." Well, if Hoddle offended six million disabled with his views; I would think Woodhouse offended double that amount of parents with his. And, like Hoddle, Woodhouse apologised for his indiscretionary remarks, but there was no big media song and dance this time.

The media dogs hang one man for his beliefs and spare another for his. The reason? Well, come now, it's obvious. To the press boys, the passion of football to its readers has more appeal than the passion of parents for their children.

CHAPTER TWENTY-SIX

Today it's March 11th and I have spoken again to the adjudication officers. Their investigation into my case has now been going on for eight months. Today I explained to them how the long time waiting for a verdict is draining me.

I have now been a bankrupt for 605 days. The adjudication management have sort of promised me that it will be finally concluded in four weeks time, when I will apparently receive the adjudicator's verdict by letter. But they will give me no clues regarding the merits of my case. All the barrack room lawyers' say, I will lose it, but I believe it's been worth all my time and effort, having a crack at quashing my bankruptcy, even as expected, I lose.

Following the first publication of my book, I received many letters from readers who had suffered similar injustices to mine in their lives. However, they had taken no action over newspaper slander or bad professional advice. One of the main reasons they cited was lack of funds. I know all too well how much it can cost to fight, say, a libel case.

If I were to win my case against the VAT, I will not hesitate to be prepared to put up hundreds of thousands of pounds to fight the newspapers for libel. If that's what it cost to get justice and my family's name cleared, so be it! And if I lose my case I will mortgage my remaining assets to raise capital to fight my corner.

Does the public have to know 90% of the scandalous newspaper stories about people's private lives, I ask? I think not. Downmarket tabloids with their lurid stories not only shame the alleged sinner but, sadly, also humiliate and shame those innocent people within the family - wives and children. Readers support these dirty washing stories by buying these grubby little newspapers, so paying towards the salaries of reporters who glory in writing the gutter press stories we seem to crave to read.

One man sadly wrote to me how his daughter had suffered a nervous breakdown following a lurid sex exposé in which the newspaper in question milked and glossed over the true facts. Such was his daughter's shame for the disgrace she had brought on her parents, brothers and sisters, that she attempted suicide. And the story? Well of interest to no one really - other than a pervert.

So, if you buy these papers and you consider yourself to be a Christian, think on! I have also been shamed and my family humiliated. My shame arose from the concoction of lies that appeared in the press.

For example: Miller of The Times wrote that, "the DTI was to knock on the doors of all witnesses to gather statements over Dawson and Classic Bloodstock." That was a lie. Radford of The Sunday People reported that, "they visited me in Spain when I had made certain comments to them." That was a lie. Cooper of The News of the World reported that, "he had tracked me down." That was a lie.

Whitfield of The North West Evening News said, "I masterminded a multi-million horse racing scam". That was a lie.

Sims of The Sporting Life reported that "Classic Bloodstock had enriched me beyond my wildest dreams." That was a lie.

I will, of course, concede that if there had been one ounce of truth in any of those stories then, yes, the public should have the right to know. But to be named as a conman and thief when I am clearly not guilty is a burden that can only be lifted in a court of law, and with huge payments for libel as compensation for all the aggravation caused.

Because of various newspaper allegations and the subsequent outcry, Maureen and I made the decision to be interviewed under caution by the DTI investigators well over a year ago now. My solicitor was horrified that we were willing to put ourselves up for this without our solicitor being present. But, as I told him: "Look, we are just going to state the truth. We have nothing to hide, as all the audited accounts will prove. So we don't need a solicitor." And, as events proved, the D.T.I. (despite all the malicious slander in the press) found not a penny piece missing from Classic Bloodstock PLC company funds.

What has grieved me is just how many trainers and other racing folk to their shame, believed all the untrue gossip. Mine and Tim's life was destroyed by the lies. And not one trainer could bring himself to say: "Sorry, I should have waited for proof before condemning you by mouth."

Sometimes I think of myself as a fox. One who has never killed a chicken in its life, only vermin, but still hounded by the hunting pack, just because he is a fox. Then he is torn to pieces, everyone is in on the kill. We want blood. Tally Ho!

It was Sky News TV pundit, Adam Boulton that confirmed what I had always suspected about media people in general. He was interviewing Jerry Springer who willingly confessed to Murdoch puppet, Boulton, that the Jerry Springer Show on Sky TV was a circus and that most of the people on it were outrageous. But, following further criticism by Boulton who was on his high horse, Springer retorted with the comment that 80% of the news stories on TV, people don't really need to know. And that many of theses are so vindictive that the fall out envelops a whole family in shame. "Do you ever think of that hurt?" Springer asked. "I believe you should do unto others as you would be done by," Boulton replied, adding that he was not a believer and had no faith. And, my reader, that is the problem.

For if you were a Christian with true Christian beliefs, as a journalist, you could not bring yourself to write articles which can cause so much pain to others. And to top that, if your reports are untrue, as they often are - then that is downright evil.

Springer drove his knife home finally when he said to a smirking Boulton. "Have you ever known a journalist pull a story because it was sure to cause grief to some innocent members of a family?" Boulton didn't answer.

I now turn back quickly to Hoddle who the press had ridiculed for his beliefs and who then welcomed Kevin Keegan with open arms as our national football team saviour - only to find out a few days later that even "our Kev" has used the services of a faith healer, the well-known physic and medium, clairvoyant Betty Shine. And the press dogs? Well, I suspect they were looking for a hole to crawl in to. For they didn't have the stomach to crucify another *'messiah'* for his beliefs; for the time being, that is!

The point I am trying to make is, if you are a Christian and believe in God, then it is a sin to hurt someone and his innocent family just for the sake of a story. Or, to victimise someone unjustly. In my opinion, much of the downmarket tabloids are the tools of Satan and try to poison the minds of millions of normal decent folk. To these reporters and their editors of spurious and libellous newspaper articles, I say read Matthew 12, verses 35-37:

> *"A good man out of the good treasures of his heart bringeth forth good things: and an evil man out of the evil treasure bringeth forth evil things. "But I say unto you. That every idle word that man shall speak, they shall give account thereof in the day of judgement. "For by thy words thou shalt be justified, and by they words though shalt be condemned."*

It is obvious to me that, by their actions, these reporter/journalists and their editors neither fear or believe in God and do the work of the devil. I found the honesty of Daily Mail journalist, Peter McKay refreshing when commenting on the so-called 'News of the Screws' latest exposure on the England Rugby Captain, Dallagio and its drug claims about this man after setting him up in a 'honey trap'. McKay wrote that moralising newspaper journalists have their quota of in-house dope heads. Anyone who believes 'News of the Worlds' exposures should, in my opinion, see a psychiatrist. I would bet a gold bar to a penny Dallagio is innocent. Wait and see!

Take the Jockey Club. I said I was sorry for a minor infringement. I begged for leniency as a first time offender. My reward was a life ban. Now no one is ever going to tell me that these people who hold so much power and abuse it so ruthlessly are without sin? Not an ounce of compassion could they find in either my case or Tim's. Why? Well, I suspect the lies by the satanic press swayed their weak minds. Mark 12, verses 38, 39 fit the stewards of the Jockey Club perfectly. Verse 38:

"Beware of the scribes which love to go in long clothing and love salutations in the market place. Verse 39: And the chief seats in the Synagogue and the uppermost rooms of the feast".

I could then add Mathew 24, verse 28:

"Even so ye outwardly appear righteous unto men but within ye are full of hypocrisy and iniquity".

This motley Jockey Club crew, of which security chief Roger Buffham is one of the bottle-washers, have managed, yet again, to end up with egg all over their face. Their suspension of jockeys from their livelihood just over a police investigation is a scandal. With all charges dropped from their alleged involvement in doping and

My Mum with our
next door neighbour,
Bob Champion M.B.E

My son Tim aged seven on his first horse ☛

Hong Kong
Too much traffic for
Maureen and I,
but I won £6,000
at the
Racecourse Sha-Tin.

race fixing by Scotland Yard, Johnnie "Hang 'Em High" Maxie tries to cover up their 'put a boot in' attitude with press statements saying, "Roger Buffham has the full support of the Jockey Club".

No, sorry Johnnie that won't wash. The Jockey Club attitude is that there is no smoke without fire - hang 'em first. Just in case they are guilty. This motley Jockey Club crew didn't give me and Tim ten years a piece for wrongly registering a couple of ponies. No, the twits believed all the rumours of the missing millions.

K.P.M.G., that multi-million insolvency firm no doubt see the directors and managers sharing a Christmas bonus. Profits are up - back slapping all round, light up the cigars. Another poor Joe Bloggs has just fallen into our lap. His business collapsed because he couldn't collect the money he was owed. Bad luck, what! Tally Ho!

To K.P.M.G. it's directors and managers, I give them Mark 36:

"Jesus said. For what shall it profit a man if he shall gain the whole world and lose his soul".

Following a further letter to K.P.M.G. to complain over various matters which concerned me and my family and the way they could, by law, punish and humiliate us, (plus the fact that I would expose to the public some of the true horrors a bankrupt had to face in my book - Conmen, Cheat and Liars), the solicitors of K.P.M.G. and my trustees in bankruptcy, Hammond Suddards once again threatened me by letter which is included hereafter:

Proposed Publication(s) We note that you intend to publish a further book. We would like to take this opportunity to remind you that both our client and ourselves will take very seriously any comments of a defamatory nature contained within any publication on your behalf. If necessary, we shall take advantage of any remedy available to us in the event of the publication of anything defamatory against this firm KPMG, or their respective partners, staff or employees.

Do they feel guilty in their work yet believe they are untouchables? In my opinion, they do the devil's work. So, I ask them this; If they consider themselves honorable men, yet they feed their families on the misery of others, shouldn't they find themselves another job! For I believe it takes a certain kind of man to do certain types of work, and I thank the Lord that whatever ducking and diving I may have done, I have never resorted to feeding from other peoples misery.

If my plate is full on my family's table, I bless the Lord before I eat. I think God will honour that blessing if your fortune was not gained from another man's family misfortune! Now, the last thing I want is to be all pious like. I have in the past sinned to feed my family. But I have repented and changed my ways. I have seen the light!

Jesus said *"But if we judge ourselves, we would not come under judgement. When we are judged by the Lord, we are being disciplined so that we will not be condemned with the World"* (1 Corinthians 11v 31:32)

I think many of the people who have sat in judgement of my family, I and many others who are considered newsworthy, and therefore without rights, could benefit from understanding that statement. I hope they will take the time to look at their motives and actions, as I have mine.

CHAPTER TWENTY-SEVEN

If you asked me, do I believe in God. The answer is "yes". But I am amazed to realise that despite everything, He believes in me!

I say my prayers. I go to church. I try do some good things. But I always seem to fall short of the mark. I am striving to do more and am delighted to say that I now choose to harm no one. I have learnt the hard way that financially and emotionally, harmful and unproven gossip is a demon we all have to distrust.

Going to church does not necessarily make you a good Christian; it goes a bit deeper than that. You must have faith and live the life, not just talk the talk.

I believe in the devil. He tries to bend my ear on a regular basis - but is having a harder time with me these days.

I have said that I believe in God. And I also believe in miracles. I have experienced them. Perhaps we all have, but sometimes choose not to see them or believe in them.

One of mine happened when I returned from Africa with my new wife Maureen, I was admitted urgently into hospital with a serious mystery illness for which drugs were having no effect. In much pain and getting weaker, I knew I was dying.

When Maureen visited me at my lowest ebb, I sent her away. I had neither the heart or could find the love for a visit. Married only three weeks, I felt guilty of my situation. I should never have gone to Africa. An act of bravado on my part against all medical common sense for an S.L.E. sufferer like me with a very low immune system.

Four days later whilst in hospital, to my doctor's surprise, I was unexpectedly over the crisis.

The registrar and professor in charge of my case related to a bevy of doctors round my bed that, with all known medical criteria, this man should not be alive. At the same time, he explained that my body had contained none of certain elements essential for life. It was a mystery.

It was only later, when Maureen visited me that I discovered that the mystery was, in reality, a miracle. Two days earlier when I had sent her away, she explained how she was convinced that I was going to die. So she went straight to the hospital chapel and prayed all day for God to spare me. Maureen has prayed to God all her life and is a spiritual believer. And she prayed her socks off for God to make me better - and I lived. So it was a miracle, not a mystery.

Since that dark, then enlightened time in my life, I have been back in hospital four times with my systemic lupis problem but I have no fear any more.

Good Friday, April 2nd 1999 and I write this part on my return from Calpe's Evangelist Church.

I joined this small congregation a few weeks previously and every Sunday service I have raised my hand to Pastor Leslie Lyons' question, "Raise your hands those who want Jesus to come into their lives." I have also prayed for that grace. And today, Good Friday, it's truly happened to me. I am a believer! I am full of happiness and joy, goodwill and Christian spirit.

Roman 5-1. *"Therefore being justified by faith we have peace with God through our Lord Jesus Christ."*

Today, the 14th April, I have received from the Adjudication office a fax which has all but destroyed any hope I had of winning my case against the VAT. But I have had setbacks in my life before and this fax warns me to expect another.

Well, I know it's not the final official adjudication letter, but it looks to me near as saying I'm finished. Oh well, I will just dust myself down and get on with my life the best I can. And yes, I will stay loyal to my new found faith.

The Adjudicator's Office
Haymarket House 28 Haymarket London SW1Y 4SP
Telephone: 0171 930 2292 Fax: 0171 930 2298

To: Ron Dawson
Fr: Andrew Fraser

Date: 14 April 1999
You may remember in a previous letter to you I said that VAT is a self assessed tax and the responsibility to get it right rests with the trader.

There is no responsibility on Customs and Excise to visit a new business within a certain period, or to visit at particular intervals, or to visit at all. They determine the timing and regularity of their visits according to the size and complexity of your business and your past compliance, they are under no obligation to visit. In their public Notice 'Visits by VAT Officers' they say you should not wait to be visited by a VAT officer if there is anything of which you are not certain.

Our local Customs and Excise offices or Business Advice Centres can provide publications to assist you, or alternatively you can write or telephone.

Your confusion arises, I believe because you think that Customs and Excise are responsible for ensuring the accuracy of your VAT declarations.

Since the commencement of VAT in 1973 this responsibility has lain with the trader and for this reason traders such as yourself employ professional representatives. This responsibility still remains even when you receive a visit from a VAT visiting officer, the officer does not perform an 'audit' on your books and records and is not normally responsible if they miss an error.

I am not aware of the government cutbacks to which you refer, but the nature of the tax has not been changed and remains your responsibility even if you never received a previous visit.
I hope this helps
Andrew Fraser

I was not downhearted, despite this fax from the adjudicators office on the 14th April which has left me now with about as much hope of winning my case as my winning the lottery with a single ticket (which I never bought!). Why? Because of my new-found spiritual beliefs. No more reaching for the bottle to blot out the reality of life. Now I just accept that, if it is God's will that I should be stripped of my wealth, then so be it. But I know that I would never revert to my old ways and will be a true Christian for the rest of my days.

This has happened following me asking for Jesus to come into my life at Calpe Evangelist Church when I worshipped there for the first time on Sunday 8th March. From that day forward I changed. I was calmer, more patient and more compassionate. Full of love for mankind and forgiveness for my enemies.

The truth is now that, if I had not already written my book up to Chapter 26 with its obvious bitterness to so many, before I became a Christian believer, I could not have written it now.

Without this book, all the lies and malicious action against my family and I would have been unheard of, and the transgressors would have been able to carry on, committing their evil, in their dark little ways.

If the truth will set you free, and I know now that it does, then these truths about what has been done need to be given the light of day, for you the reader to decide and for those who are in the wrong to have the opportunity to find their truth and also be set free.

I now just wait patiently for my official letter from the adjudicator, which will explain in full details the reasoning behind the decision she has reached. On Friday the 23rd April, St George's Day, I phoned London yet again to ask when my case would be finally concluded. Once again I was told, in another few weeks - hopefully! But it was no longer all consuming in my thoughts. No, that had been replaced by Jesus.

On the 17th May 1999 Maureen and I were baptised at Benidorm Evangelist Church by Pastor Leslie Lyons.

Me centre right at my Baptism in Benidorm, with Maureen and my two boys Tim and David.
Left to right: Renata, Kate & Coral and Davids girlfriend Kath.

After my baptism around the pool with my growing family in Spain.
My brother Rick - 'my rock' is next to me second right.

We are now both fully confirmed 'Born Again Christians'. To quote the Bible:

John 3, verses 3:7

Jesus said: "Verily, verily, I say unto thee. Except a man be born again, he cannot see the Kingdom of God.

Nicodeaus Saith unto him. How can a man be borne when he is old? Can he enter a second time into his mother's womb and be born?"

Jesus answered. "Verily, verily I say unto thee. Except a man be born of water and of the Spirit he cannot enter into the Kingdom of God."

"That which is born of the flesh is flesh, and that which is born of the Spirit is Spirit." "Marvel not that I said unto thee, ye must be born again."

Now, my dear reader, perhaps you have listened to all this sort of stuff before? I used to run a mile from those who I saw as religious freaks.

Mind you, it did puzzle me somewhat how these people could go through life with so few material things of the world, yet were so full of joy.

Oh dear, how do I tell you 'The Good News' as the Bible calls it. So to my final story and to finish my book. Please don't throw it down yet.

After I made my commitment to Jesus on Sunday, 8th March by raising my hand in church to ask for Jesus to come into my life, strange things started to happen to me.

Small miracles following my prayers. Unexplained happenings. I was so astounded I rang up a fellow Christian who had come to see me from many miles away a few months earlier with a message he had received from above. As I explained my miracles, he replied. "Oh, we just call that 'business as usual', Ronnie. Keep praying, keep faith in Jesus and ask him for the things He wants for your life. He won't let you down. Just have faith in him."

Over the next few weeks, since my baptism, I had got into some really good habits. I like to read my Bible daily, and so every morning I walk down through my orange grove to the bottom of my garden and pray to God on my garden seat under my fig tree.

This fig tree of mine had somehow drawn me there to pray. I have several other lovely quiet places in my garden where I could pray, but I always returned to the fig tree. Yet this tree was a disappointment to me this year because, unlike other years when it bore a bounty of early young fruit, this year it was still barren.

My neighbour's fig tree had branches heavy with young fruit. Daily I prayed and, as I drew closer to my church and God, I worshipped more sincerely. Then, following my Baptism on that Sunday May 17th, I was filled with the Holy Ghost as fellow Christians will tell you is the norm. So under my still barren fig tree on the following Monday I prayed for everyone, enemies and loved ones alike.

Later that day Maureen and I had a visitor, a member of Calpe Church and for five hours without interruption she talked about faith. And, as she told us the story of her life and her love of Jesus, I was a patient listener. Gone was one of my past sins, that of impatience with people.

The next morning I went down to my fig tree and prayed and with the Holy Ghost inside me helping me on, I prayed like I had never prayed before. For the first time I truly worshipped and glorified God.

When I opened my eyes, they were immediately drawn to the leaves of my barren fig tree but God with his 'signs and wonders' had filled the tree full of fruit. Yes, they were only small, a few weeks behind my neighbour's fig tree, but they will catch up.

Oh, the tears rolled down my cheeks. I was full of wonder. I found myself shouting out loud 'God's been listening to me. Praise the Lord!" I then ran to tell Maureen,

"Come and look!" "It's a miracle!" she said on seeing the once (just the day before) barren fig tree.

Now you may say that I am a religious nut. Nowadays, I will take that as a compliment. But come now, I have sinned since a young lad without thought for God or Jesus. But verily, verily Ronnie says to you - Jesus is Real. And when you find him, and believe in him, I promise you that then you will find a happiness and purpose in your life and you will also witness signs and miracles. Incidentally, how about this scripture! John 1. 48:49

Nathanael saith unto him, "whence know though me? Jesus answered and said unto him. "Before that Phillip called thee, when thou was under the fig tree, I saw thee." Nathanael answered and saith unto him. "Rabbi, thou are the son of God, thou art the King of Israel."

Jesus answered and said unto him. "Because I said unto thee, I saw thee under the fig tree. Believest that though shalt see greater things than these."

So my reader make of my experience under my fig tree what you will. But I say to you truly, I went to God as a serious sinner, from Soho to Paris, from Amsterdam to the flesh pots of Bangkok, I have sinned and dear friend, I am forgiven and born again. I have my second chance and hell will freeze over before I blow this second chance. I tell you truly, Jesus is alive. I am no religious nut. Just a guy who got the message, who would have had to be hit over the head with a baseball bat to see the light (stars) in my dark past. But brother, when you believe in Christ, you enter a whole new ball game.

I once walked hand in hand with the evil one. I enjoyed it then, but I now walk with Jesus - it's wonderful. I caught the bus to God's heavenly Kingdom, just in time. So, if I can just sow in you some faith, just the size of a mustard seed. If my message falls on good ground, it will continue to grow in you like it grew in me.

Our four faithfull Yorkshire Terriers, awaiting my prayer time to finish, so they can reclaim my attention.

My "quiet place" under our fig tree, where so many of my prayers and requests have been offered and answered.

CHAPTER TWENTY-EIGHT

At last, the long-awaited report from my adjudication has arrived although it doesn't deliver what I had hoped for. While it is critical of the VAT in some areas, it offers me little immediate hope of suspending my bankruptcy. However, a little heartened by the report compiled by the new adjudicator, Dame Barbara Mills (OBE) QC, I have filed for a late tribunal hearing on the application by the VAT of the EU 6th Directive Sport and Recreation regarding members of a racing club being liable to pay VAT. This, I argue, is against the spirit of the EU 6th Treaty. And the VAT are not in my case applying the EU rules.

Only my pride and sense of justice made me refuse to charge my racing club members VAT on top of their membership fee. For my intransigence in putting up two fingers to the penny pinching VAT interpretation of the EU 6th Directive, they have subsequently made me liable to pay all the VAT myself of my 2000 club members fees. I refused, so they made me bankrupt for the money. Me and my obscure principles have placed me in hot water yet again. The £60,000 I refused to pay has now doubled with interest. But I fight on because I believe I am right. My new accountant also now thinks I could have interpreted the EU 6th treaty correctly.

I won't go into all the details here concerning the EU 6th Treaty (Sport and Recreation), but the VAT have made my life a misery for the past 3 years and have forced my stables to be put up for sale for a knockdown price to pay my VAT debt. If I eventually win my case, I will be compensated in full, so I continue to take comfort in that.

I have informed the VAT of the fact that both the Sports Council and the Heart Foundation have written to me which supports my understanding of the EU 6th Treaty as regards my racing club members' VAT exemption. I have since received a letter from Custom and Excise. They are going to look further into this matter of the EU 6th Treaty.

Well, after my three years of continual letter and fax writing complaints to the VAT, it's about time too.

Incidentally, I have also received a letter of apology from Custom and Excise over past indifference to my business. No compensation. No admittance that they have made an erroneous ruling in my business. Not yet!

I will just add here that anyone planning to take a case to the adjudication team, beware. In my experience, they will do you no justice. They fabricate the facts and lie so that, when they put your case up in front of the adjudicator, your evidence is twisted. They do not seem able to grasp the facts and, sadly, you are not allowed to point out the lies and errors in the report they put before the adjudicator until she has ruled on the evidence they have supplied her with.

In my opinion, it's just a bureaucracy stitch up to justify a government quango with jobs for the boys who are so incompetent they would find it hard to make a living in the real word. Personally in my dealing with the adjudication team, I found them both arrogant and ignorant.

Now on to more pleasant things. I believe if I had not stood up to the VAT on a principle, I would today have been doing exactly the same type of business. Instead, because of all the turmoil which eventually led to my bankruptcy, I was led to Christianity and the truth about myself.

Being a Christian is the hardest thing you will ever do. To try and live like Jesus I find very difficult. I have not yet achieved one full day of obedience. I start off well enough, but succumb to a temptation or sin before nightfall. But I will persevere for the rest of my life in my faith to be worthy of Christ.

So I draw my book to a close with my testimony. I, Ronnie Dawson, have been a lifetime major sinner.

A conman, thief and liar like many others in this world. You don't make a million or two in the world of horse racing through being lily white. I've 'conned' book-makers; I've 'stolen' racing secrets from others and used them for my own ends and I've lied many times in the setting up of my racing coups.

Understand me when I say this. By the standards of the world, I have been as honest as the next man. But when you apply Gods measure, then I am guilty.

I have spent money like water, sinned in all the best sinning places, yachted in the South Seas, cruised in the Caribbean, gambled in Hawaii and Hong Kong. Flitted about in private planes to wherever the action was. Rev-elled in Paris and Bangkok, curried in India and boozed in Fiji, skied in Canada and clubbed in Miami and, yes, spent some time in Alcaltraz prison (as a visitor).

I've lost thousands on the turn of the card and won thousands on another turn. I've had my highs and my lows in horse racing, drank and sinned with the toffs, safari'd in Africa and sailed on the Indian ocean. And I tell you truly, not one of my exploits has given me as much joy as being a spirit filled Christian.

So to those non-believers, sinners, parasites, hypo-crites and fools, (of whom I was also once a major player), wake up, repent and see the light. No, I am not mad!

Praying under my fig tree I asked for God's forgive-ness for me for those who I have made my enemies. Be-cause I thought I was special or right or knew better. First Brian McMath I am sorry Brian. I had forgotten just how tough life can be for others. Forgive me, Brian. My pride made me a berk. I wish you future good fortune.

Anthony Kelleway, it's not your fault you appear weird to others and me. You have a tough act to follow in your Dad's footsteps. Horse racing brings out the worst in people, especially greed, self-interest and jealousy and your financial problems I know give you a miserable life of anxiety. You need help. Change your ways before it's too late. Take stock of life and control your lies and, in my opinion, a good counsellor could help.

Forgive me, Gay Kelleway, I was selfish. I had it all, but wanted more. She messed me about once only, so I sacked her. I am sorry.

Now poor Gay is having a disastrous bad run of over 80 consecutive losers. Her punters are either in the workhouse or queuing up on the top of Beachy Head. Don't jump lads! I can save you!

I forgive my devious ex-accountant, Andy Irish BA whose advice I took as gospel but it proved flawed. I thought Andy could be being less than virtuous, when he controlled Classic Bloodstock plc but even though I was the Managing Director in title, I could not find the strength or integrity to interfere. At the time, he was looking after all my personal business interests and if you sup with the devil you are his disciple.

I forgive the Jockey Club boys. They just confirmed to me what I have always suspected. The higher in life you may appear to others, often the lower your integrity. They act like a God towards unrepented sinners, or not sinners, but those who are possibly sinners in the Jockey Club boys imagination. To these modern day Pharisees of Portman Square, I forgive thee o' self-righteous ones, but take a look at Matthew 23 verse 27 and please take note.

I have found it hard to forgive the press, you can't forgive the devil at work, but these unscrupulous reporters will face their own day of judgement, before God. Jesus said *"Forgive them, they know not what they do"* when the world crucified Him. I have asked Him to help me to forgive them, and in the spirit I can.

I'll still take them to court though, for the libel and slander they have committed, but now it's nothing personal, just righting a wrong in the only way they understand - financially, and by exposing their lies.

I do forgive Bromfield and Nutting for the misery they have imposed on me. For they have no other choice but to downgrade you. They are only upholding the law and God says we must all uphold the laws of the government.

Finally, I forgive all those who believe Christians are nuts. It's hard for some to understand Christians because they are blind to the truth and unable to hear the call of God. Some people go to church but are not moved by the Holy Spirit. That's how it was for me a few years ago, going to church. Feeling no different and thinking it's the same for everyone. How mistaken I was.

Since my baptism, I have had begun to get some of the nine gifts of the Holy Spirit, visions and praying in the Spirit and if I tried to explain to you some others I've experienced, you would say, Ronnie Boy, you are away with the mixer (not one of Shuggies' cement ones).

I have always been a stoical person and staunchly loyal with my friends, so when I believe in someone, I have immovable faith. It's the same with my belief in Jesus. When He met with me and I realised that I either had to accept Him as who He is, or refuse the relationship He offered, my decision made my conviction unyielding. I simply had to believe what He says. For instance, when I heard the sixties pop singer Helen Shapiro, giving her testimony as to how a "good Jewish girl" like her recognised Jesus as the Messiah she and her people had been waiting for, I was impressed when she mentioned that one of the first proofs she received of how Gods power can change your life, was when she asked Jesus to stop her smoking, something she had tried to do many times without success – Gods grace allowed her to stop from the moment she gave Him the authority to take cigarettes out of her life. My faith accepted this, on the strength that Jesus has "All power and authority" so when I prayed for help with my alcohol problem, I knew God would deal with it – no more a "recovering alcoholic" but a healed alcoholic, freed from the bondage of addiction. It was the same with my deafness, I was absolutely certain that God would deal with it. Months ago I had orderred a special digital hearing aid, but with the bankrupcy situation was unable to buy it. Thank God! In my quiet place under the fig tree, I kept mentioning as of how I would like my hearing back, in order to hear Pastor Lesley preach, OK I may have been asking for more selfish reasons, but anyway God heard and answered my prayers - I realised suddenly that I could hear perfectly - even a pin dropping. I tell you truly faith can move mountains, but it's obvious, because Matthew 7 verse 7 states *"Ask and it shall be given to you"* and Jesus wouldn't say it unless it was true.

That's how I see life now - a simple matter of faith. The VAT made me financially bankrupt, I had made myself spiritually bankrupt, but once I gave up trying to run my own life; from the time I accepted my spiritual bankrupcy, by repenting for my sins, Jesus took over, and my faith has been sufficient, I believe in Him with all my heart. Like it says in Luke 1 verse 37 *"For with God nothing shall be impossible"*. My life has changed completely, I am running on high octane "Holy Spirit" fuel and it overflows wherever I am.

I had a visitor yesterday. Blackpool Frank a legend on the Costas who had more underworld connections than Liverpool Street subways. Blackpool Frank was brought up by the Jesuits (give me the boy and I will make you a man). No way was Frank going to put up with my Christian spiel. I tried to reach him to no avail.

Blackpool Frank has a heart of gold like so many extrovert people I know, but religion has 'innoculated' them against Christ. I pray God will use me to reach lost souls like Blackpool Frank and introduce them to the real Jesus, who's alive and still changes lives, when we let Him.

Frank tells me he is going to write a book which I suspect will burn a few. His stories are pure magic, but these days I hear them in a different way.

A lot of my time during the next year will be taken up fighting my libel actions against the press, my ex accountant and others. How can I sue these people as a Christian, I hear you ask, well I do not want to hurt them, but they still choose to live under the law, so they must be dealt with by way of the law.

I have decided to discontinue my odds service, with the changes that have taken place in my life, it isn't something I want to do anymore.

Instead, you can get all my best racing information on **09068 100 720** it will cost you 100 pence a minute, on the days I've got information I can trust, but that's still a hundred times cheaper than paying odds to a hundred quid a winner.

Most days my on line-racing message will only cost you 20 pence, because I will not keep you on line just to take your money, with a worthless tip at the end.

To safeguard the early betting market and any job coups I am privee to, also to stop the early leak of any racing information I am given by my trainers and jockey friends, I will not divulge any betting business until one hour before racing begins.

So phone me and get genuine inside info if you are a punter. My on-line message is a good will service to my loyal former clients, not a way of making money, so give me a call and stop getting ripped off.

I would love to know what you think about this book, whether you have enjoyed it or not. I promise you I will reply personally to any letter or questions you send me, and your comments will be very welcome – good or bad!

As you get older, you think more about life. Yes, I have been fortunate in many ways but my fortunes could now never be measured in material assets.

We certainly came into this world with nothing and you will certainly go out with nothing unless you have faith, then you will have riches in Heaven.

In fact the only thing we ever really own is our soul, and the only real decision we ever need to take is where we decide our soul should spend eternity, with God in heaven or without Him, which must be hell.

Now I could be happy living in a cave with a spider for company, if the sun was warm, I could hear the birds sing and look at God's beauty of nature around me.

I have lived very rough and I have lived very smooth, but somewhere between poverty and luxury is something called "basic home comforts" and for those of us with a loving wife and faith, you have riches beyond comparison. We as true men need little more, but like the fools we are like Billy goat gruff, we often think the grass is greener on the other side. It rarely is.

I have wasted 50 years of my life with the devil as my accomplice. Now, by the grace of God, I have got a free transfer to work for His side.

Two Corninthians, Chapter 4, verses 8 & 9. I think says it well for a Christian

"We are troubled on every side, yet not distressed; we are perplexed, but not in despair."

"Persecuted, but not forsaken, cast down, but not destroyed."

God Bless

Publishers Note

When Ron Dawson told me about the book he intended to publish, I was unsure as to whether I should become involved. As a committed Christian, I was wary about a project which involved a book about gambling, crooked bookmakers, corruption in high places and depravity. I was at a bit of a loss to see where the Glory was going to go to God.

In the prescribed manner, I asked God what He thought about it, and felt that I was being told to bide my time and see what came up. I have tried to be obedient and I believe I can say that now I know where God is getting the Glory from. The Ron Dawson I know as a friend and brother in Christ today, is truly a new creation of whom the old has passed (or is rapidly passing) away.

In the time between our first meeting and now, I have come to value Ron and Maureens friendship and company. When first I met Ron, I found a bitter and twisted man who was looking for retribution. From a believers viewpoint I could easily see that Ron needed a new start and could recognise that although he needed Christ as much as anyone else, he wanted his pound of flesh more than life itself.

All Christians are called to 'preach the good news' of Christ, but I was minded to keep quiet with Ron. (excepting during our prayer time, when he was a constant target) Initially I thought Ron needed to 'vent his spleen' before he could be freed from his anger, and to a degree that was right.

But in reality Rons' story is all the more powerful for having been published 'warts and all', and then finished with the testimony of his salvation. Christians and non-believers alike cannot be unaware of the change that has taken place, and like Ron says, were he to start writing today, he would write it differently, and I think it would lose impact because of his new found faith.

Perhaps his next book will prove me wrong!

Finally to all those who will scorn him and make fun for his speaking out proclaiming his faith, I say this. Ron has taken his leap of faith knowing what he can expect as a response from the world, you cannot harm him, he is no longer in your power and fears nothing that you can do.

That brand of courage and freedom cannot be bought, fortunately it comes free, as a gift of grace, when finally we see the truth of what Christ did for us.

John 3:16

> *For God so loved the world that He gave His one and only Son, that whosoever believes in their heart and confesses with their tongue, that Jesus Christ is Lord, shall not perish, but have eternal life. (paraphrased)*

I suggest you read verses John 3:17-21 also.

May God abundantly Bless you.